TRENDS IN AGRARIAN STRUCTURE IN THE HILLS OF NORTH-EAST INDIA

Trends in Agrarian Structure in the Hills of North-East India

Edited by

M.C. BEHERA
N.C. ROY

COMMONWEALTH PUBLISHERS
NEW DELHI
(INDIA)

ISBN : 81-7169-448-9

TRENDS IN AGRARIAN STRUCTURE IN THE HILLS OF NORTH-EAST INDIA

Edition : 2024

Published by :
COMMONWEALTH PUBLISHERS (P) LTD.
4831/24, Govind Lane,
Ansari Road, Darya Ganj,
New Delhi - 110002
Ph. : 23272541, 23242541
e-mail : commonwealthpublishers2016@gmail.com

Distributed by :
ARJUN PUBLISHING HOUSE
4831/24, Govind Lane,
Ansari Road, Darya Ganj,
New Delhi - 110002
Ph. : 23272541, 23242541
e-mail : arjunbooks2001@gmail.com

Laser Typesetting by :
Dimple Computers
Delhi

Printed at :
Milan Enterprises
Delhi

Preface

Post-Independence development syndrome is very much indicative of the fact that the sectoral approach to development and the associated macro-level planning could not realise desired objectives. The approach, therefore, has been shifted from the target setting approach to beneficiary oriented approach and decentralised nature of planning has been adopted side by side the centralised one, though the former is linked to and influenced by the latter through Planning Commission guidelines and involvement of bureaucratic mechanism.

Same is the case with post-independence approaches to tribal development inspite of theoretical soundness of the philosophy as envisaged by Elwin and Nehru. Because initial development doses were prescribed and administered by the planners and policy makers from outside the system. Moreover, they were not in accordance with the factor endowment and development needs of tribal population. In course of time, even when tribal people participate in development process and involve in decision making, the nature of approaches to development still remains something alien to their specific needs which they perceive in their socio-cultural set-up. The tribal planners and policy makers have to work within the centralised national framework. As a result, tribal development still remains a myth.

But plan measures introduced for tribal development, though have not achieved desired results, have set free forces of disequilibrium into their system. Their harmonious relation with nature, socio-cultural institutions compatible with economic pursuits have been passing through transition. The magnitude of deforestation in tribal areas has been alarming, the tribal sense of cooperation is being replaced by individual competition and class formation has assumed a concrete shape in the classless tribal communities. Findings of different scholars and even a cursory observation in the field reveal such a trend in clear terms.

Traditional tribal economy, more particularly that of the hill tribes, centres around primitive system of agricultural practices which has been characterised by the use of primitive technology, shifting cultivation, community ownership of land resource and a cooperative sense of appropriation of community labour force. Man-nature relationship displays harmony in terms of the mode of resources use and hence has been eco-friendly. Social institutions and organisations agree with the requirements of the agricultural practices. Agricultural activities though form a domain of economic activities in terms of production, distribution and consumption of agricultural products, the economic forces operate together with strong non-economic socio-cultural considerations such as rituals, customs, beliefs and faiths. Agriculture in a tribal community, therefore, displays more socio-cultural implications than economic significance and any measure for agricultural development should also take these factors into consideration.

But, only economic forces of change introduced from outside into traditional tribal agricultural practices through plan programmes have acted and interacted in such a way as to disturb the equilibrium of socio-cultural and economic forces. Privatisation of community/clan land, change in cropping pattern, emergence of tenancy system, competitive relation between agricultural expansion and forest resource, land alienation, growth of activities allied to agriculture have been some of the emerging trends in primitive agricultural tribal communities.

To have a detailed account of such trends in agricultural practices of different hill tribes of the north-eastern region I approached scholars, planners and bureaucrats to contribute papers for preparing a volume on 'Trends in Agrarian Structure in the Hills of North-East India.' The objective was to focus on the emerging trends for better policy implications. Of course, there are some missing links, as it happens with seminar papers and edited books, with regard to the whole spectrum of issues identified in the outline of the project. Nevertheless, some burning issues have been covered which highlight on newly emerging trends both under identical and diversified conditions existing among various hill tribes of north-eastern India. I am confident that the scholars, planners, administrators and general readers will gain considerable insight into the emerging trends in the agrarian structure in the hills of north-east India from the pages of this volume.

I had initially planned to go for editing this volume with Dr. S.P. Shukla as co-editor. But due to his assignment as the Member of APPSC and busy schedules I practically found it difficult to go ahead with my earlier plan. So, I took the help of Dr. N.C. Roy instead in this venture. I am grateful to both of them. I am also grateful to all scholars who encouraged and obliged me by contributing papers to this volume.

I owe my understanding of tribal issues to Prof. A.C. Bhagabati, Vice-Chancellor, Arunachal University. He has always been a source of inspiration for my academic pursuits. Interaction with Prof. Tamo Mibang, Head, Department of Tribal Studies, Arunachal University has also come a long way to help me in dealing with some delicate issues. I am grately indebted to both of them.

Lastly, I am grateful to Mr. B.R. Verma of Commonwealth Publishers, New Delhi, for undertaking the publication of this volume.

M.C. BEHERA
N.C. ROY

Contents

Part II—STRUCTURAL TRANSFORMATION

Part III—INSTITUTIONAL ISSUES

List of Contributors

Dr. Amitava Mitra
Reader and Head
Deptt. of Economics
Arunachal University
Doimukh,
Itanagar-791 112.

Dr. A.C. Talukdar
Visiting Professor
Omeo Kumar Das Institute of Social Change & Development
Nowzan Road,
Uzanbazar,
Guwahati-781 001.

Dr. A.K. Neog
Director for Scheduled Castes and Scheduled Tribes
National Commission for SC/ST
Shillong.

Dr. A.K. Agarwal
Reader and Head
Deptt. of Economics
NEHU
Mizoram Campus,
Aizawl-796 007.

Dr. A.K. Singh
Senior Ecologist
Anthropological Survey of India
2 Ripon Street,
Calcutta-16.

Dr. B. Datta Ray
Secretary
NEICSSR (North-East India Council for Social Science Research)
Shillong-3.

Dr. B.N. Bordoloi
Former Director
Assam Institute of Research for Tribals and Scheduled Castes
Guwahati.

Mr. B. Panda
Lecturer
Deptt. of Economics
IGG College
Tezu,
Arunachal Pradesh.

Dr. B.D. Nayak
Lecturer
Economics
NERIST (North-Eastern
Regional Institute of Science
and Technology)
Itanagar,
Arunachal Pradesh.

Dr. D.K. Dutta
District Research Officer
West Siang District
Along,
Arunachal Pradesh.

Dr. D.K. Duarah
Assistant Director (Culture)
Directorate of Research
Govt. of Arunachal Pradesh,
Itanagar-791 111.

Dr. Gurudas Das
Lecturer
Deptt. of Economics
St. Anthony's College
Shillong-1.

Dr. J.B. Ganguly
Formerly Vice-Chancellor
Tripura University
4-Minapara Road,
Azadgarh Ward No. 1
Calcutta-40.

Mr. K.K. Satapathy
Sr. Scientist (SWCE)
ICAR Research Complex for
NE Region
Umroi Road, Barapani,
Shillong-3.

Dr. K.K. Upadhyaya
D.Lit.
Reader
Economics
NEHU
Mizoram Campus,
Aizawl-796 007.

Kh. Somorendro Singh
Faculty Member
Institute of Cooperative
Management
Imphal
Manipur.

Dr. M.C. Behera
Lecturer
Deptt. of Tribal Studies
Arunachal University
Itanagar,
Arunachal Pradesh.

Dr. N.C. Roy
Lecturer
Economics
Arunachal University
Itanagar.

Mr. N.C. Nayak
Lecturer
Economics
Govt. College
Itanagar,
Arunachal Pradesh.

Mr. Prasanta Saikia
Deptt. of Economics
Arunachal University.

Dr. P.C. Dutta
Former Director of Research
Lachit Nagar,
East Chowkidingee,
Dibrugarh,
Assam.

Mr. P.K. Kuri
Lecturer, Economics
Arunachal University
Itanagar,
A.P.

Dr. P.S. Ramakrishnan
Professor and Dean
School of Environmental
Sciences
JNU
New Delhi.

Dr. Rani Hazarika Kakati
Reader, Anthropology
Guwahati University
Guwahati,
Assam.

Mr. S.K. Agnihotri
I.A.S.
Chairman
Board of Revenue
Meghalaya,
Shillong-793 001.

Dr. S.K. Verma
Faculty Member
Institute of Cooperative
Management
Imphal, Cooperative Complex,
Lamphelpat, Imphal-795 004.

Dr. Sanjukta Das
Lecturer in Economics
Arunachal University, Itanagar.

Ms. S.S. Nayak
Scholar
NERIST
Nirjuli, Itanagar.

Dr. Y.P. Kohli
Lecturer in Chemistry
J.N. College
Pasighat, Arunachal Pradesh.

NORTH-EASTERN REGION OF INDIA

Introduction

❑ M.C. BEHERA
❑ N.C. ROY

The north-eastern region of India comprising Arunachal Pradesh, Assam, Manipur, Meghalaya, Mizoram, Nagaland and Tripura is a mosaic of cultural diversities and economic disparities. About 70 percent of the region is hilly. The National Commission of Agriculture (1976) identified the entire states of Arunachal Pradesh, Meghalaya, Mizoram, Nagaland and Tripura as hill states. The hill areas in Assam account for about 20 percent and in Manipur 90 percent. The natives of hill areas are pre-dominantly tribal. The tribal population in Arunachal Pradesh is 63.66 percent, in Assam, 12.82 percent, in Manipur 34.41 percent, in Meghalaya 85.53 percent, in Mizoram 94.75 percent, in Nagaland 87.70 percent and in Tripura 30.95 percent. Except in Assam all the tribal population lives in hills. In Assam a section of tribal population is plains tribal. The hill tribes practise shifting cultivation. The task Force on Shifting cultivation, Ministry of Agriculture (1983) recorded 1.5 percent annual area (3,869 sq. kms.) under shifting cultivation and 5.7 percent (14,660 sq. kms.) minimum area under shifting cultivation one time or other.

Tribal agricultural practice is very closely associated with many social and cultural customs, patterns and even habits. Activities associated with jhum cultivation, for example, obviously display more of socio-cultural traits in terms of rituals, cooperative nature of appropriating community/clan labour force and community ownership of jhum land than economic behaviour. Findings of individual scholars and research institutes like Agro-Economic Research Centre, Jorhat, Assam Institute of Research for Tribals and Scheduled Castes, Guwahati identify above factors along with physical constraints as retarding factors of agricultural growth in the region. As a result, the hills of north-eastern region have failed to achieve the expected goal in the agricultural sector even after four and half decades of government investment with an aim to transform the traditional agricultural practices and to raise productivity. This fact has emphasised the need for the search for an optimum development strategy for the region with regard to growth, sustainability and acceptability. Such a strategy has not yet been developed. But the search is on. This volume attempts to reveal the realities in agrarian situation so as to shape the idea for the realistic plan approach on the basis of the socio-climatic geo-physical and psycho-emotional considerations.

The present volume is the collection of twenty-eight papers. The papers obviously reflect the views of the individual authors who are eminent in their own fields. The theme and area coverage is restricted to what has been presented in the papers. Of twenty-eight papers, two papers related to north-eastern region as a whole with reference to hills and four papers only to the hills. Sixteen papers discuss different trends in individual states like Arunachal Pradesh, Assam, Manipur, Meghalaya and Mizoram and two of them deal with co-operative finance in Manipur. The last six papers deal with individual tribes.

Theme-wise, the volume contains four sections, *viz.* general, structural transformation, institutional issues and environmental reflections. Among the ten papers under general section, A.K. Agarwal's paper "Agricultural Systems and Behaviour in North-Eastern States" and B.D. Nayak's paper "The Trend of Agrarian Structure and its impact on Agriculture in North-Eastern Hill Region of India" deal with the region as a whole. A.K. Agarwal has discussed various aspects of the prevailing systems of cultivation, land ownership and distribution, foodgrains production and productivity, irrigation facilities and cropping pattern, as well other related issues, in all the seven states of the region with special reference to hill areas. He has also come out with important policy issues including diversification of agricultural activities. B.D. Nayak's paper highlights on the availability of agricultural infrastructure like irrigation, credit institutions, fertiliser consumption in north-eastern region. It discusses the growth of agricultural crops in the region. The paper, though has not categorically dealt with hill areas, bears significance because of hilly nature of some individual states of the region.

Tribals live in harmony with nature at a particular level of development of their socio-economic and cultural outlook. The practice they evolve is the best and sustainable when considered in the light of their input use and interaction with environment at that point of time. In many cases, the prevalent outlook stands in their way to perceive the benefit of a new system and as a result they hesitate to give up their age old practices. Papers of Rani Hazarika Kakati, D.K. Duarah, Y.P. Kohli and joint paper of Sanjukta Das and Prasanta Saikia throw light to understand the above propositions. Rani Hazarika Kakati in her paper titled "Agriculture and Related Activities: A Study of the Rangdani Rabhas of Meghalaya" has highlighted the agricultural practices of this tribe who are living in some villages of East-Garo Hills of Meghalaya. Tradition-bound, these people use locally available input to optimise their agricultural output. Though their method of agricultural production is old fashioned and apparently that may not seem to be highly productive, yet her study shows that the efficiency level achieved by them in the given context in quite high and that is why these people are reluctant to go for the modern technology. The paper "The Traditional Agricultural System of the Apatanis" by D.K. Duarah describes the traditional method of cultivation, cropping pattern of the Apatanis, the people who are unique in the state in view of the fact that their agriculture is based on wet rice cultivation contrary to the jhuming practice predominant among the majority of the tribes living in hills. They have been practising their traditional method, perhaps because of the fact that their system is not at least less developed than what the government introduces in the state in general. However, they have accepted fish-cum-paddy culture which is compatible with their traditional system. Y.P. Kohli in his paper "Traditional Plant Protection Practices among the Adis" has analysed rituals performed by the Adis of Arunachal Pradesh as traditional ways of protecting crops from pests and diseases. He suggests a thorough study of such practices to determine and establish their efficiency. His study throws light on the practices which involved out of their outlook and perception in relation to their socio-cultural development. The paper 'Chemical Fertiliser Vs Organic Manure: Problems and Prospects in Arunachal Pradesh' by Sanjukta Das and Prasant Saikia is a micro-study on the use of fertilisers by tribal farmers of Arunachal Pradesh. The study finds that the use of chemical fertilisers is very less as compared to manure because (of some misgivings that) the use of chemical fertilisers destroys fertility of the soil. The implicit tune of the paper hints at the attitude of the people which again is a socio-cultural variable. Under such a situation, the authors have suggested for encouraging the use of manure among the farmers of Arunachal Pradesh (about which they have indigenous knowledge).

Parul Chandra Dutta in his paper "Nature of agriculture in the Hills, Problems and Prospectives: Shifting to Permanent Cultivation (with special reference to the Nocte and Wancho of Arunachal Pradesh) has described the traditional method of agricultural practices of the N.E. region in general and that of Wanchos and Noctes of Tirap district of Arunachal Pradesh in particular with some suggestive measures for transforming their traditional system. He has pointed out that the shifting cultivation is so entwined with the socio-cultural life of the people that any transformation would not be acceptable easily. The government extension workers, as he suggests, are required to be more cautious in this respect. His analysis also shows the effectiveness of jhum practice in checking soil erosion. The Wanchos and Noctes believe that spirits dwell in low lands and so when people would be persuaded to cultivate such land, their fear-psychosis should be removed. Showing the better economic advantage of permanent cultivation they would be wean away from jhumming. The introduction of new crops for demonstration should be preceded by soil testing, lest unrealisation of expected produce might have negative impact. He is hopeful that the process of transformation, though difficult, is not impossible and the government extension workers should be serious and sincere about it.

The rest of the papers in this section throws light on changes in agricultural situation and discusses present scenario. Gurudas Das's study (Agriculture in Arunachal Pradesh: Trends and Problems of Objective Assessment) analysis some aspects of agriculture like land use, achievement in land development front, cropping pattern and the problems of intersectoral linkage with the backdrop of agricultural backwardness in Arunachal Pradesh during 1980s. He has identified some shortcomings of data collected by Agricul–

ture Department of Arunachal Pradesh which he attributes to poor assessment of agricultural development in the state. Another thrust of this study reveals that very low growth of agriculture has failed to facilitate the creation of a proper linkage which might have boosted industrial development specially the development of agro-based industries in the state. N.C. Roy in his paper "Agricultural Productivity in Arunachal Pradesh" highlights the trend of plan measures and achievement in the field of agriculture. His analysis is based on secondary data. He attributes the over all growth of agriculture in the state during plan period mainly to the extension of permanent cultivation. His analysis reveals that induction of new technology, subsidised provision of capital and migration of labour from outside the state has made the expansion of permanent cultivation possible. Therefore, he argues that there is not an increase in the productivity of land rather there is the increase in total production of land. He also notes a decline in jhum cultivation and the production of land under it which counter balances the increase in production under permanent cultivation so that over all production of land has not increased significantly. Shipra S. Nayak's paper "Agriculture in Arunachal Pradesh" is an attempt to show functional relationship between area under different crops, their yields and their determinants such as fertiliser, irrigation etc. Her correlation analysis demonstrates that fertiliser consumption has a positive effect upon area under wheat and also its yield in some districts. However, in case of millet the relationship is negative. In case of irrigation the impact is not uniform.

The second section includes five papers which deal with structural transformation in the process of agricultural modernisation. J.B. Ganguly's paper "Structural changes in Jhum-based Economy and Growing Inequalities in North-Eastern Tribal Society" highlights on the growing inequalities in the jhum-based economy of the north-eastern tribal societies. The main thrust of his analysis is to show that this growing inequality is mainly a product of peasantisation of the tribal economy, a process which has been shaped by the emergence of private property rights in land and the growth of wage-labours. In the traditional jhum-based economy, there was little surplus which was not spent on productive investment. So, the traditional tribal economy was a static economy which has been broken by the introduction of incentive packages by the government to wean away the traditional farmers from shifting cultivation. As a result, settled cultivation assumed growing importance and many peasants took to both shifting and settled cultivation. This also came to establish private property rights in land and its effect was translated in the emergence of tenancy system, absentee farmers and in some cases depeasantisation. In many tribal areas of the North-East, some shifting cultivators have been reduced to wage-labourers. In some cases, tribal land is alienated to non-tribals, in others tribal elites succeeded in dis–possessing fellow tribals of their land. All these have created a high degree of inequality in the distribution of land holdings in the hill areas of North-East. A.K. Neog in his paper "Transforming Hill Agriculture in Tribal Areas of North-East India" deals with the basic characteristics of farming system in the hills of the region. He has discussed the productivity of land under jhum cultivation compared to permanent one. No doubt, jhuming is an extensive form of agriculture, but as pointed out by him, its productivity may not be necessarily lower than that of the permanently cultivated land in the hills. Some studies referred to by him tend to show the efficiency of jhum cultivation *vis-a-vis* permanent one. Another highlight of the study is the problem of transformation of jhum to permanent type of cultivation. Based on the outcome of jhum control projects of NEC he shows that rapid control of jhum may be a very difficult task. However, in this connection he suggests some measures keeping in view the short term, medium term and long term objectives for effective transformation in the agricultural system.

In his paper 'Distributive Pattern and Structural Changes in Landholdings in Arunachal Pradesh: Some Implications' M.C. Behera points out the factors which have brought about changes in the structure and distribution of agricultural holdings in Arunachal Pradesh. He also brings into focus the discrepancy between the data on land holdings collected by the government and other agencies. While the census data shows a decline over time in the inequality in the distribution of holdings, the data collected by individual researchers tends to show an increasing inequality. On the growth of land holdings his findings are that the change in the materialistic outlook of the people has led to the rise in demand for cultivable land and often this demand has been met through clearing of forests. Another factor identified for rising number of holdings is the gradual nuclearization of families and this has been brought about mainly by the spread of education, migration and urbanisation. Migration has caused the new villages to come up around urban areas. The possibility of earning profit has led the newly reclaimed land and fallow jhum land being brought under commercial crops and in the process the inequalities in holdings have been increasing. As measures against growing inequalities which have negative effect upon modernization of agriculture, he suggests carrying out of cadastral survey, maintaining land records and enacting regulation for uniform inheritance. N.C. Nayak's paper (Constraints to Agricultural Growth in Arunachal Pradesh) describes various constraints to agricultural development with reference to land tenure system, cultivation practices, land use and cropping pattern which have experienced changes in recent years. Otner constraints identified are scarcity of cultivable land, lack of manpower and irrigation facility, primitive technology and lack of transport and communication that stands in the way to link agricultural sector with an organised market. His paper emphasises on codification of customary land laws, development of horticulture and scientific use of jhum land and provision for adequate infrastructure as reformist measures for removing developmental constraints in agriculture. B. Panda's paper titled "Changing Facets of Agriculture in Arunachal Pradesh analyses changes in different dimensions of agriculture—proportion of labour force engaged in agriculture, composition of agricultural working force, size of occupational holdings and the growth of foodgrains production in Arunachal Pradesh. His paper also shows the relative decline in jhum cultivation. One interesting aspect of his study is the identification of factors responsible for the growth of foodgrains product. Because of limitation of data, he could single out only three factors, *viz.* fertiliser, HYV seeds and irrigation. All of these are found to be significantly correlated to the production of foodgrains.

The third section, comprising nine papers, deals with institutional issues which have emerged in the agricultural practices in recent years. The paper "Tribal Land Relations—A Transition to Private Ownership in Meghalaya" by B. Datta Ray deals with the emergence of private property rights in land among the Khasis and Garos of Meghalaya in the historical perspective. In the traditional societies of these tribes the communal ownership of property in land was the norm. The Khasis had a matrilineal family structure where mother was the owner of the property. On her death, youngest daughter inherits that property. The Garos also have a matrilineal type of family where wife owned the land but husband (Nokma) used to manage it as a custodian. The establishment of British rule monetised the economy leading to gradual emergence of privatisation of common resources, especially cultivable land in Meghalaya. Of course, this was a long process and so far as the hills of Meghalaya are concerned, the individualisation of common land is not yet uniform. In Jaintia Hills, privatisation process started by means of Chitta and Jamabandi when in 1901 plots of land were released to private individuals. The establishment of ADC after independence, practice of wet rice cultivation and horticulture, application of Assam Law and Revenue Regulation 1966 helped in the process of emerging privatisation of land. However, as Datta Ray has mentioned, the process of privatisation is related with the emergence of capitalist trend. Its inevitable outcome has found expression in the form of landlessness and growing inequality in landholdings. The other paper on Meghalaya is "Agrarian Structure and Land Relations in Meghalaya" by S.K. Agnihotri. He has discussed various land laws of the Khasis, the Jaintias and the Garos and has highlighted the deviations made during the British period and the post-independence period in response to the changing matrix of techno-economic and socio-political variables. It describes the current situation where under the modernisation process land has suddenly been pushed into the monetary economy and where agrarian relations are being determined by the demand and supply equation of land rather than social relationship. This trend, on the other hand, has given rise to in-equalitarian property structures. Neither the district councils nor the state government have been able to guide the land-man relationship on an equitable basis.

Of three papers on Arunachal Pradesh in this section, A.C. Talukdar has discussed customary land tenures, inheritance laws among the tribes in his paper "Land Tenure and Land Use Pattern in Arunachal Pradesh." He has highlighted on permanent cultivation, inter-migration of people and the consequent emergence of several multi-clan villages as causative factors behind the growth of privatisation of property in land. Land uses into settle cultivation, jhum land, fallow land and distribution of landholdings on the basis of Agriculture Census figures are also analysed. He holds the view on the basis of his observation that the system has led to fragmentation of landholdings, landlessness along with growing inequality in ownership of land. He has suggested some reformist measures such as cadastral survey of agricultural land, landownership laws considering gender equity, official registration of land transfers and transactions. He has suggested alternative use of jhum land keeping in view both short term and long term needs of the cultivators. The paper "Risk, Insurance and Land Reform in Arunachal Pradesh," jointly written by N.C. Roy and P.K. Kuri, is an attempt to derive the rationale of land reform mainly from the changing profile of risk in agriculture of Arunachal Pradesh. Though risk is very common in rural areas of developing countries, the market for risk is very rare. Two problems moral hazards and adverse selection—stand in the way of emergence of market for risk. These problems, though universal are more acute in developing countries. The non-existence of risk market does not mean the non-existence of social mechanism from risk trading. In fact, such non-market risk coping mechanism existed in the traditional society of Arunachal Pradesh in terms of communal ownership of land. However, with the introduction of new inputs in agriculture, communal ownership has given way to private property rights in land. The new property rights regime has caused some far-reaching changes in the form of tenant cultivation, landlessness and attenuation of mutual risk-coping mechanism. All these changes which have resulted in the high inequalities in landholdings and exposed the rural poor to new kind of risks warrant reformist measures to be undertaken in the realm of ownership distribution of land. D.K. Dutta's paper "Customary Land Tenure System and its change among the Galos of Arunachal Pradesh" discusses the traditional land tenure system of the Galos. He has focussed on recent changes also. He has pointed out that land has become a commodity due to privatisation of landed property and customary hold on the practice of land transfer has slackened. His paper also throws light on the right to inheritance, traditional system of justice to settle land disputes and some customary rituals associated with agricultural practices.

B.N. Bordoloi's paper "Land Reforms in the Hill Areas of Assam" discusses land tenure systems among different tribal communities of two hill districts—North Cachar Hills and Karbi Anglong of Assam. It also outlines the process of tenurial changes and the reformist measures undertaken by the government of Assam since pre-independence days. Specifically, the paper deals with the traditional land tenure systems of the Karbis, Dimasa Kacharis, Zemei Nagas, Hmars and Kukis. One common characteristics among these tribal communities is that limited private property rights in land exists in all of them. Land is either communally owned or it is owned by the chief. The individual in its property right arrangement derives the usufructuary right only upon the land he cultivates. These limited private rights in land exist only in hill areas where land is cultivated for jhum. But in plains, the communal ownership has been replaced by private ownership. It has, at the same time, led to the alienation of tribal land sometimes through dubious means like *Paikas* system. Various tenancy arrangements like share cropping, mortgage etc. also act as instruments of alienation of tribal lands. Reform measures undertaken tried to plug all these loopholes, but new ways were devised so as to use those tenurial arrangement as instruments of exploitation and alienation. K.K. Upadhyaya in his paper "Aspects of Land-scarce Semi-Primitive Economy: Traces of Capitalist Farming in Mizoram" has traced out that capitalism is in the process of taking a definite shape in farming in Mizoram in the forms of growing plantation crops, animal husbandry, private gardens for settled farming and Womens' property rights. Privatisation of land as he has mentioned, takes place mostly due to the new Land Use Policy of the Government of Mizoram since 1984 and the extent depends on the political connections of the holders.

Somorendro Singh ("Role of Primary Agricultural Cooperatives in Rural Credit with Reference to Manipur State") has dealt with the role of credit cooperatives in agricultural sector both in plains and hills of Manipur and has made a comparison with that of other north-eastern states. He has analysed the problem with reference to the Eight Five Year Plan. His analysis refers to some problem areas which are to be solved through effective management, proper distribution of funds, high morale of employees and reorientation of approach of development agencies to the needs of the cooperatives. S.K. Verma in his paper "A Review on Agricultural Cooperative Finance in Manipur" has discussed cooperative movement in Manipur and has analysed the role played by different agricultural credit to the farmers. The credit societies have extended some credit to weaker sections of the society though the amount advanced is hardly sufficient. The paper also discusses on the achievement and failure of the cooperative movement.

The last section consists of four papers on environmental reflections associated with agricultural practices. Earlier papers discussed in section one have related agricultural practices to the environment. In this section, environmental factor is dominant while highlighting agricultural practices and provides justification for a new look into evolving strategies in the hills. P.S. Ramakrishnan in his paper "Scientific Basis of Traditional Wet Rice Cultivation by North-East Indian Hill Tribes" has shown that low elevation wet rice agro-eco system are more energy efficient than that of at Indian plains and Western agricultural system but less efficient as compared to jhum system. He has based his findings on a number of case studies over a period of many years in Meghalaya and Arunachal Pradesh. His study at Lailad in Meghalaya has shown that mono-cropping practice of Nepalis and Mikirs, who are traditionally better organised settled agriculturists, is more energy efficient than double cropping system of the Garos who use comparatively higher energy input for each cropping. But in the context of Balijan he has found that the energy yield from double cropping by the Karbis is more than that of the Nishings mono-cropping. He further shows that the efficiency of immigrant Nepalis and of local Khasis is almost same in WRC because ecological and other operational conditions are same. Discussing on agricultural practices of the Apatanis he has prescribed some measures for the introduction of multi-cropping practice in valley system of agriculture and has suggested it as a possible model for redevelopment of wet rice agriculture in north-eastern hills. K.K. Satapatty (Watershed Management in Hills) has given the magnitude of soil loss due to non-scientific agricultural land uses. According to an estimate as much as 181 million tonnes of soil is lost every year. The factors responsible for the rise of acute soil erosion problem are various biotic interferences. He prescribes watershed approach for proper land use and conservation of water for irrigation purposes. He suggests that through proper water-shed management horticulture, agriculture, silvipasture, livestock, forestry etc. can be developed. Based on watershed management terraces in the lower portion of the hills can provide stable alternative to shifting cultivation. On the basis of the nature of hill slopes he has prescribed different structures of terraces suitable for specific crops and horticulture. He has cited some indigenous water management systems like zabo system, drip irrigation using bamboo, water harvesting structures, hill springs, etc. which have been evolved in different watersheds and has suggested innovations for some systems for better water shed management. A. Mitra's paper "Sustainable Development in Agriculture and need of Forestry Planning in Arunachal Pradesh" is an attempt to give an outline of the forest policy having bearing upon sustainable development of agriculture. Increasing demand for forest products and agriculture expansion have a conflicting relationship. The resolution of this requires that proper attention be given to such policy making as would make proper development of forestry and agriculture possible. A.K. Singh's paper "Ethnogeography and Traditional Agricultural System of the Apatanis of Arunachal Pradesh" has discussed in details the system of agriculture of the Apatanis which has evolved in their ecological setting over the years. It also highlights environmental risks and uncertainties having bearing upon their agricultural practices. The inputs used by them, though are simple, technically viable to their system. The land use pattern is well-defined in relation to the cultivation of different crops such as rice, millet, maize and vegetables. Water management system is well planned and has been developed indigenously and is most suited to their environment.

The trends in agriculture in hills as discussed in the pages of this volume suggest micro-approaches for the development of agriculture. We hope this volume will serve the purpose of developing a realistic approach to solve the problems of agriculture in the hills.

Part I

GENERAL

CHAPTER 1

Agricultural Systems and Behaviour in North-Eastern States

❑ A.K. AGARWAL

North-East Region comprising seven states namely Arunachal Pradesh, Assam, Manipur, Meghalaya, Mizoram, Nagaland and Tripura is nearly 8 percent of the country's total area and accommodates about 3.72 percent of country's population. Almost two-thirds of this region is hilly leaving the rest under the plains consisting of Assam (excluding two hill districts), and small parts of six other states. There is a wide variation in the altitude ranging from 300 to 5000 metres. The climate and so also the temperature range from tropical plains to temperate hills. The region is well known for very high rainfall combined with very high humidity. All these factors affect regional agriculture in a vivid manner.

The country has been divided into 15 agro-climatic zones and the north-east region falls in the Eastern Himalaya Zone—the most diverse, complex and resourceful region. It has been further sub-divided into five regions.

Sub region I : Himalayan Hills comprising Sikkim and Darjeeling District of West Bengal.

Sub region II : North Eastern Hills comprising Arunachal Pradesh, Meghalaya, Nagaland, Assam Hills (Karbi Anglong and North Cachar Hills).

Sub region III : Southern Hills and valleys comprising Manipur, Tripura and Mizoram.

Sub region IV : Central and Lower Brahmaputra Valley comprising Nowgong, Darrang, Kamrup and Goalpara Districts of Assam.

Sub region V : A. Upper Brahmaputra Valley comprising Lakhimpur, Dibrugarh and Sibsagar.

B. Barak Valley (Old Cachar District).

Agricultural System

The agricultural practices in the region are broadly of two distinct types, one practised in plains, valleys, foothills and terraced lands on slopes called settled agriculture, and the other followed on hill slopes of all possible gradients called "shifting cultivation" or "jhumming."

Table 1

CULTIVATED AND IRRIGATED AREA IN N.E. REGION, 1983-84 (PROVISIONAL)

(000 hectares)

State	*Total Reporting Area*	*Cultivated Area* Net	Gross	*% of Net Cultivated Area to Total Area*	*Irrigated Area* Net	Gross	*% of Net Irrigated Area to Net Cultivated Area*
Arunachal Pradesh (d)	5550	118	177	2.13	22	23	18.64
Assam (a)	7852	2696	3577	34.33	572(m)	572(m)	21.22
Manipur (b)	2211	140	184	6.33	65	76	46.43
Meghalaya (a)	2249	193	214	8.58	50(g)	51(g)	25.91
Mizoram (e)	2102	65	65	3.09	8	8	12.31
Nagaland	1099	185	195	16.83	68	73	36.76
Tripura (c)	1048	246	375	23.47	29	38(g)	11.79
Total	22111	3643	4787	16.48	814	841	22.34

(a) Relates to the year 1980-81.
(b) Ad-hoc estimates.
(c) Relates to the year 1977-78.
(d) Relates to the Agri census 1976-77.
(e) Relates to the year 1974-75.
(g) Relates to the year 1981-82.
(m) Relates to the year 1953-54
(.) Estimated on the forecast data.

Of the total gross cropped areas under cultivation, (74.7 percent) is alone in Assam leaving the rest for other six states. The net cultivated area is 16.48 percent of the geographical area ranging from 2.13 percent in Arunachal Pradesh to 34.33 percent in Assam. The area sown more than once is very small *i.e.,* 11.4 lakh hectares. (Table 1) The annual area under jhumming is estimated as 4.7 lakh hectares *i.e.,* 43.5 percent of country's area under jhum cultivation. About 4.43 lakh jhumia families are practising shifting cultivation in the region (Table 2). With the increase in pressure of population on land fallow period has shrunk to 2-9 years affecting the productivity adversely.

Table 2

SHIFTING CULTIVATION IN N.E. REGION

(Area in Sq. Km.)

State	*Annual Area Under Shifting Cultivation*	*Fellow Period (in years)*	*Minimum Area Under Shifting Cultivation One Time or Other*	*No. of Families Practising Shifting Cultivation (in 000)*
Arunachal Pradesh	700	3—10	2100	54
Assam	696	2—10	1392	58
Manipur	900	4—7	3600	70
Meghalaya	530	5—7	2650	52.3
Mizoram	630	3—4	1890	50
Nagaland	1014	5—8	6330	116
Tripura	223	5—9	1115	43
N.E. India	4693		19077	443.3
All India	10778		491250	

Source: Indian Agriculture in Brief 22nd Edn. 1988, p. 18.

Since the multi-cropping strategy for the plain areas is dominantly rice based, there is need for development and propagation of short duration, early maturing, non-photo sensitive high yielding rice cultivars particularly suited to medium to low land flood prone areas of the north east. The Assam Agricultural

University and ICAR have developed some of the short duration period rice cultivars suitable for planting in the pre-flood and post-flood situation. This needs wider field testing, co-ordinated trails, and mass scale adoption by the farmers to achieve a major breakthrough in agricultural productivity and also second time use of same land for recultivated to attain higher cropping intensity.

In the light of inherent constraints being faced in the north-eastern hilly parts it is suggested to adopt "Model Land Use Pattern" as recommended by the ICAR for jhum lands involving terracing, contour bunding, half-moon terracing etc. in conjunction with appropriate soil and water conservation measures and judicious application of proven quality seeds, fertilizers, plant protection measures. Wherever feasible, intensive wetland rice cultivation by adopting a package of improved scientific practices.

Stress should be given for adopting diversified farming practices with suitable components such as agriculture, horticulture, apiculture, sericulture, handloom and handicrafts for long term economic benefits to the hill people.

For the hill and tribal areas main problems of deforestation and growing inequality in individual land ownership have to be tackled. Conservation of forest resources can be best done with the help of the tribals. By honouring the jhumias rights over land under jhumming we can encourage them to go for agri-pestoral, horti-pestoral and or silvi-pestoral practices.

Timely supply of quality seeds of high yielding crop varieties is the prerequisite for improvement of agricultural production. Since the region has no well organised seed industry the farmers are to depend on other parts of the country. Due to extremely poor communication, timely supply of inputs to the farmers is adversely affected. In view of this it is desirable to establish a well organised seed industry to cater the needs of the region.

Fodder grasses and leguminous crops should be widely used either in dairy based or intensive farming system including utilisation of terrace risers for fodder.

Shifting cultivation is a primitive type of cultivation of hill slopes of even steep gradient, and involves cutting of forests, bushes, upto stump level in December-January, drying it and finally burning to clear the land for dibbling of seed of different crops before the onset of rains. After every crop season or two, the area is abandoned in favour of a new site for regeneration of soil fertility within a village boundary.

The loss of soil due to erosion under this cultivation is estimated at 40 tonnes per hectare as against 5 tonnes per hectare in bench terraces, besides causing reduction in organic carbon due to burning. These losses have contributed to serious decline in the productivity of hill areas. Soil erosion also cause heavy siltation in the lower reaches of major river systems of the region leading to heavy annual floods and inundation of large tracts of riverine land.

Highland paddy is the predominant crop of these lands, mixed with maize, finger-millets, fox-tail millets, beans, tuber crops, tobacco, cotton etc., to meet annual needs of the family. The choice of crop is consumption oriented, except in some hill areas exposed to modern farming methods where single crop is taken in a given piece of land.

Rice, maize, wheat and ragi are important cereals while tuber crops such as tapioca, yams and sweet potato, oilseeds primarily mustard and sesamum, jute, mesta, ramie, cotton, pulse crops such as blackgram, green gram, pea, soyabean, arhar and lentil are all important crops of the region. The importance of plantation crops such as tea, coffee and rubber are already well known. Due to unique diversity of agro-climate conditions owing to topographical variations and altitudinal differences coupled with fertile, deep and well drained soil a large number of fruits and plantation crops extending from higher temperate types like walnut, apple, etc., to typical tropical species like coconut, cashewnut, arecanut, black pepper etc., are being cultivated. The vast area in the hill slopes under shifting cultivation provides an unlimited scope for expansion of horticultural industry in a phased manner as an alternative to the shifting cultivation.

Land Ownership

In most hill areas of north-east India land is owned by the community as a whole. Individual ownership of land recognised in certain areas is usually confined to homestead and settled farm land. Of late, because of the inherent contradictions in the communal ownership of land, privatisation is gradually emerging as the main form of ownership. Short fallow land cultivated for 1 or 2 years followed by 2 to 4 years of fallow period have also become private lands. These lands exist where commercial crops like potato, ginger and vegetables are grown with closed burning system (bun method of shifting cultivation). Lands, where 2 to 3 years of cultivation is followed by 6 to 8 years of fallow period and cultivated by open burning system of shifting cultivation, are still under communal ownership. Under this system each village operates in a particular demarcated area and the power of distribution of land to individual families is vested in the headman or village council. Due to non-fixity of tenurial rights, the farmers naturally do not take interest in the improvement of land for future use. A tendency for improvement is noticed in area where land is privately owned.

Operational Holdings

The size of farm enters as a variable because the farmers owning small farm usually have poor access to the research institutions and credit etc. The management problem of the small farmers then pertains to adequate supplies of credit, increasing inputs and easy access to extension services, research institutions, etc. With the growth of population and slow pace of development of the secondary sector there has been very little diversification of employment opportunities for the rural and the hill people. Therefore, dependence on agriculture has been intensified. This is borne out by the fact that both the total number and the area of operational holdings have steadily increased during the period 1970-71 to 1985-86. However, the notable feature is the decrease in average size of area operated per holding for all the size groups. The average size of marginal holdings has declined from 0.46 in 1970-71 to 0.44 hectares in 1985-86; for small from 1.40 to 1.41 hectares (almost same during the period); for semi-medium holdings from 2.72 to 2.68 hectares; for medium holdings from 5.67 to 5.58 hectares; for large holdings from 25.71 to 24.20 hectares, and for all sizes from 1.71 to 1.61 hectares during the period.

The overall land-man ratio is relatively high in the region but the average size of holdings is quite small. Marginal and small farms dominate the agrarian scene. About 6.9 percent of medium and large size holders occupied 40.5 percent of land area whereas

78.7 percent of small and marginal holders cultivated over 35.5 percent of total operated area in 1985-86.

The operational holding data for Nagaland and Arunachal seems to be rather confusing. There is reason to believe that the whole area kept for shifting cultivation by a household is taken as operational holding. For example, 5.9 percent of large holders possess 28.3 percent of land area in Arunachal Pradesh while in Nagaland 29.1 percent of holders possess 63.9 percent of land under farming operation.

Availability of Essential Inputs

The pace of development of infrastructural facilities in agriculture in this part of the country is very slow (Table 3). Although area under HYV has increased from 5.2 lakh hectares in 1973-74 to 18.744 lakh hectares in 1988-89, but there does not seem proper management to ensure timely availability of essential agricultural inputs like quality seeds, fertilizers and plant protection chemicals etc. Fertilizer consumption per unit of gross cropped area ranges from 1.80 kg/ha in Nagaland to 30.70 kg/ha in Manipur against national average of 48.70 kg/ha in 1986-87.

Main causes for this relatively low consumption of chemical fertilizers *viz.* defective fertilizer distribution system due to short supply, inadequate transport, storage and credit facilities rising cost of fertilizers and adoption of primitive techniques of production *i.e.,* shifting cultivation in the hills.

Expansion of irrigation facilities was neglected in the earlier plan periods but got momentum after mid-sixties. As compared to the national average of 29.69 percent net irrigation area to net cultivated area, the region has 22.34 percent. The irrigation area varies from 11.79 percent in Tripura to 46.43 percent in Manipur. About 94.97 percent irrigated area was under food crops and rice alone accounted for 92.11 percent of gross irrigated cropped area while pulses account for 0.7 percent only.

Existing irrigation facilities in the region are mainly for utilising surface water fed by rains to partially supplement the requirement of water for the crop. The sources are generally rivers, rivulets, tanks and wells. Most of these irrigation schemes fall under minor irrigation and are not generally of permanent nature. In most

Table 3

BASIC DATA RELATING TO AGRICULTURE IN N.E. INDIA

State	*% of Net Irrigation Area to Net Cultivated Area*	*Average Size of Operational Holding (in ha 85-86)*	*Electrical Pumpsets ('000 no) 1986-87*	*Electricity Used in Agricultural Sector to Total Consumption (in percentage)*			*Villages Electrified (in %) 1986-1987*	*Fertilizer Consumption Per Unit of Gross Cropped Area (Rg per Hect) 1986-87*	*Area Under HYV (Lakh Hect) 1987-88*
				1970-71	*1980-81*	*1985-86(p)*			
1	*2*	*3*	*4*	*5*	*6*	*7*	*8*	*9*	*10*
Arunachal Pradesh	18.64	4.05	NA	—	—	—	33.2	NA	0.106
Assam	21.22	1.31	2.763	0.1	0.7	0.9	71.5	4.70	12.01
Manipur	46.43	1.24	0.029	—	8.5	3.0	37.6	30.70	0.980
Meghalaya	25.91	1.76	0.056	—	—	0.1	28.5	6.20	0.54
Mizoram	12.31	1.57	NA	—	—	—	28.7	NA	0.083
Nagaland	36.76	7.46	0.01	—	—	—	80.0	1.80	0.248
Tripura	11.79	1.02	0.961	0.3	8.3	15.9	46.0	18.20	1.77
N.E. India	22.34	1.61	3.819	NA	NA	NA	57.9	NA	15.737
All India	29.69	1.68	5649.105	10.2	17.6	19.1	71.6	48.70	512.263

N.A. = Not available.

of the states of the region there is no perennial irrigation facility whereby water resources can be conserved. Ground water resources in the region have generally remained untapped due to various impediments.

Rural electrification is considered to be another important factor for accelerating agricultural development. About 57.9 percent of villages in the region are electrified as against 71.6 percent for all India. But, hardly two percent of the total electricity generated in the north eastern region is used in agriculture and irrigation. Electricity used in agricultural sector to total consumption varies from 0.1 percent in Meghalaya to 15.9 percent in Tripura reflecting to a notable point of electricity consumption for agricultural purposes in plains of the region only.

Foodgrain Production and Self-Sufficiency

Rice being the major crop of this region is cultivated in widely varying situations from deep water (upto 5 metres) to upper ridges of the high hills in different periods of the year. Though there is an increase in area under rice cultivation in north-east by 25 percent during 1970-71 to 1985-86 but average yield has gone up by about 20 percent. Actually there is a negative growth in yield rate of rice in Nagaland and Mizoram during the period. Average yield of maize is high in Arunachal, Manipur and Meghalaya and hence is immense potentiality of this crop. Although potato is an important crop in Meghalaya but its average yield is not satisfactory. Jute is another important cash crop in Assam and Tripura.

About 3.72 percent of country's population lives in the north east but its share in total foodgrains production is 2.6 percent *i.e.*, 2.8 percent for cereals and 0.55 percent of pulses. According to an estimate the total requirement of cereals in 1989 was 5734 thousand tonnes and of pulses 267 thousand tonnes whereas production figures for the year show a shortage of more than 30 percent in case of cereals and of 74 percent for pulses of total requirements.

It is claimed that all the states have attained the level of self-sufficiency in the food-grains production but the deficit of 11 lakh tonnes of foodgrains in the region to be made up from the rest of the country in 1983-84 and an increase in this quantity onwards reflect either of the two possibilities: (1) large errors in actual production and estimated projected in the Annual Plans of the States: (2) hidden/transitory population and widespread smuggling of foodgrains (rice) to neighbouring countries of Bangladesh and Burma. Diversion of rice to manufacture indigenous alcohol by the tribals is not taken into account while estimating the foodgrains requirement in the region. This necessitates sincere efforts to produce additional 20 to 25 lakh tonnes of foodgrains especially rice, pulses and oilseeds.

Further, this is all the more important from view point of heavy transportation, storage and distribution charges incurred to maintain a balance between the actual demand and supply of foodgrains in the region. For achieving the goal of attaining self-sufficiency in foodgrains production a significant improvement in productivity and increase in cropping intensity are the only hopes along with the check on population growth.

Agriculture sector has also been showing signs of some diversification. There have been some noteworthy increase in the population of livestock. The production of milk has gone up to 7.33 thousand tonnes, eggs 5.54 lakh in numbers and fish 78 thousand tonnes in 1986-87 (p.). The respective share to the all India production remain 1.61 percent, 3.20 percent and 2.70 percent only much below the requirement asking for import of all these items including meat animals from other parts of the country.

Area under vegetables which stood at 10.79 thousand hectares in 1984-85 and the production touched to the level of 85.06 thousand tonnes. However, there is a dearth of vegetables in the plain areas particularly in monsoon season. Early varieties of vegetables can successfully be grown at higher altitude in hills and can be marketed in plain areas at an attractive price.

Problems

Specific problems of agriculture include: *(a)* problems of agro-climate such as acidic soil, high rainfall, humidity, very low temperature during winter and poor sunshine hours during monsoon, *(b)* wide variation in altitude, *(c)* inadequate infrastructural facilities like transport, communication, irrigation, supply and marketing net work, inaccessibility of interior areas, *(d)* dearth of adequate number of technically qualified personnel, *(e)* lack of appropriate technology and unavailability of proper training facilities, *(f)* socio-economic problems related to large number of ethnic groups, *(g)* community ownership of land, small size of operational holdings, *(h)* adverse ecological balance due to deforestation, *(i)* low cropping intensity, and *(j)* poor market intelligence, inadequate storage and sales promotion activities.

Shifting cultivation widely practised in the hills and losses caused by in the plains are two other main problems in the region. According to an estimate 2.47 lakh hectares of land is chronically flood prone in Assam alone. Besides damaging the standing crops, it has stood in the way of better utilisation of irrigation facilities.

The average farmer is still tradition-bound and the concept of local consumption-oriented agricultural operations are still prevalent over a wide area. Initiation of the average farmer to take to new and modern technique has, therefore, been lacking. The dearth of draught animals is another major problem for the farmers of this region. The cattle population in the region is non-descriptive and non-productive. Genetic improvement of local breeds of cattle needs immediate consideration.

Mechanization agriculture is badly needed in the region. So use of power tiller in this region may be encouraged and improved models of some existing farm implements such as mould board, plough, hoe etc. may be promoted further.

Future Course of Action: Some Suggestions

Cropping intensity increase is feasible if more irrigation potential is created in the region. Increase in area under irrigation will result in higher cropping intensity and better productivity. Intensive research work on economic usage of various inputs and updating of technology are also urgently called for.

Inter-cropping or mixed cropping will play a vital role in intensifying more production in the hill areas. Water harvesting through collection of run-off should be practised on a wider scale.

Human resource management needs more careful tending and evaluation before embarking upon a new model of planning. There is an urgent need to transform the technology from the laboratory to the farms. It is important to gear up the extension services to bridge the adoption gap through a suitable package of financial, technical, and supply measures.

The horticulture in the region be developed as an industry as has been the case for apples in Himachal Pradesh and Kashmir, mango in Uttar Pradesh, Maharashtra and Tamil Nadu, grapes in Hyderabad, banana in Maharashtra and vegetable seed industry in north Indian Hills. The full potential of fruit crops, and potato, turmeric, ginger and orchids has not yet been exploited fully. In order to bring the horticultural industry of the region on sound footing and to raise the economy of the farmers there is a need to adopt a multi-tier horticultural crop combination. Besides, an integrated approach of agri-horti-silvipastoral system may lead to achieve the goal which may include livestock as subsidiary source of income.

The marketing infrastructure in the form of better handling, storage, transportation and processing facilities is also a pre-requisite for increasing the production of all alternative enterprises including crops, vegetable, dairy, poultry and fishery.

CHAPTER 2

Nature of Agriculture in the Hills, Problems and Prospectives: Shifting to Permanent Cultivation

(With Special Reference to the Nocte and Wancho of Arunachal Pradesh)

❑ PARUL CHANDRA DUTTA

Introduction

The North-East India is the home land of a large number of people of different ethnic groups with both tribal and non-tribal identity. The indigenous people of different states in this region have their own tradition, socio-cultural heritage, religious faiths and beliefs, languages, customs and ways of life. The mainstay of the people of this vast area is agriculture. Nowadays, however, the people living in around the developing urban township areas in each of the seven states have endeavoured to take up to various other vocations for livelihood, such as jobs in government and other departments, Army, Police and Para Military Forces, business, contract work etc., and thus agriculture among these people has become a somewhat secondary occupation. But among the people living in the rural areas the mainstay of life is still continuing to be agriculture which forms the basis of their economy. Growth of population and low standard of living have prompted the younger generation to search for better avenues of earning money and as a result agriculture has become neglected. Due to shortage of manpower and want of technical knowhow and improved tools and implements the agriculture in the North-East and particularly in the hilly regions is still continuing in the same traditional way.

In the following pages an attempt has been made to focus the nature of agriculture in the hills of North-East India and to analyse the problems and prospectives of change from shifting to permanent cultivation.

Nature of Agriculture in the Hills

The land of the North-East India consists of hills and plains. The undulating nature of the topography of the area has compelled the inhabitants to adopt mainly two methods of agriculture, permanent and shifting, according to their suitability. The state of Assam comprises almost plain areas except two districts, the North Cachar and the Karbi Anglong which are hilly areas. In the plain areas of Assam permanent cultivation is the only method adopted by the people for agricultural operation; while in the hilly regions the nature of the land has forced the people to practise shifting cultivation by slash and burn method.

Similar is the case in respect of the states of Manipur and Tripura where shifting cultivation is practised by those people who live in the hilly regions while others dwelling in and around the plain areas, practise permanent cultivation, with the help of plough and bullock.

In Arunachal Pradesh, Nagaland, Meghalaya and Mizoram there is dearth of sufficient plain land suitable for permanent cultivation. Whatever plain land is available is far less than the requirement of the people for wholesome subsistence. Hence in these states shifting cultivation is mainly practised. In Meghalaya, however, terrace cultivation has found favour with the people and it is gradually replacing the traditional shifting cultivation. This process of transformation from shifting to terrace cultivation is working gradually in the state of Mizoram also and it is expected that in course of time the pristine method of agricultural operation will yield place to the new method which is slowly but firmly anchoring its roots in the soils of Mizoram.

In the states of Arunachal Pradesh and Nagaland shifting cultivation is still predominant. Although of late, permanent cultivation system in the areas where plain land is available has been introduced, yet it has not found favour with the people due to obvious reasons. Terrace system of cultivation has also been taken up in some areas of Arunachal Pradesh and Nagaland mainly for orchards. In the Monpa area of Tawang and West Kameng districts of Arunachal Pradesh potatoes are cultivated in terrace system and it has been taken up as one of the important crops for economic development of the people. Some of the tribes of Arunachal Pradesh, such as the Khamptis, the Singphos and the Apatanis practise permanent cultivation since sufficient plain land is available in their habitat. As a matter of fact it is the traditional system which they are following since time immemorial. The Adis of Siang, the Mishmis of Lohit and some other tribes have also taken up permanent cultivation, but have not given up jhum cultivation altogether. It is only because of the fact that sufficient land to depend entirely on permanent cultivation is not available.

In the permanent cultivation system tillage of the soil is generally done by plough except the Apatanis. The Monpas engage horses in ploughing. In shifting cultivation the tools and implements used are very simple and limited in number, Dao (broad bladed knife), spade, hoe, wooden digging stick and scrapper of either bamboo or iron are the only agricultural tools and implements. No tillage of land is done since seed sowing is done by making holes with digging sticks. The system is intimately entwined with the socio-cultural life of the people for which it is rather practically difficult for the people to do away with the system for adoption of other methods of cultivation.

In jhum cultivation many socio-religious activities are also involved which provides the people with some sort of amusements in their so called isolated life style. Every stage of operation in jhum cultivation is done after performing some socio-religious rites and ceremonies both individually and community-wise. These rites and ceremonies are the essence of the socio-religious and socio-cultural life of the people, which they are following since time immemorial. Adoption of a new method of cultivation will, therefore, not find much favour with the tradition bound people initially, but in course of time when the benefit derived from permanent cultivation becomes discernible to the people, then only complete avoidance of jhum system of cultivation may be possible. The most important aspect for introduction and advocation of permanent system of cultivation is availability of sufficient land suitable for permanent cultivation. Terracing system may not find much favour because of the very hard work involved in the process of terrace cutting. But once the people could visualise the benefit to be derived from terrace cultivation, it will then be quite easy to convince the people for adoption of the system.

With this back ground let us now examine the whole problem by citing examples from two very arduous jhum cultivating tribes of Arunachal Pradesh, namely the Wanchos and the Noctes of Tirap district.

Prior to the reorganisation by the present government of Arunachal Pradesh, Tirap district was inhabited by four tribes, Nocte, Wancho, Tangsa and Singpho. But after reorganisation it is now the homeland of only two tribes, the Nocte and the Wancho. During the days of the British administration both these two tribes found frequent mention in the Annual Administrative Reports of the British government. They were generally referred to as Eastern Nagas. The Ahom Kings also maintained friendly relations with these two hill tribes. The Ahom Kings called the Noctes by different names such as Borduworias, Paniduworias, Namsangias, Tupigongias etc., and the Wanchos—Bor Mithunias, Haru Mithunias, Bor Banchang, Haru Banchang and so on. The Wanchos came to prominence during the days of the British Government due to their involvement in the massacre of a Survey Party headed by Lt. Col. Holcomb in the outskirts of the present Nginu village, sometime in the year 1857.

The areas of habitation of the two tribes are clearly demarcated by a river called Tisa. To the west of this river and up to the eastern boundary of Nagaland live the Wanchos, while the Nocte area extends upto the western boundary of Tangsa area. The southern boundary of the entire area is marked by the Patkai hills and the northern by the districts of Tinsukia, Dibrugarh and Sibsagar of the state of Assam.

Both the tribes are basically agriculturist and it is the mainstay of their livelihood.

The entire area of their habitat is undulating with high and low hills. Towards the Patkai in the southern boundary the hills are considerably high and in some places the height crosses 5000 feet mark. There are a good number of streams and rivulets in the area. Naturally flat land is rarely visible. Under such situation there was no other alternative for the people then to adopt shifting cultivation by the method of jhumming. They have been practising this method of agriculture ever since their settlement in this area some hundreds of years ago. This system of cultivation has become a part and parcel of their life and culture. Most of the socio-cultural and religious rites and ceremonies performed and celebrated by the people have some connection with agriculture, because right from selection of a jhum plot up to harvesting and carrying home the crop for keeping in the granary—they perform some rites and celebrate the occasion and also observe taboos on occasion. Some of the rites and ceremonies assume the nature of major festivals which keep binding the entire community. Modern gadgets of amenity like radio, television, cinema hall etc. are matter of yesterday only. These amenities also do not reach the people in the far flung areas and hence can not give full satisfaction to the entire population. Under such situation the traditional festivals only provide enjoyment to the people, besides maintaining the tradition.

It is generally believed that in jhum cultivation the forest is denuded and soil erosion takes place causing great harm to the eco-system. But from my personal observation, particularly among the Noctes and Wanchos for more than thirty years since 1955. I did not see any serious soil erosion in the lands of the Noctes and Wanchos caused by jhum cultivation. Among these two tribes I observed that, while clearing a jhum plot the jungle of the topmost portion of the plot is not cut but left as it is, which helps in preservation of the soil. Moreover contour bunding is done by means of logs and stones so as to prevent erosion of the top soil by rain water. Thus, they preserve the soil by their own indigenous process. A jhum plot is cultivated for two years consecutively and then left fallow for a period varying from nine to ten years. During the fallow period the shrubs and the small plants which are left uncut here and there in the field grow sufficiently and the fertility of the soil increases. Each villages of the Nocte and Wancho has a number of jhum fields varying from nine to ten, and the jhum cycle also varies according to the number of the fields. Each jhum field has a name given either according to the nature of the soil or for its situation or for abundance of some particular variety of plant etc.

There are four types of land such as village land, agricultural land, jungle land and reserved forest land with three categories of ownership such as—land owned by individual, land owned by the clan and common village land. In absence of cadastral survey distribution of land among the individual families is done by the village council of elders. Among these two tribes also the number of agricultural worker is gradually thinning out because of dispersal of the young able bodied persons in search of other vocations for better economic condition. The agriculture is being carried out by the elderly persons only.

Shifting to Permanent Cultivation: Problems and Prospectives

It has already been discussed as to the circumstances under which the people living in the hill areas of North-East India have been compelled to undertake the shifting cultivation. Much endeavour will be necessary on the part of the agency advocating for the permanent system of cultivation. The people will have to be convinced about the advantage of permanent cultivation both in terms of operation and higher yield in comparison to the traditional method of shifting cultivation.

Secondly, availability of land suitable for permanent cultivation is another very important question for convincingly persuading the people to adopt the new system. Since large areas of plain land is not easily available, terrace cutting of the existing hill slopes will be required to be taught to the people. This will be a very tough job for the field workers. The people are not accustomed to terrace cutting which is evident from the way of construction of their dwelling houses. The Noctes and Wanchos, for example, do not level the land for construction of their houses. It is for this that the interior of the Wancho houses, particularly, are uneven and a new visitor to a Wancho house will find it difficult to move about freely inside the house. The Noctes build their houses on raised bamboo platform.

Another very important aspect of the changing process is either introduction of some new rites and ceremonies to be observed in the new method of cultivation or convincing the people to observe the same rites and ceremonies which they have been observing traditionally in jhum cultivation. After all, whatever method of cultivation is followed, the basic idea is to cultivate some crops and this idea must be brought home to the people.

The fact that the yield in the permanent cultivation is much higher than that in the jhum cultivation is another very important factor to convince the people for its adoption. After all the people are also generally interested to have enough crops to meet their requirement of food for the whole year.

Preparation of the seed bed, preparation of the land for transplantation of the seedlings, sowing of seeds etc. will be entirely new to the people and it may not be very easy to convince them for taking up the new method of cultivation involving all these operations. Much will depend on the capacity of the field workers of the concerned departments to persuade and convince the people. A band of very serious sincere and dedicate workers will be required for effective performance and desired result.

Harnessing of animal power for tillage with the help of plough will be a new item in the agricultural operation of the new method. As the people are not familiar with plough cultivation it may not be introduced in the beginning of the transformation process. More over it will also involve the problem of taking care of the plough animals to which most of the hill people are not accustomed.

Among the Noctes, the interest in wet rice cultivation was found to be growing, but lack of suitable land prevents the people from adopting this method in a serious way. The nature of the terrain does not permit a radical change from jhumming to permanent cultivation. So while introducing permanent cultivation the old method of jhumming has also to be allowed to continue simultaneously with some required improvement on scientific lines where necessary. The cultivable waste land in the Nocte and Wancho area is usually situated in the lower regions and utilization of such land for permanent cultivation depends upon several factors such as water supply, nearness to village and communication. Among some of the Wancho villages there is the belief that the low lying areas are the abode of some evil spirits and cultivation of such land will invoke the wrath of the spirits. Such belief has to be removed from the minds of the people before advocating for taking up cultivation in such low lying areas. The belief in the existence of spirits, malevolent or benevolent, is deep rooted and any endeavour to dispel such belief from the minds of the people will require very careful handling of the matter else the result may prove to be entirely negative.

Conclusion

From the discussion in the foregoing pages it is evident that transformation from the existing traditional system of jhum cultivation to permanent cultivation method in the hill areas of North-East India will involve lots of problems, such as, availability of land suitable for permanent cultivation, introduction of new technology, tools and implements, chemical manure and fertiliser, imparting of training in terrace cutting, persuading the people to give up jhum cultivation and so on. Since almost all the people living in the hill areas are generally tradition bound they will find it difficult to agree to do away with their age-old system of cultivation. There is also the deep rooted belief that there are some deities and spirits at whose good will the people have been able to raise the crops and have good harvest and as such they will not like to incur displeasure to the unseen supernatural beings connected with agriculture and invite any disaster. This will be a very delicate problem to handle with. These are some of the constraints for implementation of the process of transformation from shifting to permanent cultivation.

Even though the constraints are there, the picture, however, should not be taken as bleak as it appears. In view of the advantage and expected high yield from the permanent method of cultivation, it may not be entirely impossible to introduce the new method by overcoming the constraints discussed above. The basic and most important requirement for successful implementation of the scheme is persuation of the people and to convinced them for adoption of the new method and also some new crops. Persuation of the people to take up a new method of cultivation will also not be a very easy task. As has already been said earlier some tactful workers whom the people may take to their confidence easily would be required to entrust with this task.

Rice growing is traditional and hence introduction of some other variety of crops to replace rice may not be easily accepted, however, economically beneficial the other crops might be. Growing of pineapple, pears, apple and some citrus fruits may be introduced simultaneously as a subsidiary cultivation along with rice. In course of time, however, when the people themselves would find the benefit large scale horticultural gardens will automatically come up at the efforts of the people themselves. In Meghalaya, for example, large scale pineapple gardens owned by individual families are seen on both the sides of the Guwahati Shillong road and also in the interior areas of the state. Though the Khasis were rice growers earlier, but nowadays, seeing the economic advantage, they are giving more stress on the cultivation of pineapple, pears, plums, orange, bananas etc. Potato is a major crop of the Khasis nowadays. Khasi potatoes are sold in the markets outside Meghalaya also. Vegetable gardening has also been taken up by the Khasis seriously on commercial basis. In Arunachal Pradesh also, potato cultivation on commercial basis has been taken up by the Monpas. Orange growing is a specially of the Adis. Pineapple is also grown in large scale in the Basar area of West Siang district. Apple is grown in the higher altitude belt of Tawang, Kameng, Subansiri and Siang districts. In other hilly areas also it may not be entirely impossible to introduce some such economically beneficial crops among the jhum cultivators with a view to replace the shifting cultivation by permanent cultivation method in due course of time.

For introduction of new crops to replace rice cultivation by jhumming and also in the areas where sufficient land suitable for rice cultivation by permanent cultivation method is not available, soil testing is most essential for growing of the new crops proposed to be introduced. This is necessary because if due to some deficiency in the soil the new crops do not thrive or give poor yield, then the people will be reluctant to accept the crop. This is a prerequisite for propagation of the scheme. In this connection I would like to cite an example of my personal observation in an Adi village near Along, the headquarters of West Siang district. It was sometime in the year 1975-76 that I visited the Adi village situated some three to four kilometers away from Along. The people of that village planted a good number of areca nut plants at the instance of the V.L.W. (village level worker) of the village.

The plant grew alright but there was no fruiting. The villagers were very much disheartened. I brought some sample of soil and on getting it tested at the Areca Nut Research Centre at Guwahati it was found that due to some chemical deficiency the soil was not suitable for areca nut plantation. The remedy suggested by the Centre was conveyed to the villages but what happened afterwards was not known. This type of situation naturally have negative effect on the enthusiasm of the people. So it is highly essential that before introduction of any new variety of crop proper scientific analysis of soil and other required technical know-how should be provided so that peoples' efforts are not negativised by the failure or poor yield.

The success in the process of change from shifting to permanent cultivation will depend much on the efforts of the departments of the concerned government. There must be serious and sincere endeavour in this respect. It is hoped that a day will come when the so called devastating method of jhum cultivation will completely yield place to the permanent cultivation method.

CHAPTER 3

The Trend of Agrarian Structure and Its Impact on Agriculture in North-Eastern Hill Region of India

❑ B.D. NAYAK

Introduction

The economy of N.E. region is predominantly agrarian. Majority of the people of the region depend on agriculture and allied activities. The favourable climate for growth, the soil types, the water resources, the diversity of crops and germ plasm, etc. make the region endowed with rich potentials. Inspite of the problems such as the geographic isolation, the infrastructural deficiencies, socio-economic structures, there are vast potentialities for the development of agriculture in this region.

The agrarian structure and their changes are perhaps the most crucial issues in the discussion of agricultural development of the region. It is therefore, natural that the study of agrarian and social structure has acquired increasing popularity in recent past. This paper is an attempt to study some selected agrarian infrastructure, socio-economic factors and their relations with the peasant economy of the North-Eastern Hill Region.

The present study aims at analysing how far agrarian infrastructure and their changes have succeeded in accelerating the development of agriculture of the NEHR. It is based on secondary information and processed data.

Agrarian Structure of the Region

Agriculture, the purposeful use of soil for living, has evolved through a number of farming systems beginning with old and traditional process without tools and implements and has passed through fire agriculture *i.e.*, jhum, rudimentary plough culture, advanced plough culture to modern and scientific farming processes. Each of the systems of cultivation is associated with the definite form of land tenure system, social structure, topography, climate, etc.

The annual area under shifting cultivation in the region is about 3869 sq. kms. out of which the highest amount of area (900 sq. km.) and second highest amount of area (700 sq. km.) are under shifting cultivation in Manipur and Arunachal Pradesh respectively. About 31.5 percent families of the NEH region are practicing shifting cultivation, However, about 78% households in Nagaland, 62% families in Mizoram and 43.2% families in Arunachal Pradesh are engaged in jhum cultivation.

Agriculture as a Source of Employment

The percentage of total workers to total population in the region is 37.5. This percentage is highest in Mizoram (49.4%) followed by Arunachal Pradesh (47.5%) and Nagaland with 44.2% and it is lowest in Tripura being only 31.4%. The proportion of workers engaged in agricultural activities to total working class people of the region is 58%. This percentage is highest in Nagaland (68.6%) followed by Meghalaya (66%), Arunachal Pradesh (63%), Manipur (60%) respectively. But this proportion is less than that of the region in the states like Assam and Tripura which implies that most of the agricultural workers belong to tribal community in the tribal majority states like Nagaland, Meghalaya, Arunachal Pradesh and Manipur.

Infrastructure of the Region

The institutions concerned with rural development like banks, cooperative agencies, rural electrification, research and training in agriculture, marketing agencies, agricultural servicing centres are mainly linked up with the agricultural development. In addition to this some departments of State Governments and Central Government such as the department of Agriculture, Animal Husbandry, Fisheries, Soil Conservation, Forestry, Rural Development, the North-Eastern Council, Agricultural Universities have major programmes for development of agriculture.

The educational institutions concerned with the development of agriculture and allied sectors namely Assam Agricultural University, College of Agriculture in Nagaland, College of Agriculture, Imphal, Manipur have come up in the region. Besides these, Assam Agriculture University has started more colleges particularly in Agriculture, Veterinary and Fisheries. The Guwahati University is offering post-graduate courses in Bio-technology and applied Botany. The North-Eastern Hill University (NEHU), Shillong, in its School of Life Science offers course in ecology which is relevant to agriculture, the North-Eastern Regional Institute of Science and Technology (NERIST) in Arunachal Pradesh is offering Certificate, Diploma and Degree courses in Agricultural Engineering. The ICAR complex of N.E. hill region also has been conducting research on agriculture.

Land Use

The net area sown in the North-Eastern hills region has increased by 3.4% during the period from 1980-81 to 1988-89. The net area sown has increased by 53.6% in Arunachal Pradesh during the same period whereas in Nagaland and Tripura, the rate of increase is 17.6% and 9.8% respectively. However, the increase in net area sown is negligible in rest of the N.E. states.

In case of total cropped area, it has increased by 8%. In Arunachal Pradesh, Nagaland, Meghalaya and Tripura have experienced increases in cropped area at the rates of 52.6%. 20.7% 17.7% and 17.1% respectively and there is no change in cropped area in Mizoram whereas it has decreased by about 21% in Manipur.

The similar results are found with regard to area sown more than once. Area sown more than once has increased by 25% in the region. In case of Manipur, it has decreased and in Mizoram there is no change whereas it has increased at significantly higher rates in all other states of the region.

The net cultivated area has increased by 13.4 percent in the NEH region but it has increased by only 5.6% in the country. The inter-state comparison indicates that the highest rate of increased in net cultivated area in the reference period is 100 percent in Nagaland followed by Arunachal Pradesh and Meghalaya with 55.4 percent.

Irrigation

Irrigation is by and large a vital infrastructure for the development of agriculture. In absence of proper irrigation, double and multiple croppings are not always possible and use of fertilizer will have less effect in increasing land productivity. Thus, development of irrigation is an important objective of the government for promoting agricultural productivity of the region. The net irrigated area has increased marginally by 2% only in the N.E. region in comparison to 14% increase in India during the period from 1980-81 to 1988-89. The change in net area irrigated in all states other than Arunachal Pradesh and Tripura has not increased. The percentage change in net irrigated area to net cultivated area is also negative in all states excluding Tripura. The proportion of net irrigated area to net cultivated area has decreased by 10.2% from 22.5% in 1980-81 to 20.2% in 1988-89 in the N.E. region while it has increased by 7.5% from 28% to 20.1% in the country during the same period. The analysis shows the disappointing picture in improvement of irrigation in the region. The slow development in irrigation facilities are mainly the results of hazardous rainfalls, landslide, soil erosion and regular and frequent floods in almost all hill states as well as in plain states.

Credit Institutions of the Region

The institutions like commercial Banks, Regional Rural Banks, Co-operative Banks and Credit Co-operative Societies are the agencies providing agricultural finance. Unlike the rest of India, the contribution of agricultural credit agencies in the north eastern region is not only less but discouraging in general and the loan provided by co-operative institutions in particular is meagre and insignificant. We have therefore considered only the scheduled commercial banks and regional rural banks in the present study.

The number of branches of all these banks have increased by 62% from 1985 to 2066 in 1991 in the region whereas the rate of increase in bank branches in rural areas of the region is 70.3%. It is also observed the growth in rural branches is significantly high in the states like Mizoram (114.7%), Arunachal Pradesh (113.6%), Tripura (109.7%).

The C-D ratio (Credit-Deposit Ratio) has declined in all the north-eastern states excluding Arunachal Pradesh and Nagaland. The decreasing C-D ratio in the reference period is perhaps due to the slow growth in loan payment to the borrowers relative to the deposit growth rate. The positive C-D ratio in Arunachal Pradesh and Nagaland reflects the higher growth rate of bank advances for agriculture and allied purposes.

Fertilizer Consumption

The application of chemical fertilizers for increasing agricultural productivity is an essential input of modern agriculture. The volume of total fertilizer consumption and the per unit gross cropped area fertiliser consumption reflect the status of agriculture of a nation. The fertiliser consumption has increased from 17.05 thousand tonnes in 1980-81 to 65.53 thousand tonnes in 1990-91 in the N.E. region while the same has increased by 127 per cent in India from 5516.6 thousand tonnes to 12523.46 thousand tonnes in same time period. The annual fertiliser consumption has increased by 13 times, 11 times, 5 times, 4.5 times, 4.3 times and 4.2 times in Mizoram, Nagaland, Arunachal Pradesh, Manipur, Tripura and Assam respectively.

Development Trend of Major Crops in North-Eastern Hill Region

The impact of agricultural infrastructure on the trend of crop production in the region is discussed here.

(a) Rice Crop

The area under rice cultivation from 1980-81 to 1990-91 has increased in all N.E. states. The area under rice production has increased by 8.5 percent in N.E. region and by 6 percent in India. The increase is highest in Mizoram with 77% followed by Arunachal Pradesh with 46% and Nagaland with 25.4%.

It is further noticed that the use of land for rice crop has increased by 8.5 percent in the region as compared to the rate of increase 6.1 percent in the national level whereas the rate of increase in volume of rice output is 39.1 percent in the country in comparison to 28.4 percent increase in the region. All the N.E. states excluding Meghalaya have positive change in rice production. Mizoram, Nagaland and Arunachal Pradesh have got higher growth rates of 125.4%, 71.4% and 61.6% respectively which are substantially higher than the national growth rate of 39.1%. The output of rice in Meghalaya has decreased by 9.6% during the study period.

(b) Total Foodgrains

The area used for foodgrains cultivation (Rice, Wheat, Maize, Small Millets, Gram and Tur) in the N.E. region has increased by 8.7 percent from 3415.9 thousand hectares in 1980-81 to 3713.9 thousand hectares in 1990-91 whereas it has decreased by 1.3% in India. The area used for foodgrains has increased at substantially higher rates in the states namely Arunachal Pradesh, Assam, Mizoram and Nagaland on the other hand it has decreased marginally in rest of the North-Eastern states. The total foodgrains production during the study period had increased at higher rate (40.1%) in the region in comparison to country's growth rate (32.2%). In all N.E. states other than Meghalaya, the growth in production of foodgrains is positive and significantly high.

(c) Oil Seeds

Oil seeds are not only cash crop but also highly profitable crop and it needs less investment. The climatic condition and soil are extremely favourable for oil seeds cultivation in some parts of the region. The area under oil seeds crops in the region has increased by about 46 percent from 266.1 thousand hectares in 1980-81 to 388.7 thousand hectares in 1990-91 while this has increased by 36.4 in the country. However, the rates of increase in area for oil seeds crops is highest (511%) in Nagaland followed by Mizoram (205.6%), Arunachal Pradesh (146.5%), Tripura (102.8%), Assam (37.0%) and Meghalaya (12.7%) respectively but it has decreased by 44.7% in Manipur. The oil seeds output has increased at enormously higher rates in Nagaland with 1236.4%, Mizoram with 983.3%, Arunachal Pradesh with 219.4%, Tripura with 128.9%.

(d) Tea

Tea production is mostly concentrated in states like Assam and Tripura even though it has been extended to other hill states of the region namely Arunachal Pradesh, Manipur and Nagaland in recent years. As the data on the volume of tea output in Arunachal Pradesh, Manipur and Nagaland is not available the trend in growth of area under tea plantation and tea output of only Assam and Tripura are considered for present study.

The area under tea plantation during the period from 1971 to 1989 has increased by about 26% in Assam and by 20.4% in Tripura. The area under tea plantation in the N.E. region was 236.4 thousand hectares *i.e.*, 57 percent of the total tea producing area of the country (416.6 thousand hectares) in 1989. Similarly, the volume of tea production of the region was about 57% (385.2 thousand kilograms) of the national total tea output (688.1 thousand kilograms) in 1989.

Conclusion

The analysis shows that agricultural infrastructure has been expanded at a moderated pace. This has paved the way for agricultural growth in the region. Though the growth rate is found to be higher than that of the other parts of the country, this is mainly because the expansion started here from the narrow base. Still the facilities provided are not sufficient and it warrants further expansions of such facilities like irrigation, transport, marketing etc. The North-East Region hold greater agricultural potentialities.

CHAPTER 4

Agriculture and Related Activities: A Study of the Rangdani Rabhas of Meghalaya

❑ RANI HAZARIKA KAKATI

Introduction

In the foothills of Garo Hills in Meghalaya a large number of Rangdani Rabha villages are found along with the Garos, Pati Rabhas and other communities of the Bodo group whose traditional agricultural systems attracted the attention of the author of this paper. The Rangdani Rabhas are conservative in their ways of life and animistic in their religious beliefs and practices. But their Pati Rabha neighbours are mostly Hinduized and the Garo neighbours are Christianized in large numbers. The Rangdani Rabhas have their own dialect. They prefer to live in the foothills. Their villages are still homogeneous. They have excellent choice of selecting their village and agricultural sites. A few Rangdani Rabha villages in the Mendipather area namely Kachari Para and Harinkata which includes, New-Harinkata and Bakrapara hamlets in the East Garo Hills of Meghalaya were visited by the author from 25th November to 12th December 1994 for collecting data for this paper. These villages are under the Manikganj Mauza. The area is hilly all around with some plains area here and there with a narrow river named Tamrang. The Rangdani Rabha villages are well planned with independent big compounds for all the families. They plant trees like Teak (Sal), banana, coconut, betel nut, bamboo in their compounds. Trees are grown in such a manner that one can hardly notice the village huts. Agriculture is the main occupation of the Rangdani Rabhas. The main crop cultivated is paddy. In addition to paddy they cultivate mustard, gunji til, pulses etc. They follow their traditional agricultural methods. These activities are the result of the experiences of their forefathers enriched by well-knit village organization and close family ties. They are proud of their agricultural heritage. They use bullock plough, indigenous method of irrigation, local seeds, manure, local methods of controlling pests and storing of seeds. Their way of life reminds the way of the Amish[1] farmers in North America (The Amish are the best known for their non-conformed way of life. They are excellent farmers but refuse to use modern farm machinery) and the Kashmiri[2] farmers in the Himalayan foothills of Tehri Garhwal (A group of Kashmiris at Tehri Garhwal have started *Bij Bachao Andolon* to save their agricultural heritage. They believe that new hybrids cannot survive long without expensive chemical fertilizers and pesticides. They want to retain self-sufficiency without using modern technology).

Role of Village Council

In each Rangdani Rabha village there is a headman (locally known as *Gaonburah*) who is selected for a period of five years by the village council comprising the elderly males of the village. All the internal and external matters of the village are decided by the headman. He can call a meeting of all the village elderly male members (village council) whenever he feels it necessary. Certain rules and regulations are laid down by the headman in consultation with the village council for maintaining law and order with the village during agricultural season. These are noted below:

(i) An adult male member is appointed to look after the internal matters including the damage of crop by domestic animals within the village. This man is called *Lekhakari.*

(ii) Domestic animals like cattle, pig, hen etc. should be kept inside the compound of each family from the beginning of planting to the end of harvesting paddy.

(iii) Owners can send their cattle to the common grazing ground with the herdsmen.

(iv) If anybody finds a cow or goat grazing outside without herdsmen then he/she can inform the *lekhakari.*

(v) If somebody's field is damaged by a cow then the person can inform *lekhakari,* or

(vi) The owner of the field can directly go to the person whose cattle damaged his crops three times and then inform the *lekhakari.*

Lekhakari has the power to take immediate action or he can keep the records of the crimes throughout the year and submit the records in the village council meeting at the end of the year. The village council is held every year in the month of Magh *i.e.,* in the first part of January. In this annual meeting a new *lekhakari* is appointed for the next year. It may be the same person if the village council found him dutiful or a new person may be appointed for a year. Every member of the village council must be present in this annual meeting. *Lekhakari* submits his report and the fine he realised in one year. The members of the village council listen and discuss everything in details. Punishment is awarded if not already punished by the *lekhakari.* Punishment is called *danda* in their dialect. *Danda* is imposed on the following irregularities.

(a) If somebody allows his domestic animals to move freely during harvesting time then the fine (danda) is imposed on them at the rate of one rupee per day for each cow.

(b) Those who do not take care of their cattle even after warning face heavy *danda.*

(c) The village council issues order to an erring owner to handover one of his cattle to the village council. The animal is slaughtered in the presence of all the members and its carcas is thrown away. This is done to frighten the villagers so that nobody dare to repeat such act in future.

Appointment of Herdsmen

Two body are appointed as herdsmen by the headman in consultation with the village council to look after the cattle for the whole village. Their duty is to collect the cattle from every house early in the morning and to drive them to the common grazing ground. At noon herdsmen keep them in a closed space (bathan) made by bamboo fencing near the village and have their meal. After taking few minutes rest they take the cattle out again to the field. Herdsmen may allow them to graze near the paddy fields but keep the eyes on them so that they do not damage paddy. Cows are allowed to move freely on the paddy fields where harvesting is over. In the evening at about 5 p.m. herdsmen drive the cattle home and return the same to their owners. These herdsmen are appointed for a period of two years under the following conditions:

(1) Two boys are selected as herdsmen by the headman at the village council meeting for a term of two years. After the expiry of the term two new boys are appointed in a similar manner. If the villagers found the former boys trust-worthy then they may reappoint them for the next term.

(2) As all the villagers are very busy during the agricultural work, herdsmen are appointed from a neighbouring village. They may be appointed from the Garo community also who lives nearby.

(3) Herdsmen are each paid 20 maunds (1 maund = 40 kg.) of paddy for a year and served a free meal daily.

(4) When any one of the herdsmen is sick the village council arranges a boy from within the Rangdani Rabha village to look after the herds temporarily. That boy receive free meal from the villagers for the working days.

(5) If any cow is lost for the carelessness of these herdsmen they will have to work for another term without payment. But such a situation normally does not occur.

Provision of Agricultural Labourers

Here a unique system of engaging agricultural labourer is prevalent. A person employed by a landowner for this purpose is known as *Bhagi* in this locality. A *bhagi* is generally engaged on a short term basis especially covering the harvesting period. *Bhagi* receives payment in kind and also free food and shelter during the working period. He lives like a family member in the land-owner's house and enjoys equal facilities and social privileges. *Bhagis* are generally from the same village and also from the same community. But an outsider of the same community *i.e.,* from a distant village may also be engaged for this purpose. They are treated as assistants rather than as servants by the land-owners. There is also a long-term provision for keeping a *bhagi*. When there is no male member in the family or a temporary shortage of male members, a *bhagi* may be appointed. A widow may engage a *bhagi* for the entire agricultural season. The *bhagi* and the owner of land in that case, get equal share of paddy at the end of the season.

For a short period *i.e.*, 22 to 30 days' work the *bhagi* receives 4 maunds of paddy. The measurement is made with a bamboo basket called *dun*. One *dun* is equal to 5 kg. of paddy. The *bhagi* gets 32 *dun* of paddy after the completion of his work. If the *bhagi* is ill than the owner looks after him and manages his work with somebody's help but at the end *bhagi* will get the equal share even though he could not perform his job, during illness.

The general rule is that when there is lack of working male member in the household a *bhagi* is engaged who can do ploughing and other hard works in the field. Again, if a farmer is not having a pair of bullocks he may engage a *bhagi* who will bring his own pair of bullocks and work throughout the whole agricultural cycle and receive half of the yield at the end. A *bhagi* in such a situation may stay in his own house in the village and work in his own field side by side.

Use of Fertilizer

The Rangdani Rabhas believe that their land is fertile and possess all the qualities for good crops and therefore no need to apply chemical fertilizer. Paddy fields are situated at the low levels of the foothills. During rainy season, rain water washes the hills and brings with it red soil and other rotten leaves, grass etc. to the paddy fields which make them fertile. Sometimes, the streams are diverted to the fields by diging small shallow drains. This is the best way to make the fields fertile. They also use decomposed cowdung as manure. Manure is abundantly used in other crops as compared to paddy. Besides cowdung, the stubble along with wild grass are mixed with the soil at the time of ploughing which make the soil more fertile. The Rangdani Rabhas believe that single cropping maintains the soil fertility.

Control of Pests

No chemical pesticides are used by the Rangdani Rabhas of East Garo Hills. They worship several deities connected with these harmful animals, insects, rats or other enemies of the crop. To get rid of the evil effects, evil eyes and wrath of deities certain annual *pujas* are performed by these people. In addition to these rituals, the Rangdani Rabhas sprinkle ashes in the paddy fields to drive away cornfly, grasshopper etc. They also catch a large number of grasshoppers as this is a delicious food item of the Rangdani Rabhas. To drive away birds a bamboo instrument is used by these people which is locally known *taklok*. It is a long piece of bamboo splited at one end. The manipulator holds it by the handle in one end and strikes the splitted end in the palm of the other hand and thereby makes big sounds to drive away small birds and monkeys. Sometimes earthern balls are thrown to frighten monkeys.

Storing of Paddy

Paddy is stored in the granary which is locally called *Bhandar*. After harvesting is completed paddy bundles are brought to respective houses and placed in the corner of the courtyard. The courtyard is smeared with a mixture of cowdung, paddy husks and water. Thrashing is done with the help of 2 to 4 pairs of bullocks. After separating paddy from the straw, it is dried in the sun for few hours and then kept in the *bhandar*. *Bhandar* is a separate house made on a platform raised 1½ feet to 2 feet above ground level. Posts are made of wood and the platform is also made by using flat wood or bamboo splits. Walls are made of bamboo splits woven very tightly without any window. There is only one small door. Roof is made of thatch of C.O.I. Sheet. The floor and walls are smeared with mud-cowdung mixture before storing paddy. Grains of different varieties are kept separately inside the granary. Sometimes big bamboo baskets are placed inside the granary or bamboo or wooden walls are made for keeping different varieties of paddy.

Apart from individual granaries, the villagers set cooperative granaries where from they can borrow paddy at the time of need. There are three types of such cooperative granaries—Male Old party, Male Young party and Ladies party. These granaries are called *Mai-Bhandar*. After thrashing is completed at the beginning of the year eleven (11) old male members start the co-operative by depositing 1 maund of rice from each member. The *Mai-Bhandar* is constructed in one of the member's house. All the members help in the construction by offering free labour. The rules of borrowing paddy are that the borrower must pay half a maund of paddy as interest for each maund borrowed. The time period after which one can return the borrowed paddy is fixed by the borrower considering his future situation. Mortgage is also taken in terms of ornaments, utensils or land. But the borrower can use his mortgaged things during the whole period. The young boys co-operative is formed by 12 boys by depositing two maunds of paddy. The Ladies party also deposits paddy in the same manner but the amount of paddy is half a maund. In the Ladies Co-operative all the interested ladies without any age bar can join. The governing rules are the same in all these cooperatives. The male members organize lotteries when they have enough money which is acquired by selling paddy. But the ladies party do not organize any lottery, they buy and distribute yarn among the members for weaving their own dress.

Every family takes utmost care for preservation of seeds for the next year which is known as *bidhan.* Before thrashing is done, the best bundles of paddy are kept separately after sorting. These bundles are thrashed separately, dried up and then kept in a specially made bamboo basket called *topa.* Some long, thin and flat bamboo splits are placed criss-crossed in a round basket open at both ends. Paddy straw is spread over these bamboo splits thickly and over it paddy seeds are kept. The opening is then tightly closed with cane or bamboo splits. Each *topa* contains 20 kg. of seeds. These are piled one after another to touch the roof of the living house or kept inside the *bhandar* in one corner.

Rites and Rituals Connected with Agriculture

Performance of rites and rituals along with the agricultural activities is a must among the Rangdani Rabhas. All the villagers perform certain rituals specially for good harvest. The Rangdani Rabhas believe that whatever they get from the soil is due to the blessings of the Goddess, whom they call *Ma-Baikho. Ma-Baikho* has created the earth so it is the first duty to propitiate the Mother to get good yield. Two rituals-Hasong and Tura are performed annually to get her blessings.

Hasong is performed on a fixed day of the month of Jeth every year in which six deities are worshipped. These are: (1) Budaba, (2) Lakshmi, (3) Hasong, (4) Baikho, (5) Hacho, and (6) Rakshi Barjoada. In each village there is a priest (deuri) who only can perform *Hasong* ritual. Objects need for this ritual are five chickens, one pig, some banana leaves, earthern lamps and mustard oil. A special *dao* is required for sacrificing these animals before the deities. The place of the worship is situated at the southern side of the village. Only the male members of the village take part in this ritual. The deuri takes bath before the puja, then utters some spells. After lighting the earthen lamps he sacrifices these chickens and the pig with the *dao* and after that the sacrificed chickens and the pig are distributed among the villagers.

Tura is performed in the month of Kartik (between October and November). It is performed to protect the paddy from rodents pests and other enemies of the crop. There are seven deities worshipped in *Tura,* namely (1) Budaba, (2) Lakshmi, (3) Tura, (4) Ringaba, (5) Achu-Koncho, (6) Langa, and (7) Khusuri. The deuri sacrifies a hen and a pig by facing west or south. Out of these seven deities the first three are female and the rest are male. Ringaba is maternal uncle of Tura. Achu koncho is the deity living in the rocks of the hills. Langa is the God of elephants. It is worshipped by sacrificing two chickens, one she-goat or a pig to protect paddy from the elephants. Khusuri is worshipped by sacrificing a hen so that it protects the crop from evil eyes. Only Budaba puja is performed individually by the owner of the field whose paddy is destroyed by the rodents. When one notices the burrow of rat in the paddy field, the person performs Budaba puja by sacrificing a pair of chickens outside his house.

After the completion of harvesting paddy all the villagers perform some rituals by offering their new products to *Lakhar than.* Before that nobody can utilize his or her newly harvested paddy. There is a permanent house for worship. After completion of harvesting all the villagers offer half a maund of paddy to the village *deuri* who prepares this paddy for the puja. The things needed for this puja are: husked rice, banana, banana leaves, betel nuts and leaves, jaggery earthen lamps and mustard oil. This is called *nakhoa* and is usually performed after 9th Aghun (between November-December). All the male members come to the *Lakhar than* and take bath in a nearby pond to perform the puja. They cannot change their wet clothes during the whole period. There is an earthern altar where a lamp is lighted and offerings are placed. Thirteen deities are offered puja. These are (1) Dharam, (2) Garia, (3) Lakhar, (4) Headzamadar, (5) Saru zamadar, (6) chototuli, (7) Najarani, (8) Sonarai, (9) Ruparai, (10) Kalarai, (11) Bhangara, (12) Bura lakhar, and (13) Kaccha Thakur. Drums are beaten throughout the puja by a villager. The deuri utters some spell and offers prasad which is a mixture of wet rice and jaggery. These are placed in 13 banana leaves separately with banana, betel nut and leaf in the name of the above mentioned thirteen deities. The remaining part of the *prasad* is distributed among the villagers which they eat in the place of worship. The remaining things are taken back home. After the *Nokhoa* is over people can use their new paddy for domestic consumption.

Conclusion

The Rangdani Rabhas are very much close to their natural habitat. Agriculture is their main occupation. They strictly follow their age old methods of ploughing, sowing, transplanting, watering, manuring, harvesting and storing. Experience has taught them to rely on their own seeds, own labourers (*bhagi* system), own animals and locally made implements which lead towards self-sufficiency. Meghalaya Government is trying to introduce modern technology but these villagers are yet very reluctant to use it. Their fear is that once modern technology is introduced new training will be necessary and application of chemical fertilizer may change the quality of soil. They have developed a sense of complete reliance on their traditional methods. They also depend on supernatural powers. Their dependence on family members and village headman, internal arrangement of herdsmen and labourers, strict rules maintained by the village council help them to become successful farmers. All the village people irrespective of age and sex combine their efforts to the smooth functioning of the agricultural activities.

References

1. Carlisle, Richard. (ed.) 1984.: Amish, *The Illustrated Encyclopedia of Mankind,* Vol. 1, Marshall Cavendish Limited, New York.
2. Wright, Gillian, 1995.: The seeds of a Movement, *The Telegraph.*

CHAPTER 5

Agriculture in Arunachal Pradesh: Trends and Problems of Objective Assessment

❑ GURUDAS DAS

This paper has been written primarily to exhibit the agricultural trends in Arunachal in eighties. Arunachal Pradesh has a land mass of 83,743 sq. km. Out of the total area the broad and narrow valleys constitute about 35% each, the foothills and the plain areas cover about 10% and the snow clad peaks cover about 20%.[1]

The whole area may be classified into four belts from altitudinal point of view, *viz.*,

(i) Foot hills below 3000 ft.

(ii) Middle belt ranging between 3000-6000 ft.

(iii) High hills ranging between 6000-11000 ft.

(iv) Pastoral land and snow clad peaks beyond 1100 ft.[2]

There is no land use/land cover map of Arunachal. No exhaus–tive survey, either ground-based or remote-sensing, is undertaken in this state to assess the pattern of land use or land cover. In many cases, inference is made about the land use pattern on the basis of crude estimation of land cover. Though, there is no denying, in some cases such inference may reasonably work, but conceptually, land use and land cover—these two differ a lot. And for a society where man-nature relationship is so closed, as in Arunachal, it is more difficult to ascertain the land-use pattern on the basis of estimation on land cover. While land cover simply implies the physical nature of the land surface, *e.g.*, plain land, hilly area, river bed, forest covered land, crops covered land, snow clad land etc., which can be identified by both ground-based and remote-sensing surveys, the land use in an area, on the other hand, is a function of a number of socio-economic, political, habitual, physical and cultural parameters.[3] The same plot of land is being used by the local tribes for different purposes overtime. For example, the practise of shifting cultivation among the tribes of Arunachal requires the destruction of forest land for agricultural use. Immediately after harvesting, the same plot is converted into grazing field. After two or three consecutive years of agricultural operation, the plot is kept fallow, and in many cases, tribal groups utilize this fallow land for temporary house-site, otherwise it is left for natural regeneration. Therefore, in such cases, land cover data may explain the time-specific physical nature of land, but may not shed much light to explain the land-use pattern of the area. However, due to paucity of data, we have no option but to take land cover as an approximation to land-use.

Land in Arunachal is mainly used for two purposes, *viz.*, forest and agriculture. According to the estimation of the State Forest Department, about 62 percent of the total geographical area (51540 sq. km. out of 83,743 sq. km.) is covered with forests. The area under regular management including reserved, protected and village forests appears to constitute only about 23 percent of the total forest area. However, here we shall concentrate only on the second largest category of land-use, *i.e.*, agriculture.

Agricultural Land-Use

Though the State Agriculture Department has estimated the area under the agricultural operation being about 5% of the total geographical area of the State,[4] the 1980-81 Agricultural Census has found the total land under various land-use category being about 4%, *i.e.*, 3,35,732 hectare, of the total land surface of the State. Two distinctly different agricultural practises, *viz.*, jhum or shifting cultivation and permanent or settled cultivation, are found in the state. While the former has evolved in the long immemorial past in response to the unhospitable nature of the hilly terrain and is practised almost universally by the local tribes, the latter is, though not completely unknown to a few tribal communities like Apa Tanis,

Khamtis and the Singphos, comparatively a recent phenomenon that makes its way along with the increasing interaction of the isolation tribal communities of the territory with the outer world, penetration of the modern administration and so on. Presently, jhuming, which is thought to be uneconomic and undesirable for ecological factors, is increasingly being replaced by permanent or terrace cultivation and a large share of state aid is being directed towards this end. However, no reliable data appears to be available regarding practice-specific area of cultivation. Different study teams, individual academicians, administrators—those who worked on this frontier state—all had to depend on estimation in absence of any land records or cadstral survey.[5] National Council of Applied Economic Research (NCAER) believed that the reasonable estimates about the area under settled cultivation would be 9,486 hectares and about 246 thousand hectares for shifting cultivation. While the former is reached on the basis of village-wise information collected during 1961 Census Operation, the latter is deduced on the basis of 1961 Census Population (about 3 lakhs) and assuming per head 0.80 hectare of jhum land requirement. Assuming a eight-year jhum cycle and taking the fact into account that annual area under jhum is constituted of the fresh area brought in a particular year plus the jhum area of preceding year—the annual area under jhum is worked out at 61,500 hectares.[6]

This population of area under shifting cultivation by NCAER seems not to be absolutely absurd while compared to the estimation of the same by North-Eastern Council (NEC) in 1974. Based on the information on the total area owned by different villages practising jhuming, NEC has inferred the area under shifting cultivation in Arunachal being about 248 thousand hectare and annual area under it being 92 thousand hectares.[7] The NEC figures, in many cases, are accepted at their face-value by the academic circle. Even the National Commission on Agriculture (NCA) has taken it almost granted.[8] But Misra has rightly questioned the reliability of NEC estimates.[9] He pointed out that according to NEC estimates, given the total and annual area under shifting cultivation, the jhum cycle is reduced to two or three years which implies that shifting cultivation has lost its essence and is converging to settle cultivation. This phenomenon cannot be explained considering the vast area and relatively small population size of the state. From the factual point of view, Misra's apprehension is proved to be true by the study conducted by the Law Research Institute (LRI), eastern circle, in 1983. LRI, in course of their study, on the land system of North-Eastern Region, sponsored by NEC in order to assist the respective state governments to formulate land laws, on the basis of field data, has found the length of the jhum cycle among the different jhumia tribes. The least duration is found among the Hill Miris 5 to 6 years and the highest among the Mishmis, 15 years. The Nishis maintain a 6 to 7 years cycle, among Noctes it is 10 to 12 years and 12 to 15 years among the Adis.[10] Again the concerned state government department has claimed the annual area under shifting cultivation during 1978-79 at 101,330 hectares and the command area is about 4,20,770 hectares, *i.e.,* 5 percent of the total surface area of the state.[11] But this figure for annual area is not supported by the data published in the Statistical Handbook of the same year where it is accounted to 92 thousand hectares.[12] Thus there exists a data gap which requires serious attention on behalf of the state administration for the formulation of meaningful planning for development. Even the Directorate of Agriculture, while conducting the Agricultural Census 1980-81, does not take the difficulty to reach at some reasonable estimate on this issue. The observation, made by Misra long 15 years before, appears to be quite relevant. To quote: "There are so many other estimates that it is difficult to judge which of them is correct, in the absence of knowledge as to how they were arrived at they are often-times as good as useless."[13]

According to 1980-81 Agricultural Census, the total operated area under agriculture is estimated at 3,35,732 hectares. The conventional land-use classification is shown in the following table for 1976-77 and 1980-81 in order to have a comparative judgement.

In Table 1, the percentage rise in area under current fallow, other uncultivated land excluding fallow land and culturable waste land are in conformity with the significant percentage increase in net area sown in 1980-81 over 1976-77. The probable reasons behind such a significant decrease in the area under fallow other than current fallow in 1980-81 may be due to the combined effect of extension of irrigation facilities, a massive shift from shifting to settle cultivation, reduction of the jhum cycle to less than 5 years and so on. The available informations are, no doubt, too scanty for a reasonable conjecture of this change within such a short span of

Table 1

AREA UNDER DIFFERENT LAND-USE IN 1976-77 AND 1980-81 AND ITS PERCENTAGE TO TOTAL

Sl.No.	*Categories*	*1976-77*		*1980-81*	
		Area (in hect.)	*% to total*	*Area (in hect.)*	*% to total*
1.	Net Area Sown	1,11,914	28.30	1,18,232	35.22
2.	Area under Current fallow	24,765	6.26	23,127	6.89
3.	Fallow other than current fallow	1,05,230	26.61	57,253	17.05
4.	Other uncultivated land excluding fallow land	49,850	12.60	34,888	10.39
5.	Culturable waste land	84,540	21.37	47,595	14.18
6.	Area not available for cultivation	19,226	4.86	54,637	16.27
	Total	3,95,525	100	3,35,732	100

Source: Report on Agricultural Census 1980-81, Directorate of Agriculture, A.P., p. 30.

time. What is important is the underlying trend that the unutilised culturable lands are increasingly being brought under use. The high percentage increase of the area not available for cultivation in 1980-81 is explained by the extension of porter track, farm building and rising of rocky land due to the continuous wash out of top soil by rain, wind etc. This phenomenon appears to be a sufficient indicator to alarm the policy makers.

Apart from forest and agriculture, land in Arunachal is also used for grazing, settlement, urban development etc. Water bodies like stream, river, etc. are used for fishing and other purposes. Nearby forest areas are used by the villagers for hunting, shooting and food gathering. Many of these uses have overlapping area and it is very difficult to generate classified land-use data for such a variety of uses.

Land Development Since Independence

Since independence, the administration has undertaken the programmes of land development in order to achieve a number of goals, *e.g.*,

(i) to reduce the imports of food-grains in this food deficit land-locked territory and to achieve self-sufficiency;

(ii) to stabilise the local jhumias who were then led nomadic life which is the precondition for any development work in this territory;

(iii) to progressively substitute the jhum cultivation, which is thought to be subsistence in nature and detrimental to ecology, by settled cultivation.

(iv) to protect the rich natural forests from the destructive method of slash and burn followed by the local tribals in course of preparation of their jhum land.

Land development in Arunachal involves a huge cost due to the difficult physiographic conditions of the State. NCAER study estimated the cost of per hectare terrace building with the help of tractors at Rs. 1,700 and Rs. 3000 without using tractors.[14] Considering this cost factor and time duration necessary for building per hectare of terrace land and the socio-economic conditions of the local tribal popular, provision of State aid has been made to accelerate the task. The extent of State subsidy varies with the variation of slope and nature of land.[15] Total land developed through aids during the last three decades can be estimated from Table 2.

Table 2

LAND DEVELOPMENT UNDER PERMANENT CULTIVATION

Decades	*Area in Hectares*
1951-61	6398.00
1961-71	4529.00
1971-81	24664.51
Total	35599.51

Source : Constructed from

(i) Barthakur's compilation in "Swidden to Sedentary Cultivation", p. 9.

(ii) Statistical Handbook of A.P. 1972-73, 1978-82.

(iii) Compilation by M.C. Joshi in "Shifting Cultivation in Arunachal Pradesh," reproduced in S.D. Jha's "The Wealth of Arunachal Pradesh," p. 222.

It is to be noted that the figures, in table 2, released by the agriculture department, Arunachal Pradesh, are based on the volume of aids that have been offered for land development, not on the basis of physical verification. Moreover, in some cases where lands have been developed once for permanent cultivation are seen to have reverted again to jhum cultivation in later years. A study of a Hill Miri Village, Kicho, which was regrouped in 1974, reveals the fact that once the villagers have started WRC having subsidies from the administration but later due to the lack of irrigation facilities they have reverted again to their traditional jhum cultivation except one villager who has, somehow, managed water from a nearby spring.[16] However, no attempt has been made to estimate the area developed independently under individual effort of the local people in the State. In spite of all these lacunas, land development programmes appear to have, to some extent, successfully penetrated into the traditional tribal groups of Arunachal. Descriptive studies indicate that most of the jhumia communities have adopted WRC/TRC to the extent permissible by their socio-economic and topographic conditions and have switched over to permanent cultivation. A *prima facie* impression can be drawn about the achievement of various land development programmes from Table 3.

Table 3

NET AREA SOWN UNDER PERMANENT AND JHUM CULTIVATION*

Decades	*Net Area Sown in Hectare Under*		
	Permanent	*Jhum*	*Total*
1970-71	28,006 (26.36%)	78,220 (73.64%)	106,226 (100%)
1980-81	52,012 (43.71%)	66,979 (56.29%)	1,18,991 (100%)

Source: Constructed from unnumbered table in the Report on Agricultural Census 1980-81, A.P., p. 9.

Note: Area brought under permanent cultivation during 1973-74 is not available and hence is excluded. Land development includes both Terrace Rice Cultivation (TRC) and Wet Rice Cultivation (WRC) lands. Land Development data since 1983 are not published in Government annual publications due to some unknown reasons.

The reliability of the figures presented in table 3 is not out of question. There are so many estimates, as has pointed out earlier, that it is very much difficult to establish any consistency among them. However, the trend, that the jhuming is increasingly being replaced by settled cultivation, can be understood from these figures which gets support of a number of micro studies done recently on Arunachal.

The degree of adoption of settled cultivation depends on a number of socio-economic and cultural parameters on the one hand and the availability of suitable culturable land on the other. Due to the spatial and inter-tribal variation of these parameters, the degree of adoption also varies among the different tribes of Arunachal. The Adis have shown much interest and enthusiasm in switching over to settled cultivation. Large areas in East and West Siang districts, the land of the Adis, have been brought under permanent cultivation. Apart from the Adis, the Mishmis also have undertaken settled cultivation extensively in the available low land areas under their possession. A tribe-wise account of the proportion of jhum and settled cultivation to total cultivated area is not recorded. Nonetheless, the available information indicate that the Nishis, Wanchos and Sherdukpens have also adopted WRC/TRC to some significant extent. While the Noctes, Tagins, Tangsas Hill Miris, Sulungs, Akas, Khowas and Mijis have joined in this effort marginally.

Cropping Pattern

Mono-cropping is, by and large, the usual phenomenon in settled cultivated lands in Arunachal. Kharif is the main harvesting season when all the important crops, *e.g.*, paddy, maize, millet and wheat are grown all over the territory. In course of shifting cultivation different kinds of vegetables are also grown along with main crops. Though the extent of agricultural activities vary from place to place depending upon the nature and availability of cultivable land and other infrastructural facilities, spatially the cropping pattern remains more or less the same. In some cases, the relative importance of the main crops only varies but that too also not very significant. Important crops of each of the district, arranged in descending order according to the area under each crop, are listed in Table 4.

Table 4

DISTRICT-WISE CROPPING PATTERN IN ARUNACHAL (WITH REFERENCE TO 80'S)*

Sl. No.	*District*	*Major Crops*	*Minor Crops*
1	*2*	*3*	*4*
1.	Tawang	Barley, Wheat, Paddy, Millet, Maize, Potato.	Soyabean, Buck Wheat, Ginger, Chillies.
2.	West Kameng	Maize, Buckwheat, Millet, Paddy, Potato, Pulses, Wheat.	Cabbage, Rajma, Barley, Soyabean, Sweet Potato, Chillies, Ginger, Garlic, Mustard, Groundnut, Cauliflower, Radish.
3.	East Kameng	Paddy, Millet, Maize, Fruits, Vegetables, Pulses, Mustard.	Wheat, Potato, Ginger, Sesamum, Groundnut, Chillies, Sugarcane,
4.	Upper Subansiri	Paddy, Maize, Millet.	Barley, Pulses, Oilseeds, Spices.
5.	Lower Subansiri	Paddy, Maize, Millet, Pulses, Potato.	Ginger, Chillies, Turmeric.
6.	West Siang	Paddy, Maize, Millet, Potato, Sugarcane.	Vegetables, Wheat, Oilseeds, Pulses, Ginger, Chillies, Turmeric.
7.	East Siang	Paddy, Maize, Mustard, Millet, Aram, Wheat, Potato.	Ginger, Soyabean, Blackgram, Jobstear, Chillies.
8.	Dibang Valley	Paddy, Maize, Mustard, Millet, Fruit, Potato.	Wheat, Buckwheat, Pulses, Sugarcane, Chillies, Ginger.
9.	Lohit	Paddy, Oilseeds, Maize, Fruits, Groundnut, Vegetables, Pulses.	Millet, Wheat, Potato, Sugarcane Ginger, Garlic, Turmeric.

(cont.)

1	*2*	*3*	*4*
10.	Changlang	Paddy, Millet, Maize.	Chillies, Ginger, Potato.
11.	Tirap	Rice, Millet, Maize, Tapioca.	Wheat, Blackgram, Sugarcane, Chillies, Ginger, Garlic, Mustard, Sesamum, Groundnut, Potato, Kotchu, Soyabean.

Source: Constructed from District Statistical Handbooks of all the districts, 1984-85 to 1988-89.

**Note:* A new District, *viz.*, Papum Pare, has been curved out from Lower Subansiri district in 1922 and hence the number of district in Arunachal has gone up to twelve.

Paddy is the principal crop and is cultivated all over the tract since long historical past. Similarly, Maize and Millet are produced as traditional substitutes by the different tribes of Arunachal. Production of fruits like apple, pine-apple, orange, plum etc., and vegetables like potato, cabbage, cauliflower etc., are appeared to have been introduced in the recent past in this territory. In fact the practice of horticulture is being encouraged by the administration from the late 70s. Since then it has been emphasized due to agro-climatic and ecological factors. A national model for agricultural development in the hills has been framed on the basis of the experiences gained mainly from Himachal Pradesh and U.P. Hills and research activities conducted by Indian Council of Agricultural Research (ICAR). A three-tier vegetation has been suggested by the agricultural scientists, *i.e.,* cultivation of field crops upto 20 to 30 degree gradients, tree crops from 30 to 50 degree slopes and beyond that forest should be maintained. This hierarchical vegetational model is believed to be mutually sustainable and economically viable in the hilly region and the administration appears to have been pursuing such a model, like elsewhere, in Arunachal.

Sectoral Linkage Between Agriculture & Industry

This section involves a few general observations regarding the role of agriculture in economic growth and industrial development as well as their specific condition in reference to Arunachal's agriculture.

In an economy, regional or national, agriculture is, in most cases, the prime mover of initial growth. It contributes to the general process of economic development by releasing resources to other sectors, *e.g.*, food and raw materials, labour, capital, etc. The sequencial development of industrial society has started its journey based on the raw materials from agriculture, *i.e.*, agro-based industries.

The dynamics of initial growth process lies in the interdependence of these two principal sectors, *viz.*, agriculture and industry, of an economy. The dependence of industrial sector on agriculture has been stated in the preceding para, the similar input-output relation also holds good in case of dependence of agriculture on industry. The former has to employ the products of the latter as inputs to produce its output. This sectoral input-output linkage reinforces each other for further production and thereby accelerates the growth process.[17]

Now the relevant question that requires a close scrutiny is: What is the nature of this sectoral interdependence in Arunachal. How far it is possible to exploit this inter-sectoral dynamics for the future path of development of this territory. The answers will be more impressionistic than factual due to the insufficiency of reliable facts and statistics.

Characteristics of Agriculture in Arunachal

(i) *Primitive methods of cultivation:* Dominance of jhum cultivation precludes any use of animal or machine energy, irrigation, chemical fertilizer, etc. Even in case of settled cultivation, cultivators, in most cases, do not use ploughs and animals.

(ii) *Non-commercial mode of production:* Productions in agriculture in general and field crop productions in particular are mainly carried out on the basis of household requirement. Fragmented local market appears to have negligible influence on agricultural sector.

(iii) *Traditional cropping pattern:* This point is elucidated in section-iv and hence requires no further mention.

(iv) *Low rate of yield:* Low productivity in agriculture can be evidenced by the average yield rate of some important crops

during 1987-88. The average yield rate of rice, maize, wheat, millet, sugarcane and potato in this state is accounted to 1.13, 1.17, 1.48, 0.54, 19.16 and 8.59 tonnes per hectare respectively.[18]

(v) *Lower use of modern inputs, e.g., fertilizers, pesticides, and agricultural implements:* During 1987-88, a total of only 202 tonnes of chemical (nitrogenous, Phosphatic and potassic) fertilisers were applied all over the state.

Though in some areas surplus production was experienced, as among the Apa Tanis and Khamptis, but from aggregative view, the state suffers from food deficit. Moreover, despite the vast surface water sources, due to under-development of irrigational facilities, the agricultural sector is heavily affected by the seasonal factors. Frequent occurrences of climatic hazards, *e.g.*, floods, landslides, etc., also adversely affect the agricultural sector. All these have led to a fluctuating annual level of production which in turn acts as disincentive for the development of agro-based industries. Except some processing enterprise, *e.g.*, rice mill, oil mill, flour mill, etc., which are operated mainly at household level, no important agro-based enterprise has yet come up in the state.

So far the use of inputs are concerned, the village artisans generally supply the tools and implements to the cultivators. In some cases, the cultivators themselves make their tools. The tools generally used are iron hoe, dao, sickle, axe, plough, spade, jumper, shovel, crowbar etc. Since independence, state administration is also, in their effort to develop agriculture, supplying tools and equipments along with HYV seeds, fertilisers, pests at a subsidised rate in a limited scale. The use of improved seeds, fertilisers and equipments are mainly limited to the government firms which are organised for the purpose of demonstration and research. Demand for the modern inputs is not at all encouraging.

Thus, underdeveloped agriculture stands as stumbling block before the emergence of the set of industries that use the agricultural raw material as well as that produce agricultural inputs. Again the absence of suitable agricultural implements conducive to local agricultural practices, at reasonable price, lack of proper improvisation as to how benefits of scientific and technological innovations can be induced to such an underdeveloped agriculture, lack of market incentive, etc. allow the backwardness to perpetuate in the agricultural sector.

During last two decades, administration has emphasized on the development of horticulture. The congenial agro-climatic conditions, availability of horticultural land, and above all market incentives for such products have worked behind the quick adoption and extension of horticultural farming. Already a few food-processing industries have come up to utilize the surplus products. Thus, the inter-sectoral dynamics has set off though at a low ebb in the local economy.

The inter-sectoral interaction at present is too low to bring about any structural change in the near future and the underlying socio-economic processes do not indicate that it will be able to generate forces strong enough for the transformation of the traditional structural also in the remote future. Processing industries based on horticultural raw materials can only flourish along with the rapid pace of urbanisation and urban culture. As most of the horticultural products are perishable, the location of industries which use them as raw materials are area specific. The pace of urbanisation in the state as well as in the North-East Region is not encouraging for large-scale production. Though at the national level food-processing industries are growing spectacularly, the limited market facilities for the products of this region in general and Arunachal in particular may outweigh the resource oriented choice for location. However, extension and exploitation of horticulture along with forest resources may bring a substantial change in the subsistence agricultural sector in the long run and can accelerate the process of growth bringing the present impasse to an end.

References

1. Agricultural Census 1980-81, Directorate of Agriculture, Arunachal Pradesh, p. 4.
2. *Ibid.*
3. A.S. Mather, Land Use, 1986, Longman House, London, pp. 23, 99.
4. Highlights of Agricultural Development and Research Needs in Arunachal Pradesh, 1984, Directorate of Agriculture, p. 2.
5. I.K. Barthakur, Swidden to Sedentary Cultivation, 1975, Census of India—1971, part Miscellaneous (a), pp. 4-10.
6. National Council of Applied Economic Research (NCAER), Techno-Economic Survey of NEFA, 1967, New Delhi, pp. 20-22.

7. North-Eastern Council (NEC), Shifting Cultivation in North-Eastern Region, n.d., Shillong, pp. 2-3.
8. The Report of National Commission on Agriculture, Part-IX, 1976, p. 148.
9. B.P. Mishra, "A Positive Approach to the problem of Shifting Cultivation in Eastern India and a few suggestions to the policy makers," in Shifting Cultivation in North-East India, North-East India Council for Social Science Research, 1980, Shillong.
10. Law Research Institute (LRI), Eastern Region, A study of the Land System of North Eastern Region, Vol-II, Arunachal Pradesh, 1983, Gauhati, pp. 35, 67, 102, 150, 189.
11. *Ibid.,* p. 223.
12. Statistical Handbook of Arunachal Pradesh, 1978-79, Directorate of Economics and Statistics, Govt. of Arunachal Pradesh, p. 99.
13. B.P. Misra, *op.cit.,* p. 115.
14. NCAER, *op.cit.,* p. 24.
15. I.K. Barthakur, *op.cit.,* p. 7, noted the different rates offered during the early 70's as follows:

	TRC	*WRC*
(a) For Border/undeveloped areas and thickly jungle areas.	Rs. 600	Rs. 400
(b) For partially developed areas/middle belt area/moderate jungle and hard ground areas.	Rs. 450	Rs. 300
(c) For developed areas/lower base line areas/less jungle and soft areas.	Rs. 300	Rs. 300

16. LRI, *op.cit.,* p. 70.
17. Food and Agriculture Organisation of the United Nations (FAO), Agriculture and Industrialisation, Basic Study No. 17, 1967, Rome, p. 10.
18. Statistical Abstract of Arunachal Pradesh—1988, Directorate of Economics & Statistics, Govt. of Arunachal Pradesh, p. 25.

CHAPTER 6

Agricultural Productivity in Arunachal Pradesh

❑ N.C. ROY

Agriculture in Arunachal Pradesh experienced a boost with the launch of first five year plan in 1951-52. Prior to that, the traditional agriculture of this state which was based mainly on jhum cultivation generated hardly any significant growth. Since Jhum cultivation is low productive and lends little scope for application of modern inputs, the plan strategy saw in the extension of permanent cultivation, the possibility of modernizing agriculture (NEFA, General Administration Department). But in the way of such extension stood the topographical hurdles, the hurdles presented by the jhum fields on steeply-sloped hills which appeared incapable of being terraced for permanent cultivation. Given such topographical limitations to permanent cultivation, the alternative to jhumming was found in horticulture. Thus, orcharding on high lands and intensification of cultivation on foothills and valleys along with poultry-keeping, pisciculture and animal husbandry came to hold the promise of generating a sustained growth of agricultural income.

Agriculture in the initial plans received a moderate allocation of funds; however, the amount of allocation was raised in subsequent plans (Government of Arunachal Pradesh 1994a). Thus, from a total allocation of just Rs. 30.76 lakh in the first five year plan, the allocation to agriculture rose to Rs. 41.76 crore in the seventh five year plan. By 1992-93 the cumulative plan expenditure on agriculture amounted to Rs. 124.13 crore at 1992-93 prices. The expenditure by the Government went to build up both the physical and institutional infrastructural facilities, and to induct innovations.

New crops were introduced, chemical fertilizers were distributed gratis or at a nominal prices. An institute for training village level workers (VLWs) was established in Pasighat. The trained VLWs were assigned the role of acting as the agents of change in the agricultural sector; they were to provide various extension services to the cultivators and disseminate information as regards better seeds, chemical fertilizers and improved methods of farming.

Arunachal agriculture seems to have responded well to the various policy-incentives. Thus, by 1993-94, high yielding varieties of rice, wheat and maize came to occupy 30.64 percent of area under these crops. (Government of Arunachal Pradesh, 1994b). The consumption of fertilizers and irrigation facilities, however, did not increase significantly. During 1993-94, the consumption of different types of chemical fertilizers amounted to only 575 tonnes and the net area irrigated constituted only 2 percent of total net area sown in the State. The largest gain achieved by Arunachal agriculture has been in the realm of new crops, mainly horticultural crops. By 1993-94, the area under horticultural crops amounted to 24 thousand hectares and their production was around 51 thousand tonnes.

Agriculture in this state seems to have started growing in the fifties. However, no reliable time-series data exists for the first two decades of planning. In the absence of such data it is impossible within my present effort—to construct a growth-profile of Arunachal agriculture for the last four decades. So I confine my analysis mainly to the seventies and eighties.

The overall growth of agriculture during the past 25 years ending in 1994-95 is around 7 percent per annum. Period-wise, the growth in the seventies amounted to 6.39 percent and in the next 15 years to 7.83 percent per annum. The estimated growth rates are shown in table 1. The population in the state grew in the seventies and eighties at 3.01 and 3.14 percent per annum respectively.

If it is assumed that the growth of population in the agricultural sector was the same as that of the total population in the state, then per capita agricultural growth in the seventies amounted to 3.38 percent and in the eighties to 4.69 percent per annum. Thus over the last 25 years the per capita income in agriculture has grown almost at the rate of 4 percent per annum and this rate can be taken to be an approximate measure of the growth of average productivity of labour in agriculture.

Table 1

AGRICULTURAL GROWTH IN ARUNACHAL PRADESH

Period	*Estimated Equations*	R^2
1970-71—1979-80	logy = 6.61 + 0.0639 t	0.94
1980-81—1994-95	logy = 8.16 + 0.0783 t	0.96

N.B.—y in table 1 is net value added in agriculture at constant prices and t is time in years. Data Source: Government of Arunachal Pradesh (1995).

It would now be quite germane to shed some light on the factors which have brought about such a high growth of agriculture in this state. This can be done by considering the production function,

$$y = f(K, L, N, T) \quad \ldots\ldots\ldots\ldots\ldots\ldots \quad (1)$$

Where Y = production in agriculture

K = capital

L = land under cultivation

N = labour

T = technology.

Since in Arunachal Pradesh two types of agricultural practice—jhum and sedentary—coexist with highly differential use of inputs, the production function (1) cannot represent both. While in sedentary cultivation, all the inputs are important so that the function (1) can be expected to represent such an agricultural practice well; but in jhum cultivation capital and technology are not important. For jhum cultivation, the appropriate function would be

$$yj = fj(Lj, Nj) \quad \ldots\ldots\ldots\ldots\ldots \quad (2)$$

j in (2) refers to jhum and all other symbols have meaning as in (1). The problem with a separate production function is that for jhum cultivation no separate data on production and acreage exist. In the absence of such data, one is forced to carry out the aggregative analysis.

In Arunachal Pradesh, all inputs, L, K, N and T have grown over the last several decades and the fastest growth has been experienced by land, especially land under permanent cultivation. The growth of net area sown, the area under permanent and jhum cultivation is estimated in the following equations:

$$\text{Log LT} = 11.553 + 0.0217\,t \quad \text{.........}\ (3)$$
$$R^2 = 0.84$$
$$\text{Log LS} = 10.204 + 0.0647\,t \quad \text{.........}\ (4)$$
$$R^2 = 0.99$$
$$\text{Log LJ} = 11.285 - 0.0072\,t \quad \text{.........}\ (5)$$
$$R^2 = 0.28$$

Where LT = total net area sown

LS = area under permanent cultivation

LJ = area under jhumming

t = time in years.

No. of observations in all these equations in 5, with each observation relating to a census year from 1970-71 to 1990-91. One very startling fact emerges from the above equations: a high rare of growth of net area sown under sedentary cultivation, the yearly average growth rate being 6.47 percent. This rate of expansion of area under permanent cultivation almost approximates the rate at which agriculture has grown over the last two decades. So, the expansion of agricultural production seems to have been caused mainly by the extension of permanent cultivation of new areas. Such a possibility is strengthened by the fact that the overall productivity of land has not increased much, and this has happened because of the rather high fall in productivity of land under jhum cultivation. No doubt the productivity of land under permanent cultivation has increased—though the amount of increase may not be high—yet the gradual fall in jhum yield has been so high that the expansion of area under permanent cultivation with a higher productivity has not succeeded in raising significantly the overall productivity of land. The insignificant growth of productivity of land under the important crops such as rice, millet, maize and wheat amply demonstrates this. In fact, the average yield of land under rice, the main agricultural crop in Arunachal Pradesh does not show any increase at all during the period from 1970-71 to 1992-93.

The insignificant increase of average productivity of land indicates that the growth of labour, capital and technology has not caused intensification of cultivation, rather it has resulted in the permanent cultivation being extended to the new areas. Thus, the induction of new technology and capital, and migration of labour from outside the State have, instead of raising the productivity of land, enhanced the total production of land. In the process, of course, the productivity of labour has increased. So, the relation between area under cultivation and labour, capital and technology can be set as

$$L = h\ (N, K, T) \ \ldots\ldots\ldots\ (6)$$

Since T is mainly embodied in K, we can write the relation as

$$L = g\ (N, K) \ \ldots\ldots\ldots\ (7)$$

To conclude, Arunachal Pradesh has, in recent decades, experienced the process of gradual modernization of her agriculture; relative importance of jhumming has declined. The overall growth of agriculture is quite high and this growth has been caused mainly by the extension of permanent cultivation. Of course the expansion of permanent cultivation has been made possible by the induction of new technology, subsidized provision of capital and migration of labour from outside the State.

References

1. Government of Arunachal Pradesh (1994 a): *Arunachal Agriculture in Brief.*
2. __________ (1941): *Economic Review of Arunachal Pradesh.*
3. __________ (1995): State Domestic Product of Arunachal Pradesh.
4. North-East Frontier Agency, General Administration Department. Different Annual Reports.

CHAPTER 7

Agriculture in Arunachal Pradesh

❑ SHIPRA S. NAYAK

Arunachal Pradesh is agriculturally dominant with a large number of people depending on it. Therefore, agriculture development of the state assumes a greater significance. Various efforts have been made by the state government to develop agriculture but still agriculture development is slow and much less in comparison to some of the other states of the north-eastern region.

In this paper, an attempt has been made to study agricultural development of Arunachal Pradesh in 90s. This study is based on secondary data. The sources of information are the government publications. The data related to the agricultural indicators of the district for the year 93-94 has been compared with the 90-91 data. The agricultural performances of all the districts have been measured by assigning ranks to the districts in the ascending order. Spearesman's rank correlation method has been used to find out the relationship in between some of the agricultural indicators. The agricultural characteristics discussed in the present paper are as follows—

1. Area under rice, wheat, millet, maize and pulses crop.
2. Production of rice, wheat, millet, maize and pulses crop.
3. Consumption of fertiliser.
4. Irrigation intensity.
5. Cropping intensity.
6. Total livestocks.
7. No. of villages provided with water supply.

Consumption of Fertiliser

Table 1 shows that the largest amount of fertiliser has been consumed in the Tawang district in 90-91 and 93-94. Lower Subansiri district consumed the least doses of fertiliser in 90-91 but the position of the district in relation to consumption of fertiliser improved in 93-94. It is interesting to note that undivided Lower Subansiri district consumed least doses of fertiliser but its position improved when it was broken up and the new Papum Pare district was formed. There has been a fall in the consumption of fertiliser in the upper Subansiri and Dibang Valley districts in 93-94. A rise in the doses of fertiliser consumption has been noticed in the East Siang and Changlang districts in 93-94 in comparison to 90-91. The amount of fertiliser consumption in other districts remained same in both the years under study.

Irrigation Intensity*

In the year 90-91 West Siang, Lohit, East Kameng and East Siang districts had high irrigation intensity. Changlang, Tawang, Upper Subansiri and Lower Subansiri districts had medium irrigation intensity and Dibang Valley, Tirap, West Kameng districts had low irrigation intensity whereas in the year 93-94, irrigation intensity seems to be high in the West Siang, Tawang, Lohit and East Siang districts. It was moderated in the Tirap, West Kameng, Lower Subansiri and Changlang districts, and low in the East Kameng, Dibang Valley and Upper Subansiri districts.

Cropping Intensity

It has been observed in Table 1 that Tawang, Dibang Valley, Lohit and West Kameng districts had high cropping intensity. East Siang, West Siang and Changlang districts had moderate whereas Upper Subansiri, East Kameng, Lower Subansiri and Tirap districts had low cropping intensity. The ranking position of the districts indicates that there is no variation in the degree of intensity of cropping in the districts in 93-94 in comparison to 90-91.

---

* Districts having ranks from 1 to 4 have been classified as districts having high irrigation intensity and districts having ranks from 5 to 8 have been classified as districts having medium irrigation intensity while districts ranked from 9 to 12 have been categorised as districts having low irrigation intensity.

Table 1

RANK DISTRIBUTION OF AGRICULTURAL INDICATORS IN THE DISTRICTS OF ARUNACHAL PRADESH

Sl.No. Districts	*Rice*		*Wheat*		*Millet*		*Maize*		*Pulses*		*Fertiliser consumption*		*Irrigation intensity*		*Cropping intensity*	
	90-91	*93-94*	*90-91*	*93-94*	*90-91*	*93-94*	*90-91*	*93-94*	*90-91*	*93-94*	*90-91*	*93-94*	*90-91*	*93-94*	*90-91*	*93-94*
1	*2*	*3*	*4*	*5*	*6*	*7*	*8*	*9*	*10*	*11*	*12*	*13*	*14*	*15*	*16*	*17*
1. Tawang	11	12	1	1	6	6	10	11	11	11	1	1	6	2	1	1
2. West Kameng	10	11	2	2	5	5	5	3	4	4	2	2	11	6	4	4
3. East Kameng	7	7	8	8	11	11	8	9	6	5	5	5	3	9	9	8
4. Lower Subansiri	1	1	9	10	7	10	2	4	8	9	11	9	8	7	11	11
5. Upper Subansiri	9	10	10	11	10	8	11	12	10	10	9	11	7	11	8	9
6. West Siang	2	2	7	7	3	3	6	6	5	6	7	7	1	1	6	6
7. East Siang	3	3	3	3	1	1	4	5	2	2	4	3	4	4	5	5
8. Dibang Valley	6	6	4	5	8	9	3	2	9	8	6	10	9	10	2	2
9. Lohit	5	5	6	6	9	7	1	1	1	1	3	4	2	3	3	3
10. Tirap	8	9	11	9	2	2	7	7	7	7	8	8	10	5	10	10
11. Changlang	4	4	5	4	4	4	9	8	3	3	10	6	5	8	7	7
12. Papumpare	—	8	—	12	—	12	—	10	—	12	—	12	—	—	—	—

Impact of Fertiliser Consumption on the Area Under Rice, Wheat, Millet, Maize and Pulses

The correlation coefficient figures for the year 90-91 and 93-94 in Table 2 indicate that the high doses of fertiliser consumption had less impact on the area under rice crop in 93-94 (r = 0.148) in comparison to 90-91 figure (r = 0.543) in the districts of Arunachal Pradesh. But there seems to be a very high correlations between fertiliser consumption and area under wheat crop in 90-91 (r = 0.702). This further increased in 93-94 (r = 0.785). There has been

Table 2

CORRELATION COEFFICIENTS OF MAJOR FOOD PRODUCTS IN A.P.

1. Impact of fertiliser consumption on area under

	Foodgrains	*1990-91*	*1993-94*
(a)	Rice	r = 0.543	r = 0.148
(b)	Wheat	r = 0.702	r = 0.785
(c)	Millet	r = 0.011	r = 0.425
(d)	Maize	r = 0.072	r = 0.234
(e)	Pulses	r = 0.152	r = 0.485

2. Impact of Irrigation Intensity on area under

(a)	Rice	r = 0.455	r = 0.175
(b)	Wheat	r = 0.104	r = 0.545
(c)	Millet	r = 0.082	r = 0.683
(d)	Maize	r = 0.018	r = 0.264
(e)	Pulses	r = 0.473	r = 0.386

3. Impact of fertilisers consumption on cropping intensity

(a)	r = 0.725	r = 0.563

4. Impact of Irrigation Intensity on cropping intensity

(a)	r = 0.086	r = 0.470

a positive but very low increase in the area under millet crop (r = 0.425), maize (r = 0.234) and pulses crop (r = 0.485) with the increase in the consumption of fertiliser in 93-94 as against 90-91 figures.

Impact of Fertiliser Consumption on Cropping Intensity

The correlation in between fertiliser consumption and cropping intensity was high (r = 0.725) in 90-91 but it became less in 93-94 (r = 0.563). The impact of irrigation intensity on cropping intensity is shown in Table 2 as with the increase in the intensity of irrigation, the cropping intensity increased (r = 0.470) in the districts of Arunachal Pradesh 93-94 as against the increase (r = 0.086) in 90-91.

The correlation coefficient figures in Table 2 indicates that the impact of irrigation intensity on area under rice crop became less (r = 0.175) in 93-94 in comparison to 90-91 figure (r = 0.455). However, with the increase in irrigation intensity, area under wheat crop increased in 93-94 (r = 0.104) . Intensive irrigation had negative impact (r = 0.082) on area under millet crop in 90-91. But a positive correlation was found between irrigation intensity and area under millet cultivation (r = 0.683) in 93-94. The correlation between irrigation intensity and area under maize and pulses cultivation seems to be positive but low in both the study periods while the correlation figure in between irrigation intensity and area under maize cultivation in the year 93-94 was (r = 0.264) little higher in comparison to 90-91 figure (r = 0.018). But the correlation between irrigation intensity and pulses cultivation became much lower in 93-94 (r = 0.386) in comparison to the 90-91 figure (r = 0.473).

This variation in the correlation between irrigation intensity and area under the crops in the year 90-91 and 93-94 may be due to a change in the cropping pattern in addition to the fact that there is a decline in the net area irrigated in the state during the study period as shown in Table 3.

Percentage Change in Some of the Indicators

Table 3 indicates percentage change in some of the agricultural indicators of the state during the study period. Such as the area under the total foodgrain cultivation have declined by 51.95% from

90-91 to 93-94. But on the contrary production has increased. This explains that the area under the food crops declined must have been diverted for the cultivation of some other crops and increased production may be due to the high dose of fertilizer consumption. In addition it has been studied that the total cropped area of the state has also increased.

Table 3

PERCENTAGE CHANGE IN AGRICULTURAL INDICATORS IN 1990-91 AND 93-94

Sl. No.	*Items*	*Percentage charge*
1.	Area in Hectare	-51.95
2.	Production in M.T.	1.62
3.	Total cropping Area	0.06
4.	Cropping Intensity	—
5.	Net Area Irrigated	-5.64
6.	Irrigation Intensity	—
7.	No. of villages provided with water supply	16.60
8.	Fertiliser consumption in M.T.	30.09
9.	Fair price shop in No.	10.57*
10.	Net State Domestic Product at F.C. by industry of origin at constant price	128.8**
11.	Total Livestock in No.	16.50***

Note: * Year 93-94 over 91-92.
** Year 89-90 over 80-81.
*** Year 88-89 over 78-79.

The net irrigation area of the state decreased by 5.6% and the irrigation intensity has also declined. But the number of villages provided with water supply increased in the state by 16.60%. Decline in the net are irrigation is either due to transfer of irrigated land for the use of some other non-agricultural purposes or the most probable reason is destruction of the irrigation sources by floods and landslides. Fertiliser consumption of the state has increased. There is a 10.57% increase in the number of fair price shops in the state. Besides, it is also observed that the total livestock population of the state has increased by 16.50% during the year from 1978-79 to 1988-89. This is an important indication for it will increase the supply of meat and manure in addition to the draught capacity and transport facility of the state.

Conclusion

It may be concluded that in some districts the area under rice, wheat, millet, maize and pulses crop has increased and in some it has decreased while in other districts it has remained the same during the study period. But the figures for the state with regard to rice and maize indicates that area under rice and maize has declined in 93-94 as against 90-91.

Similar is the case with regards to fertiliser consumption, irrigation intensity and cropping intensity in the districts of the state.

The correlation between fertiliser consumption and area under wheat cultivation is high in the districts of the state. The relation with the other crops is positive but the increase is very slow. Impact of fertiliser consumption on area under rive cultivation became less in 93-94.

With the increase in fertiliser consumption cropping intensity declined in the districts of the state in 93-94 as against 90-91. But it increased with the increased in irrigation intensity. Impact of irrigation intensity an area under rice and pulses became less in 93-94 as against 90-91 but it has increased on area under wheat, millet and maize in the study period.

The total area under foodgrains declined in the state but production has increased. The total cropped area has also increased. The net irrigated area of the state has decreased but the number of villages provided with water supply has increased.

About 31 percent increase in fertiliser consumption has been noticed in the state. The livestock population of the state has also increased.

On the basis of above analysis made in this paper it can be concluded that the agriculture of the state has made some progress in certain aspects. But the progress is very less. Much more effort has to be diverted towards agricultural development.

References

1. Borthakur, Dhirendra Nath: Agriculture of the N.E. Region.

2. Gurjar, R.K.: Irrigation for Agricultural Modernization.
3. Kourtsoyiannis, A.: Theory of Econometrics.
4. Sarkar, S.: Agricultural Development of Madhya Pradesh.
5. Directorate of Economics & Statistics, Govt. of Arunachal Pradesh: Statistical Abstruct of A.P. 1989, 1991, 1992, 1993 & 1994.
6. Estimates of State Domestic Product of Arunachal Pradesh 1970-90.
7. North-East Council, Shillong: Basic Statistics of North-Eastern Region, 1985.

CHAPTER 8

Chemical Fertiliser Vs. Organic Manure : Problems and Prospects in Arunachal Pradesh

❑ SANJUKTA DAS
❑ PRASANTA SAIKIA

Maintenance and improvement of the fertility of the soil is probably the main concern of the people attached to agriculture. More and more doses of chemical fertilisers, pesticides, insecticides are used for this, particularly in the modern farming. The main purpose is to reap maximum output immediately. In modern society the farmer is considered simply as a producer, who must enhance his productivity and efficiency, cutting his cost by every possible device, "even if he thereby destroys the fertility of the soil." He considers land as a factor of production which should be used efficiently. However, in case of Arunachal Pradesh, the situation is much different.

The eastern most state with a predominantly tribal population is still far away from this profit motive. The people here live as part of the Nature, observing all its laws and rules. Here they think of maintaining the natural fertility of the soil. All of them use organic manures to fertilise the soil. Sometimes they leave the soil fallow to regain its fertility. A few of them use chemical fertilisers, pesticides etc. Their traditional belief influences them to live in harmony with the Nature, and not to over exploit it to satisfy their greed.

A field study was conducted in Doimukh Block in the district of Papumpare to collect information on the relative importance of different types of fertilisers used by tribal peasants to maintain and improve the productivity of soil. In this district gross cropped area is 8445 hectares and the land under permanent cultivation in 7400 hectares (87.6 percent) in 1993-94. Because of the Government encouragement, more and more lands are being brought under permanent cultivation. Food grain is the main crop and its production was 5108 tonne in 1994. Peasants in the area studied use organic manures as fertiliser. However, recently some changes in the outlook and attitude of the people have been noticed. Some of them have started using chemical fertiliser. The official data show some area under the use of chemical fertiliser.

Four villages Midpu, Nonpu, Emchi and Doimukh were selected by purposive sampling. From these four villages 15 households were selected by simple random sampling for interview, the sample unit being the individual farmer household. Data were collected from the heads of the households, with the help of structured questionnaire.

Findings

It was found that all of the sample households were doing permanent cultivation although 20 percent of them were simultaneously practising jhum cultivation.

All of them are producing food grains. Only a few of them were doing cash crop cultivation side by side. Only adequate rainfall is necessary to maintain the stability in output at a high level. About 40 percent of the interviewees believed, perhaps ignorantly, that fertility depends mainly on rainfall. Uncertainty and fluctuation in rainfall causes fluctuation in output. High fertility of the soil is mainly due to the comparatively less use/exploitation of the soil. This is again mainly due to the low density of population and thereby low food demand. Besides, the soil component and the existance of different nutrience in it also indicate the high fertility. There is not much need of the injection of more and more doses of chemical fertilisers like phosphorous, nitrozen etc., to maintain the soil fertility.

However, they are using all the available resources to maintain fertility of the soil. The cultivators leave the stubble in the fields to get decomposed in soil. However, some of them have started using chemical fertilisers. But their number is few. The following table represents the different crops produced and the use of various fertilisers by different respondents. It is found that all the respondents are producing rice but only about 80 percent of them are producing vegetables. It is observed that irrespective of the cropping pattern all are using cowdung in their fields. Only 2 (*i.e.*, 13%) were found using chemical fertiliser in rice production and one person chemical fertiliser in the vegetable production.

Type of Crops	*Fertiliser Total*	*Cowdung*	*Stubble*	*Chemical Fertiliser*
Rice	15 (100%)	15 (100%)	15 (100%)	2 (13.33%)
Maize	6 (40%)	6 (100%)	6 (100%)	
Chilly	4 (26.6%)	4 (100%)	—	
Marva	5 (33.3%)	5 (100%)	3 (60%)	
Vegetable	12 (80%)	12 (100%)	6 (50%)	1 (8.33%)

About 60 percent of the respondents are against the use of chemical fertilisers. They told that they had negative experience of using chemical fertiliser as application of chemical fertiliser resulted in high growth of plants, but output was less. Again a few respondents expressed that if chemical fertiliser was to be used, it had to be used regularly. But their income constraints and unavailability of fertilisers in their areas caused problem.

It can be concluded that owing to low density of population, high fertility of the soil, traditional method of cultivation the use of chemical fertilisers is not yet popular in the study area. Given the technical know how of the cultivators it is recommended that use of organic manure be encouraged. Recently, it has been studied and proved by a number of researches (mainly by CRIDA AND ICAR) that the use of organic fertilisers is very much beneficial (mainly high yielding both in short as well as in the long run). 'One Straw Revolution' of Dr. Fukuoka provides the guiding example of it. In India also a number of such instances like 'Gloria Farm' of Pondicherry, 'Sambhav' in Nayugarh (in Orissa) are there. Hence, this method should be encouraged. More and more efforts should be made by the Government in the form of "Demonstration Farming" to make the people aware of the natural method of farming by using organic manure. It seems to provide a big prospect for Arunachal Pradesh. In the near future, the crop produced without the chemical fertilisers, pesticides etc. are expected to have a demand because of increasing health consciousness of the people.

References

1. Schumacher, E.F.: Small is Beautiful, Sphere Book Ltd. 1988.
2. Kumarappa, J.C.: Economics of Permanence Sarva Seva Sangh Prakashan, Rajghat, Varanasi, 1984.
3. Somani, L.L. (ed.): Recent Advances in Dryland Agriculture, Vol. I & II Scientific Publisher, Jodhpur, 1993.
4. Seetharaman, Saothers: Handbook on fertiliser usage—The Fertiliser Association of India, New Delhi, 1986.
5. Patnaik (ed.) Kishan: Vikalpa Vichar (Oriya) Forthnight Vth Vol., Vikalpa Prakashan, Bargarh, 1993.
6. "Papumpare District at a Glance"; Statistical Branch of Papumpare District, Naharlagu, 1993-94.

CHAPTER 9

The Traditional Agricultural System of the Apatanis

❑ D.K. DUARAH

Introduction

Agriculture is the mainstay of livelihood of the twenty five major tribal groups of Arunachal Pradesh. Traditionally most of the tribes used in practise Jhumming on hill slops by slash and burn method. The Apatanis have been practising WRC and TRC with their indigenous irrigation system since time immemorial which solely depends on human labour. Their technique of utilization of land and water is unique which enables them to enjoy a comparatively better economic life. In other aspects of their culture too, the role of agriculture is notable. The advanced methods of agriculture are however, introduced by the Government among the traditional jhummias since late sixties which they have taken up with enthusiasm.

Land and Agriculture

The traditional economy of the Apatanis is solely based on agriculture. For a settled agricultural community land is the primary resource. The Apatanis consider land as the main item of individual wealth, and as matter of fact a man's status and influence in society is mainly counted on the size of his holdings. The 25 sq. kms. (appox.) area of hilly terrain and valleys under occupation of the Apatanis can be divided into three categories, *viz.,* privately own land, clan land and common village land. The privately owned land comprises all categories of cultivated land such as irrigated rice fields, dry fields, vegetable and fruit gardens, groves of bamboo *(bije)* and pine *(puse)*, as well as house and granary sites. The clan land consists of the area used for public assembly platform *(Lapang)* inside the village, pasture and burrial grounds scattered on the outskirts of the village and tracks of the forest where only the owner clan have the right to hunt and trap. Common village land which is gradually shinking in the valley due to growth of population, usually consists of few insignificant stretches of pasture for rearing of animals like mithun, hunting ground in the forest, fishing spot in the river and rivulets and unused land between private land and clan land. These lands are properly demarcated with either some natural sings, errection of fencing or by putting posts, which are known to and honoured by all people. As the area is not cadastrically surveyed and there is no standard unit of measurement of land prevalent in the society, it is difficult to get a clear picture of nature of land holdings by each household. However, an idea of individual holding of land may reflect from the Table 1 (1978).

Table 1

DISTRIBUTION OF LAND BY SIZE-CLASS OF OWNERSHIP HOLDINGS AND THEIR PERCENTAGE OF DISTRIBUTING (BAMIN VILLAGE-1976)

Size class (acres)	*Households*		*Area (in acres)*		*Average (in acres)*	
	Nos.	*P.C.*	*Owned Area*	*P.C.*	*Total Area*	*Paddy Area*
Below 2.0	14	19.48	20.91	8.83	1.49	0.79
2.0-4.0	40	54.79	115.16	48.63	2.88	1.35
4.0-5.0	13	17.81	59.12	24.95	4.55	1.96
6.0-8.0	5	5.85	32.91	13.89	6.58	3.00
8.0-above	1	1.37	8.83	3.73	8.83	2.50
Total	73	100.00	236.93	100.00	3.25	1.48

Haimendrof (1980) stated that—"Ever since the Apatanis established themselves in their present habitat rice cultivation on irrigated terrace fields has been the main base of their economy." As per the legends, the area occupied by the Apatanis was once a lake inhabited by acquatic reptiles mainly buru. In course of time, the silt brought down by the streams from the surrounding hills, had transformed the lake to a flat land. The energetic early settlers built up dams and dug channels and developed the valley bottom to an unbroken series of rice fields. The streams originating from the surrounding hills were used to irrigate the terraced rice fields.

(a) Indigenous Irrigation System

On the indigenous irrigation system of the Apatanis, Haimendrof (1980) described that "Every one of the streams rising on the wooded heights that ring the Apatanis country is utilized for irrigation purpose soon after it emerges from the forest and reaches a gully wide enough to accommodate series of terraces. A short distance above the terrace the stream is tapped but here only a small amount of water is deflected and channelled to the highest field. By opening or blocking the connecting ducts any field can be flooded or drained as required. At the head of the valley the terraces are on an average narrow: they are partly carved out of the hill side and partly built-up, with a difference in level of one to three feet between the individual terraces. As the valley broadness the terraces grow in size and the difference in level dwindle to an little as half a foot." The layout of terraces reflects a high degree of technological advancement together with co-operation and considerable skill. Generally the water is not allowed to overflow the dams and terraces are drained through wide wooden or bamboo pipes let into the dam. The channels are often dug deep into the soil in the main valley and the dams are built-up by rows of wooden stakes and sometimes reinforced by strong bamboo matting to secure against the onrush of flood water. A major part of their time and energy is spent to up-keep the terrace fields, dams and channels.

(b) Type of Rice Fields

There are two types of rice fields, *viz.*, permanently irrigated and seasonal irrigated. The former is kept under water or at least in a very wet condition throughout the year, and considered more valuable. Late variety of rice, locally called *emo* is the principal crop grown in these plots. The other type of fields are dried out and harden soon after the harvest. These are cleared and dug over everytime before the cultivation and then water from channels is allowed to flow over slowly to make the soil loose for puddling. Early variety of rice *(Mipiya)* is grown in these fields.

(c) Agricultural Operation

Soon after the celebration of the Myoko festival in the middle of March, the season for agricultural operation begins. At the first stage repairing of dams, clearing of channels and preparation of nurseries for rice seedlings are taken up. Those plots which are under water throughout the year and manured regularly are usually considered for nurseries. The soil is pudded into thick paste of about a knee deep and seeds are broadcasted dry over the plot. Proper care is taken to get healthy seedlings.

In the middle of April, most of the fields are ready for transplantation. Each of the terrace plots is puddled for 2 or 3 times with an interval of 3 to 4 days and properly irrigated. Normally, by mid of May transplantation is over throughout the valley.

The weeding of the fields is taken up thereafter and this is done with great throughness. Each plot is weeded for 2 or 3 times but there are instances of weeding for five or more times.

In mid of June, dry crops like early millet *(Mipe)* are planted mainly alongwith the bunds of rice fields and in garden plots too. The late variety millet *(Sarse)* is cultivated on highland garden plots. Maize is however, sown exclusively in gardens alongwith other vegetables.

Harvesting of early varieties of rice begins in later part of August. The main harvesting is done in mid of October and continues for 2-3 weeks depending upon the land holdings and availability of workers. The harvesting pattern of the two varieties of rice is different. While in early varieties the grains are stripped from the ear by hand, and in other varieties the straws are cut with either sickles or knives, tied into sheaves. The seeds are then thrashed out on the spot by beating against a slanting wooden board. The seeds are stored in carrying baskets which are later shifted to the owner's granary. The seed grains are kept aside from those stored for day to day consumption.

(d) Workers and Implements

The whole agricultural operation of the Apatanis is based entirely on human labour. Both men and women, young and old join their hands together in the field. Role of the women is, however, more prominent than their male counterparts. From the construction of the dams to that of the harvesting the women render commendable service. Their main tasks are, of course, in transplanting, weeding harvesting and to a little extent in preparation of the terrace for cultivation. The menfolks, on the other hand do the jobs like construction and repairing of dams and channels, preparation of nurseries, wet and terrace plots; and in thrashing and carrying of rice grains from the fields to the granery. All able body persons of a family participate in agricultural activities with the objective to earn and enjoy a prosperous life. Yet, besides the companion of family members, the young Apatanis find it more comfortable to work in the fields in a group of contemporary agemate. This co-operative habit enables them to form and develop a unique organization of agricultural workers locally called as *Patang*. A patang is usually constituted of youngsters of equal age group, preferably unmarried boys and girls representing a cluster of families or a clan. The service rendered by these patangs is generally confined among the members. They work on rotation in their fields and host member only has to entertain other patang members with mid-day meal and drinks *(Opo)*. A patang may often rendered is service to the distressed families of the village. Often such services are extended to other families of the valley too having close affinity to any members of the group. In tradition, there is no agricultural labour on wage basis, but slavery system was prevalent among the Apatanis.

The main implement used in agriculture is a hoe. They have not practised ploughing and used other machinery. The sickle and knives are used in harvesting. A dao is also an implement used for multiferous works. Another tool is a flat wooden tray of oval shape. used for carrying lumps of mud at the time of development and remodelling of terraces. Remodelling is done generally if a terrace plot is not evenly watered or yield of the plot is not up to expectation.

The manuring and controlling of pests and insects also form part of their agricultural activities. Apart from decomposed stubles and weeds they also use materials collected from below their pile-dwellings, where they keep pigs. Similarly, to control the insects they use some wild plants locally available. Moreover, they also perform a ritual called *yapung* in the field during July and August for protection of the crops from insects and natural calamities like hail storms and thunder.

Agricultural Crops

The system of double cropping is not normally practised. They cultivate paddy along with dry crops such as maize and millet of different varieties. The three varieties of maize, *viz.* mire, mit and tani are dibbled in garden plots (bula) situated in and outside of the village. The early variety millet *(mipa)* is planted along the bund of terrace rice fields, and the later variety *(sarse)* is cultivated in open dry plots *(lapro)* adjoining the bamboo and pine groves.

The other garden items are beans, chillies, cucumbers, tare, ginger, marrow, tobacco and a croase leafy vegetable, commonly known as *laipat.*

Agricultural Production

The Apatanis have the habit of determining the size and value of a plot of particular plot of rice field from its output, the expression of which is usually made in terms of baskets. The more common basket used in measuring paddy is termed an *anti-yagi,* which contains about 25 kg. unhusked paddy. The total land owned by a family is often expressed through the size of its traditional granary which is of two types, namely *suchinesu* (small) and *suro-nesu* (large); while former can accommodate 100 to 120 anti-yagi and 200 to 220 anti-yagi by the later. However, an idea of per capita production of paddy, millet and maize in their fields can be had from the Table 2.

Changes and Development

Although no remarkable changes and development have been noticed in their traditional agricultural system as well as indigenous irrigation system, it may be mentioned that the Apatanis are not content with merely maintaining an established system but seek to develope. With the implementation of minor irrigation projects by the Government, they can now utilise the water resources in a more scientific manner with less physical labour which they have diverted in opening of new terrace fields on hill slopes. High yielding varieties of paddy fertilizers and pesticides have been introduced in recent years. Double cropping is however, not yet practised. The paddy-cum-fish culture is very much successful among them. Some high yielding common varieties of fish are left in the permanently watered paddy fields just after transplantation and grow simultaneously with the rice plants. This enables them to earn a substantial amount of cash money. Silviculture *i.e.*, plantation of bamboo and pine groves form an integral part of their culture and horticultural gardening of apple, plum and other fruits are though newly introduced this seems to have deeply penetrated into their society.

Table 2

DISTRIBUTION OF PER CAPITA PRODUCTION OF CEREALS BY OPERATIONAL SIZES (BAMIN-1976)

Size-class (acres)	*Number of households*	*Per capita Paddy*	*Production in kilogram Millet*	*Maize*
Below 1.0	11	225	45	8.5
1.0-2.0	35	320	42	5.6
2.0-3.0	25	440	28	5.9
3.0-4.0	1	572	43	14.3
4.0-5.0	1	1000	60	8.0
Overall	73	337	33	5.6

The ploughing with bullock or use of any other machinery is still out of their culture. The traditional patangs are being respected by wage labour.

With the growing population the pressure on agricultural land has increased. But the possibility of terracing new areas for cultivation is limited because of topography.

The traditional agricultural system of the Apatanis has been planned enough to check soil erosion and deforestation. The Apatani farmers are mainly progressive and maintain the tradition even after a lot of changes and development in their culture have taken place.

References

Haimendraf V.F., 1980: *A Himalayan Tribe from Cattle to Cash,* Vikas Publications, New Delhi.

Phukan, U., Buragohain, S.N., Barthakur, G.C., 1978: *Bamin:* A Socio-Economic Survey of an Apatani village in Subansiri District of Arunachal Pradesh. Agro-Economic Research Centre for N.E. India, Jorhat-13, Assam.

CHAPTER 10

Traditional Plant Protection: Practices Among the Adis

❑ Y.P. KOHLI

The rituals of Adi tribe of Arunachal Pradesh to protect crops from pests and diseases have been discussed. The present paper forms the hypothesis that the sound frequency produced during the chanting of hymns/verses by an ethnic priest and the odour produced from the altar smoke may be the reason which prevents mating of insects/pests away and thus keeps the crops safe from the diseases.

There was a time, when man used to take uncooked meat of animals. In the lap of mother nature, playing with plants, dancing with creepers and living under trees, he learnt about different crops to get food. When he found that the crops in his fields were threatened by emergence of pests and disease, he thought it to be because of evil spirits..To get rid of evil spirits in the form of pests and diseases, he prayed to the Almighty, chanted the hymns in the praise of different gods and goddesses and performed different rituals to please the protectors of the crops.

In Arunachal Pradesh, PADAMMINYONG ADI society observes different rituals when their field crop is attacked by pests and diseases. In one of the rituals, an altar is erected in one of the corners of the field and following articles are used during the rituals.

(a) Small branches of a few selected trees,

(b) Leaves of the jungle creeper TALO,

(c) Leaves of KOW tree (in making a groove),

(d) A bamboo tumbler.

The whole altar is decorated by different types of bamboo festoons.

Near the altar 10-15 big containers of APONG (fermented beverage/Beer), sufficient quantity of rice, small pieces of freshly cut ginger and one red coloured cock are placed. In front of the altar, small amounts of rice, APONG, meat and ginger are taken after which fire is lit and the priest starts chanting the verses in the praise of the Goddess of Crops, KINE-NANE:[1]

Engo riknyoe rigo so
Anyi oboe dupor binem
Anyi nekoe tenga dola
Kilung Kamebe kebbo bulu
Ambang lebangem kebbang tumilo

....

Kine layings, dende layinge
Asi besim
Asi sigoem jome tula
Kine gyayinge jemi gyaying

....

Koje ludume kamsum besik
Jemi ludume kamsum besik

....

Yarem gyapange polek tesik
Dunggo yollongem uottola
Sobo loginge kamring tesik
Etkam ponadem natula

....

Delok rongem
Minur murmue gitung tesi
Bonong sepue murmu dunaike
Boyik sepur murmu dunaike

....

Delok rongem
Pedo domi miti omum no

....

Omum kibe pete biyepe
Anyi kibe pete biyepe

(*i.e.*, at the time, when our crops have been threatened by unknown enemies, O Goddess Kine-Nane, protect our crops and drive away the enemies.

This young plants are withering, it may be because of not getting food from the soil. O Goddess Kine-Nane; we pray to thee; bless our tender plants to receive nutritious food from the mother earth and ever flourish.

O Goddess Kine-Nane; may our tender Plants enjoy the protection from malevolent forces. Slay the hostile evil-doers who torment our crops.

May the morning and evening dews provide fresh water, energetic water to our tender crops.)[2]

IRII RITUAL

The Adis of Pasighat area perform another ritual IRII, when young paddy plants just grow up. In the centre of every paddy field, one bow and one arrow decorated with bamboo festoons are placed. The young boys of the village with their bows and arrows, go around every paddy field and sing:

Ribo ribo .... ribo ribo
Ribo ribo .... ribo ribo

i.e., (O our young friends—(young paddy plants)—smile as we smile and laugh as we laugh. We pray the Goddess Kine-Nane for your good health.)

Finally, all young boys go out of the village and throw arrows in different directions (in order to keep the evil spirits away from the village.)

Likewise the GALLO-ADI society performs AMPU-YOLU ritual for the protection of their crops from the pests and diseases. The priests chant the verses in the glory of different gods and goddesses like AMPIR, MOPIN, PIKKU, PIRTE, PIRLIN-NGURLIN etc.

"May the Goddess listen to our invocations and bless our crops with a healthy growth, may mother nature be kind to our paddy plants and so on ....

In folk-lores, there are an unconscious effort and vitality that seems to spring from a timeless relationship with the past and an innocent relationship with the environment around. Should we see this heritage as only a ritualistic way to keep away evil-spirits or a combination of the earlier man's aspirations and his necessities? Should we discard this ancient practice as unwanted in view of today's scientific and technological advancement or it should be seen as far as possible, as man's adventurous journey for going ahead. Let us analyse such folklores stored and possessed by the forest dweller-ethnic groups in the context of modern advances in science and technology.

According to a W.H.O. survey,"In the Third-World, one person is poisoned every minute by imported pesticides and each year over 5,000 die due to the side effects of their indiscriminate use." This is the reason, man has been searching an alternative to chemical pesticides.

According to the discovery made by Prof. K.N. Saxena and his team of Delhi University Zoologists, playing harmonium or notes from a 'Shruti' box prevents mating among green leaf-hoppers (Amrasca devastans) a serious cotton pest and brown plant hopper (Nilaparvatalugens), a major pest of rice plants.

If the music is played for several hours, the males simply quit the leaf in disgust and die.[3]

It is possible that the chanting of verses by an ethnic priest in a typical way may produce a note of required frequency of sound waves to prevent mating. It is not only music that turns off sex in these pests, Dr. Saxena's team also discovered that the smell from certain volatile chemicals is also capable of jamming the communications between the male and female insects.

It is possible that ginger, some particular creeper, branches of selected trees etc. used in the altar, may give particular odour capable of keeping the pests away from the plants. A thorough scientific research of the sound frequency produced by chanting the verses and the scientific analysis of the things used in the altar should be made to determine the degree of efficacy of the ancient practices for controlling the insects and pests.

References

1. Rukbo, T.: Solunġ gidi adi ke tùrkeng; 1977.
2. PTI Science Service, Nov. 16-30, 1981.
3. The Assam Tribune, March 10 '92.

Courtesy

1. Shri T. Rukbo, Secretary, Adi Cultural and Literary Society, Pasighat.
2. Dr. T. Nyori, Controller of Examinations, Arunachal University, Doimukh.

Part II

STRUCTURAL TRANSFORMATION

CHAPTER 11

Structural Changes in Jhum-Based Economy and Growing Inequalities in North-Eastern Tribal Society

❑ J.B. GANGULY

Shifting cultivation as a method of producing agricultural crops including the main staple, rice, is still widely adopted by the tribal people in the North-Eastern Region (NER) even though right from the First Five Year Plan several schemes of offering incentives and financial grants for inducing the jhumias (shifting cultivators) to give up this practice and take to settle cultivation have been in operation. According to the Report of the Task Force on Shifting Cultivation appointed by the Ministry of Agriculture, Government of India (1983), all-told 4,43,336 families in the NER practised shifting cultivation. Total estimated area under this system of cultivation measured 14,660 sq. km. although annually 3,869 sq. kms. of this area was actually subjected to jhuming (Statewise details are given in Table 1).

Such macro-level data, however, conceal much of the changed structural features of this system, without knowing which effective plans of actions for controlling jhum practices, stopping the process of growing ecological imbalances and helping the hill people to attain higher levels of living cannot be formulated. In this paper an account of the process of structural changes in the jhum-based tribal economy associated with the on-going process of peasantization of the tribal farmers and growing inequalities among them is given.

Table 1

SHIFTING CULTIVATION IN THE NORTH-EASTERN STATES

State	*Total Area (sq. km.)*	*Annual Area Under S.C. (sq. km.)*	*Fallow Period (Years)*	*Minimum Area Under S.C. at One Time or Other (sq.km.)*	*Proportion of Total Area (%)*	*No. of Families Practising S.C.*	*Average Area Per Family (hectare)*
1	*2*	*3*	*4*	*5*	*6*	*7*	*8*
Arunachal Pradesh	83,743	700	3—10	2,100	2.5	54,000	1.3
Assam	78,438	696	2—10	1,392	1.8	58,000	1.2
Manipur	22,327	900	4—7	3,600	16.1	70,000	1.3
Meghalaya	22,429	530	5—7	2,650	11.8	52,290	1.0
Mizoram	21,081	630	3—4	1,890	8.9	50,000	1.3
Nagaland	16,579	190	5—8	1,913	11.5	1,16,046	0.9
Tripura .	10,486	223	5—9	1,115	10.6	43,000	0.5

Source: Report of the Task Force on Shifting Cultivation, Ministry of Agriculture, Government of India (1983), as quoted in Basic Statistics of North-Eastern Region, 1992, North Eastern Council, Shillong, p. 28. Data in Columns 6 and 8 have been compiled the writer.

The primordial system of shifting cultivation as practised by the hill people of the north-east covered all aspects of their life, namely, production, distribution and consumption (or the so-called economic aspects), inter-personal and individual—community relations (or social dimensions of life), performance of rituals, enjoyment of leisure, music and dance, etc. (or cultural aspects of life), and the authority and power structure determining individuals' access to productive assets, mainly land, forests and water resources and maintenance of tribal solidarity, administration of justice, etc. (or the political aspects of life). Briefly, social, cultural, economic and political aspects of tribal life were all linked with the system of shifting cultivation. Such an economy was based on subsistence farming which is a non-surplus generating system. It is not that in the physical sense no surplus was produced. Whatever surplus was produced it was distributed among the co-villagers in the form of organising feasts and festivals by those having surplus stock of grains, poultry, pigs, *mithuns,* etc. However, no accumulation and no capital formation was involved in the process. The economy was a stationary one without any growth. The people were therefore susceptible to sufferings and food insecurity at the time of natural calamity and crop failure on account of ravages by pests, etc.

The system has, however, been undergoing changes over a long period of time under the impact of both endogenous and exogenous changes (Ganguly 1993, pp. 303-306). At the present moment the practices of shifting cultivation in different parts of the north-east are basically quite different from what it was in the remote past. Many hill farmers to-day practise both shifting and settled cultivation at the same time. In the non-privately owned and non-reserved forests, they raise some crops by following the method of shifting cultivation, while in the individually owned or, in some cases, even in unsettled government lands in the plains the same individuals practise permanent plough or wet rice cultivation. "According to a recent study by NIRD (National Institute of Rural Development, North-Eastern Regional Centre, Guwahati), about 40 percent farmers in Meghalaya, Assam hill districts and hill districts of Manipur practised permanent cultivation along with shifting cultivation" (Seven Sisters, Vol. 3, No. 1, January 1996, p. 1).

These cultivators as also those tribal farmers who have taken to the exclusive practice of settled cultivation are in a position to produce surplus and take place as transactors both in the input and output markets.

Besides the mixed jhum-cultivators there are still many tribal households which are exclusively jhum-cultivators. But not all of them can fully subsist on this system of cultivation. A growing number of these households have to supplement their income by working as wage-labourers on the farms of well-to-do tribal households, public-works projects of the government or on works of the forest department.

Growth of a class of absentee jhumias represents another aspect of structural changes in the hill farmers' economy. In Tripura, Meghalaya and Mizoram, cases have been reported where non-government but formerly community controlled land have been let out by Tribal salaried urban-dwellers and/or land-owning resourceful tribal households to the poor *jhumias* for jhuming mainly on crop-sharing basis.[1]

To-day, the tribal villages in the north-east generally consist of the following classes of households:

1. The exclusive jhumia households. They wholly depend on jhuming for subsistence. Their number has been falling steadily.

2. The mixed farmers. They partly practise shifting cultivation and partly settled cultivation. Their number has been rising over the years.

3. The pure settled cultivators. These households exclusively practise wet-rice cultivation. No income is earned by such households from shifting cultivation.

4. Tenant shifting cultivators who raise crops by adopting the method of jhum cultivation on forest lands over which they do not have any direct right of use either sanctioned by the community or the government. The tribal households having right of use over such lands for shifting cultivation let out this right to the poor tribal households on crop sharing or payment of cash rent basis. Some of such tenant jhumias may have also their own community-sanctioned access to forest lands for jhuming but they cannot raise enough crop therefrom to meet fully their subsistence needs.

   Some poor jhumia families become tenant jhumias being unable to meet their food requirements from their stock of foodgrains carried forward from the last season's harvests during the period of 'jhum-cutting,' clearing of debris, sowing of seeds, weeding, watching and harvesting and processing of crops. These households accept payment of advance wages/shares of crops for cultivation of others' jhum lands.

5. The wage-earners. Some landless tribals, who have not yet migrated to urban areas, are agricultural labourers. They work for wage on fellow-villagers' farms—either settled or shifting—public works, forest departments' projects, etc. and under various employment generation schemes of the government.

There are two sub-categories of this class of families. *(a)* Some practise jhuming in small plots and supplement their income by working also as agri-labourers during the slack season. *(b)* But there are some tribal households which earn their income solely as wage-labourers.

The above categorization does not fully account for all means of earning income by the rural tribal households. Collection of minor forest products, (such as fuel-wood, various edible roots, leaves, nuts and fruits, building materials, etc.); catching fish; rearing poultry, piggery, etc.; production of baskets, mats, etc. and weaving of cloth, etc. provide non-farming sources of income to almost all rural tribal households, Of course, the proportions and total magnitude of income yielded by such activities vary from household to household and account for in some measure the growing inequalities in tribal villages.

These developments are somewhat reflected in the agricultural census of these states. In Table 2 estimated number and area of operational holdings of all sizes by tenancy status for 1985-86 are given. From the table it will be seen that total number of holdings in the predominently tribal states of Arunachal Pradesh (85 thousand), Meghalaya (171 thousand) Mizoram (52 thousand) and Nagaland (125 thousand) are quite substantial. In the remaining states of Assam, Manipur and Tripura peasantization process among the tribals started much earlier as there are large areas of plains-land. The number of holdings operated by tribals and non-tribals respectively are not readily available excepting for Tripura. In that state total number of holdings operated by scheduled tribe farmers were 94,809 out of a total number of 3,07,732 holdings in 1980-81. The numbers were 1,19,917 and 3,12,080 respectively in 1985-86. This means that operational holdings of scheduled tribe farmers increased from 30 percent of the total number in 1980-81 to 38.4 percent in 1985-86. Total area of operational holdings of tribals increased from 1,22,781 hectares in 1980-81 to 1,43,284 hectares (State Report on Agricultural Census 1985-86 of Tripura, Vol. 1, p. 18).

Distribution of operational holdings of the scheduled tribe operators according to tenancy status in 1985-86 was as follows (*ibid*, p. 30).

From Table 2 it will be seen that in Meghalaya there are 9000 wholly leased in holdings with an area of 14000 hectares. Such

Table 2

ESTIMATED NUMBER AND AREA OF OPERATIONAL HOLDINGS BY TENANCY STATUS (ALL SIZES)

(Number in 000 Units)
(Area in 000 hectares)

State	*Total Holdings*		*Wholly Owned and Self Operated Holdings*		*Wholly Leased in Holdings*		*Wholly Other-wise Operated Holdings*		*Partly Owned, Partly Leased in & Partly Otherwise Operated Holdings*				
	Number	*Area*	*Number*	*Area*	*Number*	*Area*	*Number*	*Area*	*Number*	*Owned Area*	*Leased in Area*	*Other-wise Operated*	*Total Area*
1	*2*	*3*	*4*	*5*	*6*	*7*	*8*	*9*	*10*	*11*	*12*	*13*	*14*
Arunachal Pradesh	85	344	84	341	Neg	Neg	—	—	1	2	1	Neg	3
Assam	2,412	3,161	2,162	2,843	64	58	26	30	159	109	62	60	230
Manipur	140	174	130	163	7	7	Neg	Neg	2	2	2	Neg	4
Meghalaya	171	302	141	240	9	14	7	12	15	22	11	3	36
Mizoram	52	82	52	82	—	—	—	—	—	—	—	—	—
Nagaland	125	933	124	924	Neg	1	—	—	1	6	2	—	8
Tripura	312	318	175	182	3	2	68	57	65	49	3	24	76
All India	94,907	1,64,529	91,348	1,57,760	526	654	694	678	2,339	3,910	921	606	5,437

Source: All India Bulletin on Agricultural Census—1985-86; Department of Agriculture & Cooperation, OOI.
(Quoted in Basic Statistics of North-Eastern Region, 1992, North-Eastern Council, Shillong, p. 34).

holdings are negligible in Arunachal Pradesh and Nagaland. For Mizoram figures are not available. Numbers of partly owned and partly leased in holdings in Arunachal Pradesh are 1000 (with leased in area of 2000 hectares); in Meghalaya 15000 (with leased in area of 11000 hectares) and 1000 in Nagaland (with leased in area of 2000 hectares).

	Owned and self-operated	*Leased in*	*Otherwise operated*
Total number of holdings	79,435	29,091	67,274
Area in hectares	89,718	1,649	51,916

Underlying these structural changes in the tribal village economy one basic fact stands out. It is that the process of peasantization has been spreading across the tribal villages in the entire NER (Ganguly, 1989, p. 44-47). And, of course, in some pockets even a process of depeasantization, or what is commonly termed as alienation of tribal lands, has set in. But alienation of tribal lands, generally, the transfer of lands by the tribals to non-tribals is understood. But such transfers also do take place among the tribals themselves. And the process of depeasantization covers both types of transfer. One of the sure signs of the process of depeasantization is the steady growth in the number of agricultural labourers in the region as revealed by the Census Reports (Table 3).

Table 3

NUMBER OF AGRICULTURAL LABOURERS IN DIFFERENT STATES OF NER

State	*1971*	*1981*	*1991*	*% increase in 1991 over 1971*
Arunachal Pradesh	5,292	7,796	19,074	260
Assam	4,05,440	—	9,19,386	126.7
Manipur	13,525	28,613	63,350	368
Meghalaya	44,131	57,899	95,895	117
Mizoram	558	5,118	10,835	1841
Nagaland	3,797	2,979	23,889	529
Tripura	86,340	1,46,089	1,86,671	116

Source: NEC, Basic Statistics of North-Eastern Region, 1980, 1990, 1992.

The numbers of agricultural labourers quoted in Table 3 above do not exactly represent the numbers of tribal agricultural workers. Yet as the economies of the different states have been evolving as a consequence of the ongoing processes of peasantization, specialization, monetization, commercialization, urbanization, modernization and economic stratification of tribals, etc., the distinct identities of tribal and non-tribal economies have been waning. And the steady increase in the number of agricultural labourers includes tribal workers also.

The structural changes outlined above marking growing inequalities in the tribal society have been the outcome of the transition from shifting cultivation to peasant farming. The most striking difference between the earlier order and the emerging one is that while under the former the producers were not required to produce surplus for others, under the latter they are constrained to do so. Robinson and Eatwell have aptly stated: "In some tribal societies, the agricultural surplus is shared by the community and there is no compulsion on any family to produce more than it wants to consume. The superstructure of what is known as 'civilization' has been built on compelling the cultivators to work for others" (1974, p. 323).

Who are compelled to produce surplus and how; and who appropriate that surplus and for whom, etc. are determined by the institutional arrangement of private ownership of property, such as, lands, forests, water resource, other inputs of production like equipment, loanable funds etc. In the early stages of transformation from tribal to peasant economy, ownership of natural resources, namely, land, forest and water is the critically most important determinant. In the jhum-based economy these resources were, with some rare exceptions, not privately owned. Individual family's access to these resources for productive purpose was controlled and regulated by the traditional authority of the community. But the peasantization process starts with awarding individual ownership right over land to individual households. Land becomes a transferable commodity. A piece of land can be bought and sold. The whole system is defined by law. It also involves the process of conducting cadastral survey of land, identification of individual plots of land and documentation of ownership of surveyed plots of land. But excepting for Assam, Tripura and plains of Manipur cadastral survey of land has not yet been conducted. This has enabled the tribal elites to grab large tracts of village lands and bring them under their individual *de facto* ownership. The NIRD N.E. Regional Centre has highlighted this development as follows:

"After independence all the State Governments of North-East launched a vigorous programmes of controlling shifting cultivation. The response for this programme from among the elite class has been quite enthusiastic who seized the opportunity to privatise the community land..."

"In the absence of any cadastral survey, the private ownership of the community land is being enjoyed freely by the elite. The process is on and has led to increased internal differentiation and widening of the gulf between the rich and the poor within the tribal communities" (Seven Sisters, January 1996, p. 1).

The *modus operandi* of grabbing land seems to be that as and when the practice of jhuming in any area is restricted and jhumia families are given land for taking to settled cultivation, some areas of land earlier subjected to jhuming are marked as fallow land and ultimately waste land which neither the Government nor any individual jhumia takes up for any farming operation. The educated and influential elites being aware of the fluid status of ownership rights over these waste lands establish their rights of occupation by fencing in and starting some operations—like agricultural and/or horticultural, farming, plantation, animal husbandry or where feasible, even by starting some small manufacturing units. The scope of such grabbing of land exists mainly in respect of so-called jhum fallow lands. If we look at the land-use classification data as given in NEC's Basic Statistics, 1992 (p. 29), we may note that there is still a total area of 698000 hectares of 'fallow land other than current fallow' in the North-Eastern States excluding Manipur and including Tripura's 1000 hectares. In Tripura the pressure on land is extremely high and the average area of jhuming per family is the lowest among the North-Eastern States (see Table 1). There is also the significant fact that all such so-called fallow lands (that is, land kept fallow as a sequence of jhuming of plots by turn) have been converted to *Khash* land under the Tripura Land Revenue and Land Reforms Act, 1960 (for fuller details, see, Ganguly 1992, p. 303).

The process of unequal distribution of land hits the pure jhumias, who wholly depend on jhuming for subsistence, the hardest.

In the emerging socio-economic scenario in the tribal villages they are the poorest of all. Because of extension of area under forest reservation, under road construction and power projects, etc. and also urbanization besides passing away of 'jhum-fallow' land from under their use, the jhumias are unable to have enough land for jhuming. Fallow period is also shortening. As a result yield per hectare of jhum land has been steadily falling. The jhumias of Tripura are the most adversely affected by such developments. No wonder, the average area of jhum land per family is the lowest (0.5 hectare) and gross return per jhum is only Rs. 1658.64 which is utterly inadequate for sustaining the jhumia family.[2]

The happenings in Tripura should serve as a warning for the tribal communities in the other North-Eastern States. The explosive growth of population mainly on account of migration of a large number of non-tribal displaced persons from East Pakistan, now Bangladesh, has accelerated the process of growing landlessness among the tribal farmers. But the institutional changes, such as, appropriation of community lands and common property resources as privately owned lands and enactment of law for declaring all 'jhum fallow' lands as *khash* (government) lands, commercialization of farming activities, operation of market forces, erosion of authority of the community, etc. are also responsible for growing inequalities and deprivations of a large number of rural tribal households.

The adverse impacts of such changes on the environment and bio-diversity are also quite alarming. Most of such institutional changes have been taking place in varying degrees in other states of the region also. For equitable and sustainable development of socio-economic conditions of the tribal peoples the community should be empowered to have control over resource use. Also, open and active participation of the people in the decision-making process must be ensured. Necessary institutional structure may be built up on the model for Panchayat Raj bodies as envisaged in the 73rd Constitution Amendment Act, 1993. For this to happen there must be the necessary political will for effecting genuine decentralization of power and investment of resources for the equitable development of the social sector comprising education, health services, food security, social security, etc.

References

1. According to Agarwal (1991:295), about 15 thousand Mizo government employees get land allotted to them for cultivation in their respective villages. They obviously engage local tribal farmers or wage labourers for cultivation of their land on crop-sharing or cash rent payment or wage payment basis. He has also quoted R. Thanga as stating: "about two-thirds of harvest of local rice goes out of the state because absentee landlordism is the areas of Saiphai, Buchep, Chawnpui, Chemphai, Buchangphai, Phaisen, Zawlnum and Bungthuam bordering Cachar district of Assam and some parts of Tripura. Hired labourers work in the fields on share-cropping basis and are given a share of 2/3 of harvest."

   Tiplut Nongbri of Meghalaya writes (1987, p. 78): "In the present day Khasi society it has become a status symbol among town dwellers to own such lands as fruit orchard, paddy field and fisheries. Such people are usually the middle class and upper-middle class who themselves continue to live in the towns and give their land for cultivation to share croppers for a share in the production."

2. The National Sample Survey Organization conducted a study in the economies of Jhum cultivation in Tripura in 1976-77. According to this study average size of a jhumia family is 6.24 and the average area of land available for a family is 0.5 hectare. Gross return from such a jhum is Rs. 1658.64 only which is quite insufficient for meeting the subsistence needs of a family. The utterly uneconomic return from jhuming is further proved by the fact that for getting this return the family members are required to put in eight months of labour. (These data have been quoted by Shanker Chatterjee, 1993, p. 3).

Bibliography

1. Agarwal, A.K., 1991: 'Shifting Cultivation in Mizoram,' in *Shifting Cultivation in North-East India,* D.N. Majumdar (ed.), Omsons Publications, New Delhi.
2. Chatterjee, Shankar, 1993: '*Shifting* Cultivation in the *North-Eastern Region of India:* A Brief Review,' in *South Asia Forum Quarterly,* New York, Vol. 6, No. 4: Fall, 1993.
3. Ganguly, J.B., 1989: 'Economics of Development of the Tribal Villages of North-East India,' in *Sequences of Development in North-East India,* J.B. Bhattacharjee (ed.), Omsons Publications, New Delhi.
4. _____, 1992: 'The Process of Transition from Communal to Individual Land Tenure System in Tripura,' in *Tribal Transformation in India,* Buddhadeb Chaudhuri (ed.), Inter-India Publications, New Delhi.
5. _____, 1993: 'Development of Peasant Farming in the North-Eastern Tribal Region: A Study in Tribal Continuities,' in *Continuity and Change in Tribal Society,* Mrinal Miri (ed.) Indian Institute of Advanced Study, Shimla.
6. Government of Tripura, 1992: *State Report on Agricultural Census, 1985-86, of Tripura,* Volume I.

7. North-Eastern Council, 1992: *Basic Statistics of North-Eastern Region*, Shillong.

8. National Institute of Rural Development, North-Eastern Regional Centre, 1996, *Seven-Sisters:* Bi-monthly Newsletter, Guwahati, Vol. 3, No. 1.

9. Nongbri, T., 1987: 'The Khasi Land Tenure System' in B.B. Dutta and M.N. Karna (eds.), *Land Relations in North-East India*, People's Publishing House, New Delhi.

10. Robinson, J. and Eatwell, J., 1974: *An Introduction to Modern Economics*, Tata McGraw Hill, New Delhi.

CHAPTER 12

Transforming Hill Agriculture in Tribal Areas of North-East India

❑ A.K. NEOG

Introduction

The North-Eastern (NE) Region of India comprising Arunachal Pradesh, Assam, Manipur, Meghalaya, Mizoram, Nagaland and Tripura accounting for 7.7 percent of the country's geographical area and 3.72 percent of the population, falls under the mountain zone. About 70 percent of the region is hilly and 86 percent people live in villages. The National Commission on Agriculture (1976) identified the entire states of Arunachal, Meghalaya, Mizoram, Nagaland and Tripura as hill areas. The hill areas in Assam account for about 20 percent and in Manipur 90 percent. Arunachal, Meghalaya, Mizoram and Nagaland are not only hilly but also predominantly tribal, tribal population ranging from about 64 percent in Arunachal to about 95 percent in Mizoram and lying between the two in the other two states. The tribal population in Manipur and Tripura is above 34 and 30 percent respectively. In Assam it is 12.82 percent including both hill and plain tribes. The aim of this paper is to investigate the problems in the transformation of hill agriculture in tribal areas and suggest measures. The analysis is primarily based on official data from the hilly tribal states. Tribal scenario is given in Table 1 which is based on 1991 census.

Though the tribal population in the country accounts for 8.01 percent of the total population, the proportion is highly significant in the N.E. Region. However, the tribal society in the region is not

Table 1

TOTAL POPULATION, SHARE OF TRIBAL POPULATION AND THE NUMBER OF TRIBES, 1991

State	*Total Population (lakh)*	*Tribal Population (percentage)*	*No. of Tribes and Sub-tribes*
Arunachal Pradesh	8.65	63.66	110
Assam	224.14	12.82	60
Manipur	18.37	34.41	49
Meghalaya	17.75	85.53	54
Mizoram	6.90	94.75	61
Nagaland	12.10	87.70	39
Tripura	25.57	30.95	35

Source : Census of India.

homogeneous. The complexity in the number of tribes including sub-tribes, having distinct language, dialect, customs and institutions, and being in different stages of socio-economic development is a challenge to our development planners. While some of the tribes are sizeable in number the others are marginal and some are commonly found in more than one state.

Characteristics of Hill Cultivation

Though agriculture is the principal occupation of the hill tribals of the N.E. region, the cultivated land is limited, being confined to the valleys and hill slopes. Despite low population density the pressure on land is heavy as only a very small proportion of the geographical area is culturable. In this context the Report of the National Commission on Agriculture (1976) in Part XIII (p. 69) makes the following observation:

"Owing to the preponderance of forests and barren and uncultivated land, per capita availability of land for cultivation in the hill areas is lower than the all India average of about 0.3 ha. The lowest is in Arunachal Pradesh and Mizoram (0.12 ha.). Cultivation has been extended to marginal lands, through extensive deforestation, resulting in low productivity and soil erosion."

What is important for hill cultivation is the proportions of net area sown to geographical area on the one hand and fallow land (both current and others) and culturable waste land on the other, that have got bearing on shifting cultivation (called jhum). Forest area in the hill states in 1988-89 varies from 42.31 percent of geographical area in Meghalaya to 61.81 percent in Mizoram. Proportion of net area sown to geographical area is negligible in Arunachal (2.05 percent in 1988-89) and Mizoram (3.08 in 1988-89). It was 10.86 percent and 8.74 percent respectively in Nagaland and Meghalaya in the said years. Proportion of fallow and cultivable waste lands is extremely low in Arunachal Pradesh (0.88 percent in 1988-89) and Tripura (0.28 percent) but high in Nagaland (21 percent), Mizoram (24.5 percent) and in Meghalaya (32.77 percent in 1988-89).

Structure of Tribal Holdings

The tribes of the N.E. hills live in some kind of 'natural area' with boundaries demarcated through 'natural laws' called customary law. Cadastral survey has not been done nor land records exist. By and large the hill areas belong to the tribal people, the clans and the communities. Land ownership and the individual right to use it is almost exclusively determined under the customary laws. Land allotment to individual families, though varies from tribe to tribe, in general is done by the village council or elders or by the chief on the basis of the size of family and working members. Law of inheritance for most tribes is patriarchal except for the matrilineal tribes of Meghalaya, where inheritance is matriarchal. In the absence of land records a question may be raised *viz.* how the size of holdings is determined in tribal areas. This is simplified by the Agricultural Census which records operational holdings without regard to the title or legal form. Table 2 presents data on tribal holdings in the region. It may be mentioned that marginal and small production units predominate in Meghalaya and Mizoram while medium and large units are relatively high in Arunachal and Nagaland.

It can be inferred from Table 2 that the percentage share of the tribal farmers in the area operated is highly or fully associated with their share in total holdings, the correlation coefficient (r) being 0.9984. The average size of tribal holding is much lower

Table 2

NUMBER AND AREA OF OPERATIONAL HOLDINGS FOR TRIBALS, 1985-86

State	*No. of Holdings (thousand)*	*Area Operated (thousand hect.)*	*Average Size (hect.)*
Arunachal Pradesh	81(95.29)	336(97.67)	4.16
Assam	315(13.02)	443(14.01)	1.41
Manipur	56(40.00)	76(43.68)	1.35
Meghalaya	171(100.00)	302(100.00)	1.76
Mizoram	52(100.00)	82(100.00)	1.57
Nagaland	125(100.00)	933(100.00)	7.46
Tripura	120(38.46)	143(44.97)	1.19
All-India	7637(7.81)	17205(10.50)	2.25

Note: Figures in bracket are percentage to total including tribal and non-tribal holdings and areas.

Source: GOI, Indian Agriculture in Brief, 1990.

than the national average in the five states other than Arunachal and Nagaland (highest in India). It may be added that land availability to tribal farmers in these hill areas is not a problem. This is due to the safeguards given under the Sixth Schedule to the Indian Constitution empowering the District Councils to make laws for land use and allotment, and protection under Article 371 with respect to tribal customary laws and land resources.

Farming System in North-East Hills

There are two distinct farming systems *viz.* shifting cultivation, called jhum or jhuming and permanent or settled cultivation. The former is widespread, practised by the farmers called Jhumias in the forest areas and steeper hill slopes; the latter is limited to plains, valleys and gentler slopes (terrace farming). Tribal farmers slash the forest and burn it to make it fit as jhum land to raise mixed crops for one or two successive years. Then they abandon the land and move to new areas. After some years farmers return to the original plot. The periodicity after which cultivation is again taken up in the jhum land is called jhum cycle. Jhuming is land and labour extensive. Technology is primitive consisting of traditional seeds and use of implements like chopping knife, axe, hoe, spade, sickle, dibble. Topography does not permit the use of farm machinery. Though precise data are not available, the incidence of jhuming in the region can be gauged from the data in Table 3.

Table 3

TOTAL AND ANNUAL AREA UNDER JHUMING AND THE JHUM CYCLE

(Area in '000 hectares)

State/Area	*Area Under Jhuming*		*Jhum Cycle*
	Total Area	*Annual Area*	*(Years)*
Arunachal	210.0(2.51)	70.0	3—10
Assam hills	139.2(9.14)	69.6	2—10
Manipur hills	360.0(17.92)	90.0	4—7
Meghalaya	265.0(11.81)	53.0	5—7
Mizoram	189.0(8.97)	63.0	3—4
Nagaland	633.0(38 18)	101.4	5—8
Tripura	111.5(10.63)	22.3	5-9

Note: Bracketed figures are percentages to geographical area except for Assam and Manipur where percentage is to hill areas.

Source: Ministry of Agriculture and NEC.

From Table 3 it is seen that the incidence of jhuming is very high in Nagaland, accounting for 38.18 percent of its geographical area and is very low, 2.51 percent, in Arunachal Pradesh. However, the proportion of annual area to total area under jhuming is low in Nagaland being 16 percent and high in Assam hills being 50 percent. The jhum cycle has reached the critical limit in parts of Arunachal, Assam and Mizoram where it is as low as 2 to 3 years even though on the maximum it ranges from 4 to 10 years. A minimum cycle of three years is necessary for vegetation and next crop. Jhuming is a way of life for about 4,43,336 tribal families of the entire region, of which Nagaland alone accounts for 26.18 percent.

Input Usage

Inputs used in jhuming are traditional. Use of modern inputs like fertilizers on hill slopes is not feasible as rain may wash them away. Whatever little quantity is applied is in settled farming, by the large farmers. For instance, according to Input Survey (1986-87), only 7.62 percent and 2.47 percent of the operated areas are respectively irrigated and treated with chemical fertilizer in Nagaland, the treated area in Meghalaya is 4.58 percent. Both supply and demand factors like lack of purchasing power, indifference, risk and uncertainty, ignorance are responsible for not using improved seed and fertilizer by the tribal farmers as observed from the N.S.S. 33rd Round Report (1978-79) in Meghalaya.

Crop Yield

The yield rate of crops in the hilly tribal states is highly unstable mostly reflecting the instability of jhum yield. In 1990-91 the yield per hectare of principal crop rice varied between 1155 kg. in Meghalaya to 1244 kg. in Mizoram against all-India average of 1751 kg. Comparable yield and cost data for jhum and settled farming are not reported separately by the Agriculture Departments. The proportion of area under permanent cultivation is not totally insignificant in some states. For instance, it was 39.45 percent in Arunachal during 1988-89 and 48.16 percent in Nagaland during 1985-86. Though jhuming has been condemned for its low yield, it is debatable. Survey reports (1973) of Agro-Economic Research Centre, Jorhat reveal that per hectare yield of principal crop under jhuming compares favourably with settle farming. It can be argued that since jhuming involves mixed cropping with common cost, so its per hectare productivity and return is likely to be more than under settled farming. The said N.S.S. report shows that in Meghalaya jhuming has got considerable comparative advantage over settled farming in the production of sweet potato and other vegetables.

A Case Study

The high incidence of jhuming caught the attention of the North-Eastern Council (NEC), which launched Pilot Projects during the Fifth Plan to settle the Jhumia tribal families in settled farming. The project in Arunachal was completed in 1978-79 and the rest in 1983-84. Their particulars are given in Table 4.

The benefits under the projects included offer of developed land and infrastructure, irrigation facilities, free or subsidised seeds and fertilizers and financial assistance to construct houses.

Table 4

JHUM CONTROL PROJECTS UNDER N.E.C.

State	*Project Site*	*Project Area (Hectare)*	*Families Settled (No.)*	*Project Cost (Rs. lakh)*
Arunachal	Siang	1603	1613	123.30
Manipur	Iril	1379	1369	81.39
Meghalaya	Dedram	1315	819	87.08
Mizoram	Dhaleswari, Palak and Chandur	2082	1150	128.70
Nagaland	Mangleu	295	132	16.33
Tripura	Howrah and Manu	1118	594	61.75

Source: N.E.C.

These projects were evaluated by the Administrative Staff College of India, Hyderabad in 1988-89, selecting 300 (5.42 percent) households by random sampling out of 5537 beneficiary households. Its most important findings included inadequate supply of land, irrigation and other assets to households; lack of inputs like seed, fertilizer, credit and extension services to farmers. The report finds that even though the jhum cycle in project areas declined from 7 to 11 years in 1977-78 to 3 to 7 years in 1988-89 the jhum area remained the same, thereby defeating the very purpose of the projects. The main reason was that settled farming could not provide all the crops except paddy to the households; for other crops they had to return to jhuming. Improper selection of some project sites could be another reason. As a result, the settled families except in Mizoram continued to practise jhum. The percentage of such families reverting to jhuming are as given in the brackets—Arunachal (100), Meghalaya (91), Manipur (67), Nagaland (34) and Tripura (28). Thus, the NEC experience showed mixed success.

Problems in Transformation of Hill Agriculture

Transformation of hill agriculture is a challenging task, challenges coming from topography, technological alternative, economic backwardness of the tribals and socio-cultural factors. Plain areas being limited, it is a problem to settle a sizeable proportion of the jhumia families in permanent cultivation. The aim of settled farming being maximisation of marketable surplus through multiple cropping cannot be attained in the absence of complementary inputs. Even if there is surplus the cost of transporting to markets will be prohibitive. Though jhuming is subsistence, risk and uncertainty in it is relatively less due to crop diversification. Of course, jhum lands give crop only once in several years depending on the cycle. Compared to 'born free living free' jhum culture, settled farming demands management culture to which tribals are not adept. Reaching every community living in far-flung villages is also a problem for the extension machinery.

Though alternative land and use models are available from ICAR and technology is available for HYV paddy they same are not easily transferable without socio-cultural break-through. Some tribes believe that land fertility and crop productivity are divine blessings. Jhum rice is suitable for brewing, often required by the tribals for drinks and performance of rituals, where HYV rice is not suited. The ICAR experience in tribal village adoption to settled farming with free/subsidised inputs reveals that farmers prefer cash to kind assistance.

Settled farming is highly capital intensive. But tribal land system is a problem to banks as it lacks mortgage-ability for want of written record of ownership rights. Hence tribal farming remains 'untouchable' to banks and capital formation in hill agriculture goes by default.

Suggested Strategy

Efforts made by the government to develop hill agriculture are not sufficient by themselves. Following measures can be suggested:

(a) ***Short-run measures***—Where the jhum cycle is longer, measures should be taken to increase productivity through popularisation of optimal practices and improved varieties. Areas where the cycle is critical, attempts should be taken up on a priority basis for settled farming. Extension machinery should be strengthened both qualitatively and quantitatively. Rewards for best performance should be given to both extension workers and farmers.

(*b*) ***Medium term measures***—Areas having scope for horizontal and vertical development of agriculture should be identified to set up Agricultural Growth Centres offering infrastructure, physical, financial, marketing and training inputs to farmers through single window concept.

(*c*) ***Long-term measures***—In case the Banking Laws cannot be amended to finance jhuming, village councils and Tribal Chiefs should be persuaded to go for cadastral survey and conferring right of individual ownership. In semi-monetised tribal areas setting up of 'Input Banks' offering farm inputs, credit and marketing can be suggested. To facilitate inflow and outflow of inputs and outputs, and new ideas road communication should be expanded. As settled farming will not be able to absorb the entire surplus manpower so plans should be launched for urbanisation and industrialisation (preferably agro-based). Since pressure on land is high so population growth should be checked. Measures should also be devised to make jhuming environment-friendly.

Concluding Remarks

In view of the diversities in tribal social structure, land system and communication the approach to modernisation of hill agriculture would have to be multi-dimensional. Alternative to jhuming would have to be technologically viable, economically efficient and socially acceptable. In the execution of agricultural development projects at the village level, particularly in hilly tribal areas, involvement and active participation of the local people from the stage of project formulation to final execution should be ensured. In the earlier days, at the initiative of the village councils and headman, people came forward voluntarily to participate in such works. After the disappearance of the traditional village leadership the development work in the village has become an imposition by the government officials and so-called elected representatives. The old system of arriving at consensus has virtually disappeared. Hence in our urge to develop hilly tribal areas we should not ignore the traditional systems, and proceed cautiously to introduce the projects.

References

1. Alam, K., (ed.): Agricultural Development in North-East India (1993).

2. Goswami, P.C., (ed.): Agriculture in Assam, Assam Institute of Development Studies (1989), Gauhati.
3. Goswami, P.C.: Economics of Shifting Cultivation in North-East India, Agro-Economic Research Centre (1973), Jorhat.
4. Goswami, P.C.: Problems of Rural Sector Development in N.E. India, Journal of the North-Eastern Council (May-June 1986), Shillong.
5. Roy Burman, B.K: Institutional Finance and Development of Tribal Areas and Anthropological Perspective, Journal of the NEC, *ibid.*
6. Administrative Staff College of India: Evaluation of Pilot Projects (Jhum Control Scheme) North-Eastern States, Vol. I (1989), Hyderabad.
7. Indian Society of Agricultural Economics: IJAE, Conference No. (Oct-Dec., 1978), Bombay.
8. North-Eastern Council: Basic Statistics (1992), Shillong.
9. North-East India Council for Social Science Research: Shifting Cultivation in North-East India (2nd edition 1980), Shillong.
10. Directorate of Agriculture, Govt, of Arunachal Pradesh: Arunachal at a glance (1985-89), Naharlagun.
11. Directorate of Agriculture, Govt. of Meghalaya: Agricultural Census (1985-86); Input Survey (1986-87), Shillong.
12. Directorate of Economics and Statistics, Govt. of Meghalaya: Some Statistics of Jhum Cultivation (1988), Shillong.
13. Directorate of Agriculture, Govt. of Nagaland: Report on Agricultural Census (1985-86); Report on Input Survey (1986-87), Kohima.
14. Directorate of Economics and Statistics, Ministry of Agriculture, Govt. of India (GOI): Indian Agriculture in Brief, 23rd Edition (1990), New Delhi.
15. Ministry of Agriculture, GOI: Report of the National Commission on Agriculture (1976) Part-XIII, New Delhi.
16. Planning Commission, GOI: Report on Development of N.E. Region (1981), New Delhi.

CHAPTER 13

Distributive Pattern and Structural Changes in Land Holdings in Arunachal Pradesh: Some Implications

❑ M.C. BEHERA

The structure of the agricultural operational holdings undergo drastic changes in a primitive community that exposes itself to modern forces of development. With the limited agricultural land and the ever rising pressure of population on it, the process of changes assures greater significance in view of policy implications and environmental considerations. Agricultural development leads to changes in the structure and distributive pattern of land holdings which, on the other hand, have an important bearing on agricultural development through its influence over employment, productivity and income. Any agricultural planning, therefore, has to take into consideration the dynamics of the structure and distributive pattern of land holdings to promote sustained agricultural growth with social justice.

The present paper aims at an explorative analysis of the distribution and structure of land holdings in Arunachal Pradesh *vis-a-vis* their plan implications. It also attempts to focus attention on the need for land reforms to ensure twin objectives of equality and optimality in land ownership for efficient land use.

Agricultural development marked a beginning in the territory after independence through plan measures. But the planners were cautious enough not to interfers in the customary land tenure systems and practices of the multi-ethnic groups living here. The state has no cadastral land records so far. Land is still a free gift of nature to many tribal groups except in administrative centres. For this, the institution of tenancy was absent in the traditional agricultural system. Except few tribes, shifting cultivation was the traditional system of agricultural operation. Though land was an agent of status symbol among many tribes, occupation of land was need based. The village and community chiefs, of course, had command over more land resources; but the extent of inequality (discussed for a community practising same type of agricultural operation) in land ownership among households was, more or less, the result of family structure. There was, no doubt, a tendency to occupy more land, (this has been learnt during field study among different tribes in connection with research works) but socio-cultural bindings, the then materialistic outlook, limitation of the supply of labour force, non-existence of market economy were detracting forces which did not favour "land occupation for accumulation."

The analysis of present paper is based on agricultural census data of the state. Two statistical tools, *viz.* Lorenz curve and Gini-concentration ratio are used to interprete the data. Lorenz curve is fitted to examine the extent of inequality in the structure and distribution of holdings, while Gini ratio is calculated to measure the extent of uniformity in the distribution over years.

Agricultural census data in Arunachal Pradesh have some inherent limitations because of the prevailing agricultural situation. Results obtained from the analysis and interpretation of these data have been verified in the light of field observations to uphold the objectivity of the purpose for which the study has been undertaken.

Arunachal Pradesh has a predominantly agrarian economy. It provides direct employment to about 65 percent of total main workers of the state (1991 census figures) and shares 31 percent of the net state domestic product at 1980-81 prices during 1994-95. Presently 4.06 percent of the area of the state is under agricultural operations and net area is 44.12 percent of the total area of operational holdings. As per government records, area under different land-uses of the state for the year 1985-86 is as follows:

Sl. No.	*Land Use*	*'000 Ha*	*Percentage to Total Area*
1.	Forest Area	515	61.53
2.	Operated Area	34	4.06

(a) Net area sown	15	44.12	% to total operational area
(b) Area under current fallow	2	5.88	
(c) Fallow other than current fallow	3	14.71	
(d) Other uncultivated land excluding fallow land	5	8.82	
(e) Cultivable waste land	4	11.76	
(f) Area not available for cultivation	5	14.71	
3. Unreported area	288	34.41	
Total (1+2+3)	837	100.00	

Structure and Pattern of Holdings

Farm-size is classified into five categories as per the census classification, *viz.* marginal farm size (below 1.00 ha), small (1.00-2.00 ha.), semi-medium (2.00-4.00 ha.) medium (4.00-100.00) and large (10.00 ha and above). Table 1 shows that semi-medium and medium-farms dominate the agrarian scene as the two together accounts for 62.3 percent of total holdings in 1970-71, 56.2 percent in 1980-81 and 59.3 percent in 1990-91. But the concentration of land area is recorded in medium and large farm sizes and this accounts for 84.9 percent in 1970-71, 72.8 percent in 1980-81 and 64.4 percent in 1990-91. Percentage of holdings and land area under marginal and semi-medium farms sizes have shown steady increase. Percentage share of land area under small farm size also has shown constant increase, in case of land holdings it has increased during the period under steady but the trend has been erratic. Under medium and large groups percentage share of holdings has been declining, but this has increased in case of land area under medium group and has decreased under large group.

The average size of land holdings for all class size is Arunachal Pradesh has shown a decline from 6.18 ha in 1970-71 to 3.62 ha in 1990-91. During this period average size of holdings has increased in marginal and small farm sizes, decreased in medium and large sizes. But it is same in semi-medium size, though the trend has been erratic except the first two farm sizes.

The average size of net area sown (Table 2) has been erratic among all category of holdings except the large farm size that has registered a steady increase. But a comparison over a period of 15 years shows that the average net are sown in 1985-86 over 1970-71 has increased by 20.55 percent in the state. Table 3 also shows

Table 1

PERCENTAGE DISTRIBUTION OF HOLDINGS AND AREA OPERATED BY SIZE CLASS AND AVERAGE SIZE OF HOLDINGS DURING 1970-71, 1980-81 AND 1990-91

Year	*Size Class of Holdings*															
	Marginal Below 1.00 ha			*Small (1.00-2.00)*			*Semi-medium (2.00-4.00) ha*			*Medium (4.00-10.00) ha*			*Large (10.00 or above)*			*Average Holdings for the state (ha)*
	H	*A*	*AH*	*H*	*A*	*AH*	*H*	*A*	*AH*	*H*	*A*	*AH*	*H*	*A*	*AH*	
1970-71	7.7	0.7	0.57	12.0	2.8	1.43	25.9	11.6	2.78	36.4	35.0	5.94	8.0	49.9	17.06	6.18
1980-81	16.5	2.3	0.58	20.7	6.9	1.43	28.1	18.0	2.73	28.1	39.2	5.96	6.6	33.6	22.12	4.27
1990-91	17.5	3.0	0.62	18.9	7.9	1.51	32.1	24.7	2.78	27.2	43.0	5.74	4.4	21.4	17.55	3.62

Source: Computed from various reports on Agricultural census, Deptt. of Agriculture.

H = Holdings, A = Area, AH = Average size of holdings.

that there is a substantial increase in net area sown in medium and large categories while it has declined in marginal and small farm sizes during the same period.

Table 2

DISTRIBUTION OF AVERAGE NET AREA SOWN ALONG WITH PERCENTAGE OF VARIATION

Sl. No.	Category of Holdings	Average Net Area Sown 1970-71	76-77	1980-81	85-86	% Variation in 1985-86 Over 1970-71
1	2	3	4	5	6	7
1.	Marginal	0.49	0.51	0.41	0.42	(-) 14.29
2.	Small	0.93	1.03	0.93	0.89	(-) 5.38
3.	Semi-medium	1.27	1.53	1.45	1.51	+ 18.90
4.	Medium	1.47	2.03	1.91	2.54	+ 72.79
5.	Large	2.48	2.72	4.64	5.99	+ 141.53
6.	All categories in Arunachal Pradesh	1.46	1.68	1.51	1.76	+ 20.55

Source : Same as Table 1.

Table 3 reveals that for all size class in Arunachal Pradesh number of holdings has increased by 19.95 percent whereas land area has decreased by 29.70 percent in 1990-91 over 1970-71. During this period both holdings and area have declined for medium and large categories while for other three categories they have increased.

The tenancy status as shown in Table 4 depicts erratic trends. The change in 1985-86 over 1976-77 shows that there is an increase in holdings but a decline in land area under first two categories of tenure. Area under wholly leased in holdings has increased during this period while number of such holdings has declined.

With reference to 1990-91 agricultural census, it is estimated that 97.90 percent of operational holdings and 99.13 percent of area operated belong to tribal communities. The distribution of land

Table 3

PERCENTAGE CHANGE IN THE NUMBER OF HOLDINGS AND LAND AREA. IN 1990-91 OVER 1970-71

Size Class of Holdings											
Marginal		*Small*		*Semi-medium*		*Medium*		*Large*		*for all size class in the State*	
H	*A*	*H*	*A*	*H*	*A*	*H*	*A*	*H*	*A*	*H*	*A*
170.49	191.43	89.47	99.26	48.78	49.03	-10.42	-13.49	-70.63	-69.80	19.95	-29.70

Source: Same as Table 1. H = Holdings, A = Area.

Table 4

PERCENTAGE DISTRIBUTION OF HOLDINGS AND AREA BY TENANCY STATUS ALONG WITH VARIATION

	Year						*Percentage of change*					
	1976	*1977*	*1980*	*1981*	*1985*	*1986*	*In 1980-81 Over 1970-71*		*In 85-86 Over 80-81*		*In 85-86 Over 1976-77*	
Category of Tenure	*H*	*A*	*H*	*A*	*H*	*A*	*H*	*A*	*H*	*A*	*H*	*A*
1	2	3	4	5	6	7	8	9	*10*	*11*	*12*	*13*
A. Wholly owned & self operated	98.26	98.97	97.89	98.63	98.70	99.10	17.67	(-) 15.41	8.84	3.03	28.08	(-) 12.86
B. Partially owned & partially leased in	1.51	1.00	1.70	1.27	1.21	0.84	32.77	(-) 8.10	(-) 23.11	(-) 32.41	2.07	(-) 26.94
C. Wholly leased in	0.23	0.03	0.41	0.10	0.90	0.06	109.87	225.49	(-) 75.55	(-) 40.36	(-) 48.68	94.12
D. Total	100.00	100.00	100.00	100.00	100.00	100.00	18.11	(-) 5.11	7.96	2.53	27.51	(-) 12.97

Source: Same as Table 1. H = Holdings, A = Area.

holdings, it is supposed in such communities, assumes a greater degree of equality. Land holdings are absolutely equitably distributed if 'n' percent of the number of holdings has 'n' percent of the area operated.

Lorenz curves shown in Fig. 1 depicts the extent of inequality in the distribution of holdings. The measure of the deviation of actual distribution from the line of equal distribution has become less during 1990-91 over 1976-77. Values of Gini concentration ratio as shown in Table 5 substantiate to the point, as is otherwise depicted through Lorenz curves, that the distribution of land holdings is becoming less inequal over periods.

Table 5

VALUE OF GINI CONCENTRATION RATIO

Year	*Value of Gine C/R*
1976-77	0.52386
1980-81	0.52320
1985-86	0.49032
1990-91	0.46158

Table 6

VALUE OF GINI C/R FOR CATEGORY OF HOLDINGS (1990-91)

Category	*Value of Concentration Ratio*
Marginal	0.00471
Small	0.04476
Semi-medium	0.00180
Medium	0.06712
Large	0.12868

Table 6 reflects value of concentration ratio for category of holdings of eight blocks-four with settled cultivation and other four with jhum cultivation selected on purpose from government records to study concentration of land holdings in class size. The concentration is recorded high under large category followed by the medium and small sizes. Under semi-medium and marginal sizes the ratios are small.

Explanation and Implications

The foregoing analysis of the structure and pattern of land holdings gives a picture which has been explained in this section with reference to empirical evidences.

1. Consequent upon the decline in operated area from 4.9 lakh hectares to 34 lakh hectares and increase in the number of operational holdings from 0.8 lakh to 1.0 lakh hectares over two decades from 1970-71 to 1990-91, the average size of land holdings for all class size has declined from 6.18 hectares to 3.62 hectares. Area under jhum cultivation has dropped from 4.6 lakh hectares in 1970-71 to 2.7 lakh hectares in 1985-86.

The plausible explanation for increases in the number of operational holdings is, of course, the increase in population pressure on land. But the pressure on land, as is observed, is more due to the change in land-man relationship than population growth. The emergence of private right in land consequent upon the changing materialistic outlook has led to investment on land. Educated youths and tribal elites migrate from hills and interior villages in plains, they invest their money income on agricultural land in suitable locations in plains and establish their own households. This is a general feature in and around Pasighat Tezu, Namsai and Bordumsa areas. The village forest land in between 32 miles and Airfield and beyond towards Lohit Pur have beer converted to agricultural fields mostly by migrant population from hills to Tezu area. Shortage of agricultural land (in some villages, a few families belonging to elite group occupy culturable land for plantation crops. They also occupy more agricultural land with a "motion to accumulate" which they lease out) in the village area leads to division and shifting of families to other places. New villages recorded in census reports substantiate to the point. In areas where jhum cultivation is the practice, family members shift to distant jhum fields (shifted families occupy distant jhum fields with a motive to own and accumulate landed property.) Fallow jhum fields, which belong to the community, are being converted to the tea estates by individual families in Changlang and Tirap districts. They establish their individual rights in such land. Remaining jhum fields for supplying food requirements are used with less intervals. All these account for the decline in the duration of jhum cycle and shifting to new places. Consequently, number of operational holdings go on increasing.

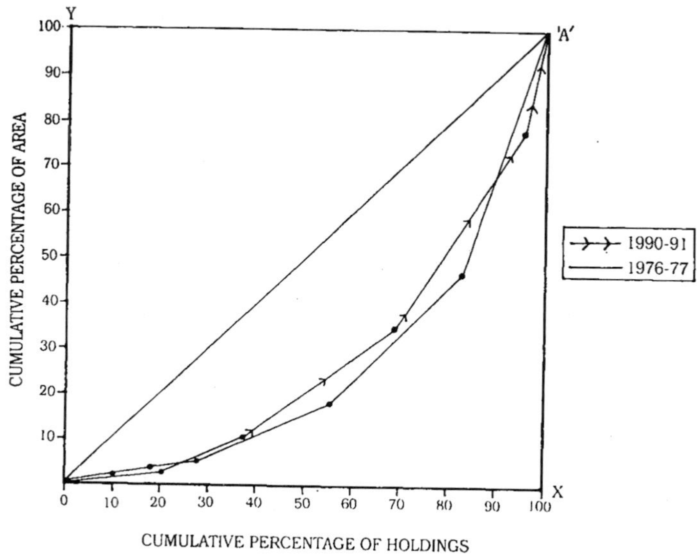

Fig. 1 : LORENZ CURVES For 1976-77 & 1990-91

The decline in area-under shifting cultivation has taken place owing to the conversion of jhum fields into permanent uses like terrace farming, horticultural gardens etc. Another explanation paints to rural-urban migration. Many rural people migrate to urban centres because of pull factors like the availability of educational institutions, job opportunities etc. The people mostly depend on market and Fair Price Shops to meet their food requirements. In some interior villages of West-Siang and Lohit districts, it is observed, some families spend the money, remitted by their relations from urban centres, on purchasing C.P.O. rice. Moreover, due to spread of education female population is found working in non-farm activities and children earlier constituting a part of the work force are schooled. All these have led to the decrease in the supply of labour force at the peak time of jhum activities and to less dependence on jhum cultivation for food supply.

During the period from 1970-71 to 1985-86, average net area sown for all class sizes in Arunachal Pradesh has increased by 20.55 percent. Due to change in land-man relationship fallow lands have been brought under cultivation. The emerging tenancy system, production of commercial crops, and decline in current fallow land from 0.8 lakh hectares to 0.2 lakh hectares and fallow land other than current fallow from 1.2 lakh hectares to 0.5 lakh hectares during the period of reference substantiate to the point.

Number of holdings and land area have declined in 1990-91 over 1970-71 (Table 4) for medium and large class size while these have increased in other categories. Official records attribute the reason to break up of medium and large holdings to the division of families and infer that the fragmentation of holdings ensures equal distribution of land. The degree of inequality is gradually declining as can be seen from Gini concentration ratio and Lorenz curve analysis. But findings of scholars like Roy and Kuri, Talukdar, Das and observations of the present author stand contrary to official reports.

There is inequality in the distribution of land holdings between areas with permanent and shifting cultivation. Marginal and small holdings are not viable to meet food requirements of the jhumias. Value of Gini concentration ratio as shown in Table 6 for different categories of land holdings of eight blocks-four each from permanent and shifting cultivation areas reveals concentration of land holdings of large and medium sizes. Tribal elites are found investing on agricultural land either by purchasing or by occupying fallow lands and forest lands for commercial crops. The primogeniture rule of inheritance in many tribes does not favour the division of operational holdings. Increase in the number of new villages as mentioned earlier is the result of concentration of village land in large and medium categories. The field study in Chowkham area has revealed that the areas along both sides of NH-52 from Kherem to Gunanagar (about 7 kms.) and to the western bank of river Bering (about 6 km.) have been brought under mustard cultivation by eight families, mostly belonging to traditional elites, with the help of tenants. Some cases of earlier fallow land being converted to private land in the districts of Tirap, Changlang and West Siang were noticed. Data collected for agricultural census, as the author feels, lack accuracy. Because lands have not been cadastrally surveyed nor ownership right is clearly defined. Informants tend to hide facts (the author has come across many such instances) because of a sort of apprehension regarding land revenue after Arunachal Pradesh attained statehood. Information is either fabricated or understated in different agricultural census reports; area of agricultural land once exceeding that of the territory is a case to the point.

Concluding Remarks

In the absence of land records, data on land holdings have their own shortcomings. It not only affects the effective implementation of measures for agricultural development but also impedes the effectiveness of development programmes as a whole. Estimation of income from agriculture and agricultural productivity though are quantitatively expressed, they lack reliability and provide weak base for launching development programmes. It has been observed in villages that many families with apparently more landed property become manipulative to get income certificate with low income figure to avail subsidies and other facilities meant for marginal farmers and families below poverty line. Provision for free ration to families below poverty line is found being availed by some contractors who have leased out their land. Behind the shadow of the primogeniture rule of inheritance, other brothers of the family living jointly became the agents of grabbing government benefits. Such families who have acquired more landed property than fellow villagers, enjoy a position in village/community and this brings them in between government schemes and real beneficiaries identified. Development schemes of the government do not percolate down to the bottom.

Even if we believe in the authenticity of official figures, there still exists inter and intra tribal inequalities in the distribution of land holdings on account of the nature of agricultural practices in hills and plains. The process of privatisation associated with emerging tenancy system is a factor for accentuating inequality. Land–lessness, in some communities like Apatanis as a result of both customary land and present process of transformation is on the increase and Das has recorded it around 30 percent of households.

The process of agricultural transformation has brought about some institutional changes as has been discussed. Such changes along with customary practices do not create base for efficient implementation of development programmes for agricultural modernisation. The process of modernisation assumes pre-conditions for achieving desired goals. Reformist measures in the form of cadastral survey, maintaining land records and enacting regulation for uniform inheritance in the state should be the priority at this juncture to ensure equality and increase productivity.

References

1. Reports on Agricultural census, 1970-71, 1976-77, 1980-81, 1985-86.

   Report on Provisional Number and Area of operational holdings 1990-91. Directorate of Agriculture, Government of Arunachal Pradesh, Naharlagun.
2. Draft Annual Plan 1994-95, P and D department, Govt. of A.P., Itanagar.
3. Report on Agricultural Census 1985-86, p. 23.
4. Roy N.C. and Kuri P.K. (1995): Risk, Land Reform and Agricultural Productivity in Arunachal Pradesh.

   Paper presented at the International Seminar on "Environment, Bio-diversity and Sustainable Development in North-East India" (NEHU, AIZAWL, Mizoram, 26-27th September, 1995).

   (1995): Traditional Institution of Land Ownership and Risk coping Mechanisation in Rural Arunachal. Resarun, Vol. XXI, No. 1 & 2 1995, Director of Research Government of Arunachal Pradesh, Itanagar.
5. Talukdar, A.C. (1995): Land Tenure Land Use Pattern in Arunachal Pradesh: A Review. Paper presented at the workshop on A Land Reforms: Agenda for North-East (Guwahati, April 3-5).
6. Das, J.N. (1989): Land System of Arunachal Pradesh, Guwahati Land Research Institute, Guwahati High Court.
7. Borpatragohain, C.K. (1987-88): Struggle for Freedom from the Economic Bondage' in Arunachal Review Sept. 87 to Feb. 88. Vol. III, No. 1, DIPR, Government of Arunachal Pradesh, Naharlagun. P. I.
8. Das J.N., *op.cit.*

CHAPTER 14

Constraints to Agricultural Growth in Arunachal Pradesh

❑ N.C. NAYAK

Arunachal Pradesh, a thinly populated mountaineous tract (density of population being 10 per sq.km. in 1991 census) on the extreme north-east India, is largely dominated by tribals (tribal population constitutes 63.66 percent of total population). Agriculture is the main source of livelihood of the people of Arunachal Pradesh. As per 1991 census, out of 390,979 main working population nearly 63.34% are cultivators and 5.12% are agricultural labourers comprising together around 69% of the total working population engaged in agricultural sector. Agricultural sector shares around 35 percent of the NSDP at 1980-81 prices during 1993-94 and provides direct employment to around 67 percent of the working population. Hence, the development of agriculture assumes greater significance in the overall developmental strategies of the state.

In this paper, an attempt has been made to have an overview of the nature and working of agrarian structure in Arunachal Pradesh and constraints arising therefrom. The whole analysis is based on the secondary data and some primary information.

Land Tenure System

The ownership of land and the individual right to use it are determined by the traditions and customs of the people of Arunachal Pradesh. Despite variations in the traditions and customs and prevalence of uncodified customary laws, and land tenure system practised among the different tribes may be classified into *(a)* village or community land, *(b)* Clan land, and *(c)* individual land.

In the areas where shifting cultivation is practised, the ownership of land is conferred either on the village or on the clan. However, the individual right to cultivate and possess land also continues through the cycle of agrarian operation and remains suspended during the fallow periods.

The village land includes outlying forest land used for hunting and forest produce. Sometimes, they are also earmarked for clans and sub-clans. Individual possession is also granted for the land under permanent cultivation.

On the other hand, individual ownership of land is conferred either by inheritance or by purchase. The inheritance of individual land also varies from tribe to tribe. However, normally the eldest son of the family inherits the parental property. In some other tribes, land is equally distributed among the sons and no land is inherited by a daughter. In the absence of a male member, the land may be inherited by the widow. But after her death, the land goes to her nearest clan member. The selling or purchasing of land can be made within the village community only.

Cultivation Practices

There are mainly two types of cultivation practices prevalent on the state *viz.* *(i)* Settled cultivation, *(ii)* Jhum or Shifting cultivation.

The settled cultivation is a type of permanent cultivation practised by a small fraction of population. The net area sown under permanent cultivation is only 7,6759 hectares on 1985-86 out of total net sown area of 149314 hectares of land. Paddy, maize, wheat, pulses, vegetables and oilseeds are the crops grown in the land depending on the climate and soil.

However, shifting cultivation is considered to be still important vocation of the people of Arunachal Pradesh. It is not only a source of earning livelihood but is very much connected with the existing social structure and any dislocation may lead to economic and social inequalities.

Shifting cultivation in Arunachal Pradesh is an age old practice. A good number of food crops are grown in the jhum field. The tropical humid forest of the state high rain-fall and low land-man ratio are conducive to practise shifting cultivation in place of any other alternative method of cropping.

Land Use and Cropping Pattern

The total operated area in the state is 344,254 hectares in 1985-86 against 335,732 hectares in 1980-81. This gives a slight increase of 2.53 percent of the operated areas within a span of five years. Out of this the net area sown in the state is 149314 hectares against 118232 hectares in 1980-81. This gives equally a positive picture of increase in the net sown area by 26.29 percent over the same period.

Table 1

Sl. No.	*Particulars*	*1980-81*		*1985-86*		*Change in 1985-86 over 1980-81*
		Areas (in Hect.)	*% to Total*	*Area (in Hect.)*	*% to Total*	
1.	Net area sown	118232	35.22	149314	43.38	(+) 26.29
2.	Area under current fallow	23127	6.89	24700	7.18	(+) 6.80
3.	Fallow other than current fallow	57253	17.05	49008	14.24	(-) 14.40
4.	Other uncultivable land excluding fallow land	34888	10.39	28655	8.32	(-) 17.87
5.	Waste land	47595	14.14	44426	12.90	(-) 6.66
6.	Area not available for cultivation	54637	16.27	48129	13.98	(-) 11.91
	Total	335732	100.00	344232	100.00	(+) 2.53

Source: Agricultural Census, 1985-86, Directorate of Agriculture, Arunachal Pradesh.

In Arunachal Pradesh, generally two types of cropping patterns are prevalent, *viz.* mono cropping and mixed cropping. The former is practised mostly in settled area where as the latter is practised both in settled and Jhum areas.

Paddy is the major crop grown in plains followed by mustard or potato or vegetables or pulses. In upland areas pulses, vegetables, oilseeds, spices, different fruits and other food and non-food crops are raised. On the other hand, on jhum fixed, mixed cropping of paddy, maize, millets, kharif pulses, vegetables etc. are grown. However, in jhum's second year paddy is raised by majority of the cultivators along with other crops.

Paddy being the major crop of the farmers in the State is grown over 93.72% of the total operational holdings covering 53.86% of the total cropped area. Maize occupies the second position covering 12.99% of the total cropped area and 81.25% of the operational holdings. The coverage of area under vegetables is 5.73% with 56.27% holdings and pulses 1.26% of area with 23.53% holdings. Under oilseeds (mostly mustard), area covered is 6.09% with 31.03% holdings. Table 2 gives the idea of coverage under different crops.

If we look at the percentage change in number and area under different crops in 1985-86 over 1980-81, we find that there are substantial decrease of holdings recorded in other non-food crops (98.24%), tobacco (79.14%) and barley (37.87%) along with the decrease in cropped area by 41.44%, 75.41% and 78.09% respectively. On the other hand, there has been a decrease in the cropped area growing millet, other cereals, sugar cane and fibre crops, although the number of holdings growing the crops have increased. Rice, maize, wheat, pulses, fruits and vegetables have shown increasing trend both in number and cropped area over the same period.

It is observed that agricultural sector in Arunachal Pradesh is based on mainly subsistence production. The marketable surplus generated in this sector is small. Food crops are raised by majority of the cultivators. Very few of them grow cash crops for commercial purpose. Therefore there is significant change in the cropping pattern in Arunachal Pradesh in some areas but not in all places.

Constraints

From the above analysis of landuse and cropping pattern, it is worthwhile to mention that agricultural sector in Arunachal Pradesh has not registered significant development despite planned afforts made in different plan periods, how-so-ever casual and half-hazard they may be. Various social, economic and institutional factors can be held responsible for the low performance of agriculture in the state. Many of them are inter-linked and act and react upon one another to hamper agricultural growth. However, an effort is being made to highlight those factors which have a direct bearing on the growth of agriculture in Arunachal Pradesh.

In this context, a report of techno economic Survey of NEFA, 1967, prepared by the National Council of Applied Economic Research listed three main constraints of agricultural development in the then NEFA, *viz.,* scarcity of cultivable land, lack of man-power and primitive technology. After about three decades of planned development, the above projected factors still persist to hold good in the state. Besides them, certain other equally important factors responsible for the backwardness of agriculture in the state are also those as cited below.

Scarcity of Culturable Land

Arunachal Pradesh in full of mountains and hilly terrains. Very negligible arable flat lands suitable for settled cultivation are available in the state. Settled cultivation is practised in the foothills comprising a very insignificant portion of the total land area. Conversion of Jhum lands to settled lands requires the construction of terrace in the slopes of the hills. This demands large scale man-power whose supply is limited in the State. Moreover, the development of cultivable land requires infrastructural facilities, such as roads, transport and communications, power supply, etc. which are also lacking. Absence of human labour is also accompanied by the lack of appropriate technology and scientific methods. All these factors combined together impede the growth of cultivable land in Arunachal Pradesh.

Lack of Manpower

On account of economic diversification a portion of the people both male and female previously dependent on agriculture have shifted to non-farm activities. Moreover, the children who also used to participate in traditional agricultural activities are schooled. Those who are educated have shifted to activities other than agriculture leaving unskilled and illiterate workforce in agriculture. Thus, the agricultural sector suffers from the death of skilled man-power which is necessary for agricultural modernisation.

Primitive Technology

Arunachal Pradesh is one of the few backward states in the North-east, which still used primitive and absolute technologies in agriculture. Use of plough and bullock in certain areas of the state is just a recent phenomenon. Cultivators continue to use dao and dibling stick as their agricultural implements for most of their agricultural operations. Use of modern technologies like tractors, power tillers, harvestores, etc. is limited to few rich farmers.

Lack of Irrigation Facility

Though the state has vast potential of irrigation projects, due to the peculiar terrain only minor irrigation schemes are introduced. Moreover, the necessity of irrigation facilities in the state was perhaps, never felt by the planners in the earlier plan periods. Only after the introduction of HYV cultivation from 1960s, the importance of irrigation was largely realised and certain minor irrigation schemes were introduced. However, the state is still lacking in irrigating agricultural sector to a significant level. As per 1990-91 date, only 31000 hectares of land have been irrigated by the sources other than chanals, tubewells and other wells. While the state has the potential of utilising both ground and surface water, irrigation facility has so far been extended mainly by utilising surface water. Moreover, use of electricity for agriculture is necessary which is also lacking in the state.

Less Use of Fertiliser

Agricultural productivity is mainly dependent on the use of fertilisers, pesticides and insecticides. However the use of fertiliser in Arunachal Pradesh is lowest in the north-east. As per 1992-93 data estimated by Planning Commission the consumption of nitrogen in Arunachal Pradesh in both kharif and rabi seasons is only 300 tonnes. Similarly, the consumption of phosphate and potash in only 140 tonnes and 50 tonnes respectively in the year 1992-93. In Arunachal Pradesh, the consumption of plant nutrients per unit of gross cropped area is only 1.9 kg/hect. The consumption of pesticides also shows a grim picture. As per the estimation made by the Centre for monitoring Indian economy, Bombay, the consumption of pesticide in 1987-88 was only 168 gms/hect as against 377 gms at the all India level.

Due to less use of fertiliser, the agricultural productivity is low in Arunachal Pradesh. It is necessary to increase the use of fertiliser to enhance soil fertility and intensify production.

Lack of Transport and Communication

Lack of transport and communication poses a big constraint for overall development. Road communication facilities are lowest in India. As per the report of the Planning Commission, Transport Division, July 1994, the total length of road in Arunachal Pradesh as on 31.3.92 in only 8.9 per 100 sq.km.

The total length of road in Arunachal Pradesh is only 7250 km. The state is not yet provided with railway lines except Bhalukpong. Due to lack of communication facilities, agricultural experts and extension officials do not like to visit the interior places. Without inspecting the cultivated areas and knowing the problems of the cultivators, the planners and agricultural extension officers prepare plans for agriculture, allocate funds and thereby disburse useless seeds, fertilisers etc.

Poor Marketing Accessibility

In Arunachal Pradesh, the marketable surplus generated from the food crops is almost negligible. However, cash crops like fruits and vegetables generate large volume of marketable surplus. Cash crops like tea, rubber, coffee, apples, oranges produce marketable surplus. But the farmers face difficulties in marketing these crops due to many reasons. There is lack of post-harvest technology to preserve and protect the crops for a longer duration. Absence of proper processing forces the farmers to sell the surplus produce at lower prices. Products are not properly graded and standardised. Due to lack of proper storage facilities, the fruits and vegetables are damaged in quantities. Coupled with this, lack of better transport and communication facilities compels the farmers to dispose off their produce in the local market at a lower price. Though, certain food crops have got export potential, farmers are unable to export them due to the above reasons. As per the data collected from the Central Warehousing Corporation, New Delhi, Arunachal Pradesh is the only state in the north-east which does not possess a single central or state warehouse. As on 31.3.93 only 5 co-operative godowns with a capacity of 2500 tonnes have been set up in the state for marketing purposes.

Shifting Cultivation

Shifting cultivation as an agricultural practice leads to deforestation, soil erosion and loss of soil fertility. It thus creates ecological imbalances in the region. The perennial occurrence of landslides in the hills is largely due to the practice of jhumming. How-so-ever,

Table 2

NUMBER AND AREA OF OPERATIONAL HOLDINGS, GROWING CROPS AND PERCENTAGE OF TOTAL CROPPED AREA

Sl. No.	*Crops*	*Total Operational Holdings*	*Holdings Growing the Crop*	*% of Holdings Growing the Crop*	*Total Cropped Area (in hect)*	*Area Under the Crop*	*% of Area Under the Crops to Total Cropped Area*
1.	Rice	84792	79471	93.72	167469	90204	53.86
2.	Maize		68896	81.25		21760	12.99
3.	Millet		62225	73.39		15392	9.19
4.	Wheat		7124	8.40		2645	1.58
5.	Barley		3163	3.73		280	0.17
6.	Other cereals		3695	4.36		370	0.22
7.	Pulses		19952	23.53		2117	1.26
8.	Spices		14861	17.53		2105	1.26
9.	Fruits		21306	25.12		9049	5.40
10.	Vegetables		47715	56.27		9589	5.73
11.	Sugarcane		1438	1.70		232	0.14
12.	Other food crops		37095	43.75		3197	1.91
13.	Oil seeds		26310	31.03		10205	6.09
14.	Fibre crops		127	0.15		8	0.005
15.	Tabacco		117	0.14		15	0.009
16.	Other non food crops		56	0.07		301	0.18
						167469	100.00

Source: Agricultural census, 1985-86, Directorate of Agriculture, Arunachal Pradesh.

social important jhumming might be, agricultural productivity would suffer, if the farmers can not put a check to this age old practice.

Conclusion and Recommendation

The following are the possible strategies that need to be developed:

1. Codification of customary landlaws to regulate the individua–lisation of property rights in land.
2. Efficient and scientific use of land and implementation of scientific jhumming.
3. Development of horticulture in the jhumming land.
4. Provision for institutional finance and extension programmes.
5. Adequate infrastructural and marketing facilities.

References

1. Alam, K. (ed): ''Agricultural Development in North-East India; Constraints and Prospects'', Deep and Deep Publications, N. Delhi.
2. Saikia. P.D. & Borah Durgeswari (ed): ''Constraints of Economic Development in North-East India (Problems and Prospects)'', Omsons Publications, N. Delhi.
3. Mazumdar, D.M. (ed): ''Shifting Cultivation in North-East India, Omsons Publications, N. Delhi.
4. Basic Statistics of N.E. Region, 1995, North-Eastern Council, Ministry of Home Affairs, Govt. of India, Shillong.
5. Report on Agricultural Census, 1985-86, Directorate of Agriculture, Arunachal Pradesh, Naharlagun.
6. Arunachal Pradesh at a glance 1995, Directorate of Economic & Statistics, Govt. of Arunachal Pradesh, Itanagar.
7. Gopalakrishnan, R.: The N.E. India : Land Economy & People, Har-Anand Publications in association with Vikas Publishing House, Pvt. Ltd.

CHAPTER 15

Changing Facets of Agriculture in Arunachal Pradesh

❑ B. PANDA

The economy of Arunachal Pradesh continues to be agriculture dominated. Out of a total geographical area of 84,000 sq.km. (approx), about 70 percent constitutes broad valleys and narrow valleys, 10 percent foothills and plains and 20 percent forms the snow clad peaks. Agricultural operations are undertaken in only five percent of the total geographical area. Even then it provides direct employment to about 67 percent of total main workers of the state as per 1991 census. However agriculture in the state has undergone significant qualitative and quantitative changes over the past two decades. This paper highlights some such important changes in the state of agriculture and makes an endeavour to quantify such changes wherever possible so that further intensive and extensive research can be carried out on those aspects by subsequent researchers. However, non-availability of data in many cases, non-availability of comparable data in some cases and limitations of space and time, etc. have denied the author to explore the possibility of undertaking certain fruitful quantification exercises. With these limitations, the following percipient changes have occurred in the agricultural sector of the state over the last two decades.

Decline in the Proportion of Working Population Engaged in Agriculture

A noticeable change has taken place in the pattern of total main working population engaged in agriculture over the past two decades. Table 1 below depicts such changes in the occupational structure and labour force composition in the state with the help of figures derived from 1971, 1981 and 1991 census reports.

Table 1

PROPORTION OF WORKING POPULATION ENGAGED IN FARM AND NON-FARM ACTIVITIES IN ARUNACHAL PRADESH (1971-1991)

Year	*Total Working Population*	*Percentage of Main Workers to Total Population*	*Labour Force in*	
			Farm Sector	*Non-farm Sector*
1	*2*	*3*	*4*	*5*
1971	269542	57.65	216452 (80.30)	53090 (19.70)
1981	313445	49.61	231164 (73.75)	82281 (26.25)
1991	399782	45.20	256041 (64.05)	143741 (35.95)

Source: Various census reports.

Note: Figures in brackets indicate percentage of workers.

Table 1 states that there has been a gradual fall in the proportion of main workers to total population from the level of 57.65 percent in 1971 to 45.20 percent in 1991. In 1971, 80.30 percent of the total main workers were engaged in farm sector, it declined to 73.75 percent in 1981 and finally to 64.05 percent in 1991. On the other hand non-farm employment as a percentage of total main workforce has increased from a level of 19.70 percent in 1971 to 35.95 percent in 1991 census. In view of more or less constant contribution of agriculture to Net State domestic product (NSDP) (it has remained more or less constant at about 33-34 percent) in the early nineties and the quantum rise in non-farm employment the noticeable fall in the percentage of workforce in farm sector indicates the huge under-employment and disguised unemployment prevailing in agriculture in the yester decades.

So far as the reasons for this fall are concerned one plausible reason is the presence of under employment. Another important reason is the increase in stress on land reflected by the gradual fall in the average size of operational holdings. (See Table 2).

Table 2 shows that the average size of operational holdings has declined from 6.19 hectares in 1970-71 to 4.27 in 1980-81 and

Table 2

AVERAGE SIZE OF OPERATIONAL HOLDINGS

Year	*Size of Operational Holdings (Ha)*
1	*2*
1970-71	6.19
1976-77	5.95
1980-81	4.27
1985-86	4.00
1990-91	3.62

Source: Arunachal Agriculture in Brief, Govt. of Arunachal Pradesh.

to 3.62 hectares in 1990-91. With the decline in the average size of operational holdings the land-man ratio has worsened bringing stress on the existing land. This along with general developmental activities (which have opened up alternative employment facilities) has been instrumental in pushing up increased percentage of main workers to find employment in non-farm activities. Further, this decline in the percentage of farm employment and the rise in the percentage of non-farm employment over the past two decades can also be partly ascribed to the increased profitability of alternative non-agricultural occupations, preference for white-collar jobs among the educated youths and rise in intensive and permanent cultivation, etc.

Rise in the Percentage of Agricultural Labour

Another development discerned is the sharp rise in the percentage of agricultural labourers in the total workforce engaged in agriculture which is explained in Table 3.

Agricultural labour as a percentage of total main workforce employed in agriculture has increased from 2.44 percent in 1971 to 3.37 percent in 1981 and to 7.83 percent in 1991, and as a percentage of total main working force has increased from 1.96 percent in 1971 to 2.49 percent in 1981 and 5.02 percent in 1991. Simultaneously a decline is noticed in the percentage composition of cultivators in total main workforce (it has declined from 78.34 percent in 1971 to 71.26 percent in 1981 and to 59.03 percent in 1991) and in the total main agricultural workforce (it has declined from 97.56

Table 3

COMPOSITION (IN PERCENTAGE) OF AGRICULTURAL LABOUR IN THE TOTAL WORKFORCE AND AGRICULTURAL WORKFORCE IN THE STATE (1971, 1981, 1991)

Year	*Agricultural Labour as a Percent of Total Main Workforce.*	*Agricultural Labour as a Percent of Total Agricultural Main Workforce*	*Cultivators as a Percentage of Total Agricultural Main Workforce*	*Cultivators as a Percentage of Total Main Workforce*
1	*2*	*3*	*4*	*5*
1971	1.96	2.44	97.56	78.34
1981	2.34	3.37	96.63	71.26
1991	5.02	7.83	92.17	59.03

Source: Computed from different census.

percent in 1971 to 96.63 in 1981 and to 92.17 percent in 1991). The rise in agricultural labour is more pronounced if we look at the decadal percentage growth during the last three censuses in agriculture labour, cultivators and non-agricultural workforce as given in Table 4 below :

Table 4

DECADAL PERCENTAGE RISE IN AGRICULTURAL LABOURERS, CULTIVATORS AND NON-AGRICULTURAL WORK-FORCE

Decade	*Percentage Growth*		
	Cultivator	*Agril. Labourers*	*Non-Agricultural Workforce*
1	*2*	*3*	*4*
1971-81	5.78	47.32	91.00
1981-91	5.65	157.23	41.75

Source: Computed from different census.

From Table 4, it is noticed that during 1981-91 decade the growth of cultivators has declined to 5.65 percent from 5.78 percent during the decade 1971-81, whereas, the decadal growth of agricultural labourers has increased from 47.32 percent in 1971-81 to 157.23 percent in 1981-91.

The stress factor, migration of labourers from outside the state in view of reluctance of educated youths to undertake to agricultural labour and their shift to non-agricultural occupations (esp. white collar jobs) etc. are some of the underlying reasons for this development. Owing to want of space and time, it is not possible here to go into the details of the causes.

Increase in Net Area Sown Under Permanent Cultivation

Another positive development marked is the continuous rise both in absolute terms and percentage terms in the net area sown under permanent cultivation *vis-a-vis* shifting cultivation. Shifting cultivation which has been the way of life of tribal people is gradually being discouraged. Table 5 below explains this trend.

Table 5

NET AREA SOWN UNDER SHIFTING AND PERMANENT CULTIVATION

(Area in Ha.)

Year	*Net Areas Sown*		*Total Area Sown*
	Permanent Cultivation	*Jhum Cultivation*	
1	2	*3*	*4*
1970-71	28006 (24.31)	87220 (75.69)	115226 (100)
1976-77	40013 (35.75)	71901 (64.25)	111914 (100)
1980-81	52012 (43.99)	66220 (56.01)	118232 (100)
1985-86	76759 (51.41)	72555 (48.59)	149314 (100)

Source: Computed from Annual plan, Govt. of Arunachal Pradesh, 1995-96.

From Table 5, it is seen that net area sown under permanent cultivation as a percentage of total net area sown has increased from 24.31 percent in 1970-71 to 51.41 percent in 1985-86, whereas, the percentage share of net area sown under shifting cultivation has decreased from 75.69 percent in 1970-71 to 48.59 percent in 1985-86. What is remarkable about this development is that such percentage decrease is net area sown under shifting cultivation and percentage and absolute increase in net area sown under permanent cultivation has been a continuous trend over last 15 years (1970-71 to 1985-86) for which period data are made available. This is no doubt a welcome sign for agricultural growth in the state. This healthy trend has been the result of spread of agricultural extension services even to the remote areas of the state-mechanisation of agriculture, stress factor, increased availability of infrastructural facilities including marketing and communication, irrigation use of HYV seeds and fertilisers and above are general socio-economic development of the state.

However, what worries the planners is that although in percentage terms there has been a precipient fall in the share of net area sown under shifting cultivation, but in absolute terms there has not been any appreciable decrease in the total area sown under this form of cultivation as soon from this table.

Table 6

FOOD GRAINS PRODUCTION IN ARUNACHAL (1970-71, 1990-91)

Year	*Foodgrains Production (MT)*	*Average Annual Percentage Growth*
1	2	*3*
1970-71	75915	—
1976-77	106339	5.78
1980-81	131026	5.36
1985-86	185000	7.14
1990-91	214308	2.98
1991-92	219780	2.55
1992-93	226050	2.85

Source: Computed from Arunachal, Agriculture is brief using the formula $r=(Pn/p)^{1/n}—1$.

Increase in Food Grains Production

Since the beginning of the fourth plan, considerable importance has been attached to increase crop production especially food grains production. Table 6 reveals the volume of increase in foodgrains production.

It is noticed that foodgrains production has increased over the past two decades from a level of 75915 in 1970-71 to 214308 in 1990-91. The decadal growth rate has been 72.60 percent and 63.56 percent respectively for the decades of 1970-71 to 1980-81 and 1980-81 to 1990-91. However, the annual percentage growth rate has slowed down in the first three years of early nineties. This is to some extent because of the diversification of agricultural activities.

The increase in foodgrains production has been possible mainly due to increase in extension services, increase in area coverage, transfer of technology (increase in irrigation infrastructure, HYV seed utilisation, fertiliser utilisation etc.) This author wanted to have estimations of the correlation of some such variables with food production non-availability of data/comparable data with regard to extension services and irrigation facilities necessitated the need to exclude these two important determinants of foodgrains production from the model of partial correlation. Even then a partial correlation analysis is undertaken involving the following variables:

Y (depended variable) = Foodgrains production.

X_1 (Independent variable) = Fertiliser used.

X_2 (Independent variable) = HYV seeds used.

In this model,

r_{yx1} = Simple correlation coefficient between Y variable and X_1 variable.

r_{yx2} = Simple correlation co-efficient between Y variable and X_2 variable.

r_{x1x2} = Simple correlation co-efficient between X_1 and X_2 variables.

r_{yx1x2} = Partial correlation co-efficient between Y variable and X_1 variable eliminating the impact of X_2 variable.

$r_{yx2.x1}$ = Partial correlation co-efficient between Y variable and X_2 variable eliminating the impact of X_1 variable.

$r^2_{\cdot yx1.x2}$ = Coefficient of partial determination between y variable and x_1 variable eliminating the impact of x_2 variable.

$r^2_{yx2.x1}$ = Co-efficient of partial determination between Y variable and X_2 variable eliminating the impact of X_1 variable.

Data for these sets of variables pertain to the period 1988-89 to 1992-93. The results are summarised below :

RESULTS OF PARTIAL CORRELATION ANALYSIS

Simple Correlation Coefficient	*Value of the Coefficient*	*Partial Correlation Coefficient*	*Value of Partial Correlation Coefficient*	*Coefficient of Partial Determination*	*Value*
r_{yx1}	0.55	$r_{yx1.x2}$	0.65	$r^2_{yx1.x2}$	0.42
r_{yx2}	0.65	$r_{yx2.x1}$	0.72	$r^2_{yx2.x1}$	0.52
r_{x1x2}	0.10	—	—	—	—

Both the co-efficients of partial determination are significant. The implication of a high $r^2_{yx2.x1}$ is that in days to come more em phasis should be given on HYV seed use.

Besides this excercise a attempt is made to study the correlation between food production and land under irrigation with data pertaining to a different period *i.e.* from 1970-71 to 1985-86 and the zero order co-efficient of determination (r^2) is found to be 0.83 which suggests that food production and irrigation are highly correlated. Hence, increase in irrigation facilities should continue to be on the top of measures to be adopted in coming years for increasing food production. (Irrigation should not be put into the partial correlation model since data for it could not be made available for the same period of time.)

Conclusion

Over the last two decades and some odd years agriculture in Arunachal has undergone a metamorphosis in various fields. In the present paper, changes with regard to the pattern and composition of main workforce employment in agriculture, net area sown under shifting and settled cultivation and foodgrains production were taken up for a detailed study. It is found that farm employment as a percentage of total main workforce has gone down and non-farm employment has increased significantly during this period. Net area sown under settled cultivation in absolute and percentage terms has increased continuously. Net area sown under shifting cultivation as a percentage of total net area sown has declined but in absolute terms there has been no marked fall in the net area sown under this head. Food production has increased at a high rate during the seventies and eighties, whereas, during the early nineties it shows a marginal growth. Food production although show a significant positive correlation with the growth of irrigation facilities, HYV seeds utilisation and fertiliser use, its correlation is highest with irrigation, higher with HYV seeds use and comparatively low with fertiliser consumption. Hence, the planners should attach highest importance to irrigation and HYV seeds use for further acceleration in food production in addition to other measures. Due to various limitations a number of other aspects of transformation, in the state of agriculture in Arunachal could not be dealt with. It will be in the best interest of the state, if researchers come forward and undertake further studies on these untreated aspects of agriculture in this State.

References

1. Annual Plan 1995-96, Planning and Development Department, Govt. of Arunachal Pradesh.
2. Arunachal Agriculture in Brief (Series-3) 1980-83. Directorate of Agriculture, Govt. of Arunachal Pradesh.
3. Economic Review of Arunachal Pradesh, 1994. Directorate of Economics and Statistics, Govt. of Arunachal Pradesh.
4. Visaria, Pravin and Rakesh Basant (Eds) 1994. "Non-Agriculture employment in India, Trends and Prospects", Sage Publications India Pvt. Ltd., New Delhi.

Part III

INSTITUTIONAL ISSUES

CHAPTER 16

Tribal Land Relations— A Transition to Private Ownership in Meghalaya

❑ B. DATTA RAY

J.B. Shadwell, a junior Political Officer stated in 1871 while stationed at Cherrapoonji, that land had been of no great importance and value in Khasi Hills. Each villages had possessed its own which any one of the villager was free to cultivate. He and his family after him had the right over this land by such cultivation. (Note by J.B. Shadwell on the Inhabitants of the Khasi and Jaintia Hills, 1871, Published in 1900 by Secretariat Press, Shillong).

In the upland plateau of Khasi hills land is classified as *(a)* public, and *(b)* private land, the *Ri Kyntis*. There are different formulations of *Ri Kynti*. One variety is *Ri Kur*. Ri Kur is private clan lands which are co-jointly held by a clan or a group of clans. Chie Nakane (1967) reports that the Khasis consist of a number of matrilineal clans or Kurs whose members consider themselves decendants from a common ancestress. Major Kurs have no definite geographical distribution. Each is scattered over a wide area. Such a group of matrilineal kins is usually confined to one domestic family, having common ancestral property. The membership of the family or *ling* is determined through the mother. According to Chie Nakane, the core of the family comprises two persons, one holding the authority and the other owning the property. Succession is strictly matrilineal. The authority is transmitted from mother's brother to sister's son, while the property is held by the daughter from the mother. Youngest daughter by social convention does not leave the mother's house like her brothers and other sisters. The married brothers and married sisters branch off, although they continue to be members of mother's family, all their life. The most intimate intransic force in Khasi society is family or Iing. The number of households that are included, according to Chie Nakane, in a single and actual kinship ties through female, is strictly small. According to Chie Nakane, in the Khasi matrilineal society, ling is a social security to a man he may demand his place at his natal house. Net the individual but clan or jait is the unit of traditional Khasi society in which the eldest maternal uncle is the head. Family property can not be disposed, of without the consent of senior male members of the house.

In the traditional Khasi society mother's residential house is inherited by the youngest daughter. But there are variations. In War areas, all children equally inherit the ancestral property. In the traditional Pnar society, all lands acquired by inheritance must follow the custom by which, property descends from the mother to the youngest daughter. Males cultivate lands, but they bring the produce to the mother's house who would distribute it among the members of her family. This is being slowly changed due to population growth, external contact, media exposures, slow urbanisation and a slow emergence of private property.

Among the Bhoi Khasis, the sons succeed to all property, whether acquired or ancestral. The Lynngam law of inheritance is the same as that of Khasis of the central plateau. The sons do not get any share unless definitely willed. Amongst the Khasis, according to tradition, all property acquired by a man before his marriage is considered belonging to his mother or to his clan, theoretically speaking. The wife and children would inherit the post-marriage property, the youngest daughter getting the largest share of such property on the death of the mother.

According to P.R. Gurdon (the Khasis, 1907) no Khasi in upland Khasi Hills can possess landed property, unless it is self-acquired. In Jaintia Hills, if a man dies and leaves acquired property, his mother,.if alive would be his heir. If the wife does not remarry, she would inherit half of her husband's property, which at her death would devolve to her youngest daughter. If there are no daughters, the acquired property would be equally divided among all children. In Lynngam areas, lands have clan ownership. Some big and rich Lynngam families rent out plots of their land to the people of the village on payment of money. It indicates the growing landless peasants in the Khasi Hills with the rise of private land holdings.

In the War area Ri Seng prevails over a large sections of the descendants of the particular founder. They follow joint cultivation and the management is entrusted to a community council. The land cannot be sold or disposed of, but is reserved for the use of the descendants of the founder of the clan. This has not prevented the rise of landlessness of the peasants in the War areas. But in recent years land has become a saleable commodity.

Ri Raid are lands which belong to the whole community or to a particular village. Ri Shnong is village land belonging to the first occupants, which can be inherited and occupied by the members of that community. Ri Khains is a plot of land owned and cultivated by the members of a village folk. The ruling families like Syiems and Lyngdohs, Myntries have their own land holding reserved for their maintenance. According to Ka Riti, the Sytems do not have right to impose taxes on the people.

In Khasi Hills, the land by tradition, belongs to the community or to the Kur. The land holdings of the individual farmers have not been surveyed and no title or documents of the land have been issued to them. No cadastral survey is allowed in Khasi Hills by the elites. But every parcel of cultivable land now has been, for all practical purposes, under the possession of individuals, even absentees. Early private capitalism has arisen in the Khasi Hills by surreptitious means in the rural and urban areas as well. Community land has now been privatised there.

In the Jaintia Hills, the land tenure system is different. There is records by means of Chitta and Jamabandi documents. In 1901, plots of land were released to private holders who paid rent for their holdings, The use of land on the Patta method of holding was introduced and the traditional village authorities, the Dolois, were allowed to collect revenue on commission basis. The basis of privatisation of land and early capitalism out of feudal setup are well founded.

In Shillong town, the system of patta or document of title is in vogue since its introduction by the British in 1864-66 onwards.

No where else in Khasi Hills, the documents of title to private land prevail, though informal documentation could be seen. As a result, the villagers cannot so easily sell plots of land under their possession—which they hold with a customary right to tillage. If he leaves the plot of land and does not claim it for a specified period, he may forego his rights on the land. But it is passing phase. Land once under occupation, continues with the holder and for all purposes, in course of time, is considered to be his personal holding—to be taken over, if any by paying heavy compensation to him, which is not feasible in ordinary circumstance.

This Khasi land tenure system has caused much confusion. Whose is the land? It can not be so easily answered. This confusion in the absence of uniform land legislation has hindered agricultural reform and modernisation of it. There is a declining productivity of land. The forestry and mineral extraction is equally primitive.

Chie Nakane in 1967 reported the development of private property in the dying Khasi shifting cultivation. This is a glaring exception in shifting cultivation. In Khasi Hills, people of the same clan cannot claim the right to use the land, unless they are direct matrilineal descendant of the women who first owned the land. (Chief Nakane's Garo and Khasi Comparative Study, 1967 Montan Co., Press, Pahis). The newly possessed land is always owned by the individual family (iing).

This conception of land ownership gives a picture of essentially a private ownership. It seems that even the Ri Kur, the clan land, has been alienated or sold and has been developed into small holdings of private land for direct materlineal descendant groups. When the entitled owners move away to another village, the land is invariably sold. The private ownership has taken a firm root. Powerful persons of the community, occupy and claim as much as community land, Ri Raid, as they can. David Roy, a Khasi intellectual in 1946, prior to the Khasi States' merging with the Indian Union, remarked that the Raid land was being increasingly transformed into private land. As a result poor cultivators have been reduced to the status of tenants or hired labourers and the phenomenon of increasing landless rural labourers has emerged. There is a distinct trend to private ownership of land in Khasi Hills in a formative stage of private capitalism. The collection and limited trade in tezpata, broomstick and potato and exaction and trade in limestone, coal, silliminate and Govt. monopoly in Uranium and generation of hydel power and Cherr a cement have brought winds of change in the social and economic structure in Khasi and Jaintia Hills. With the advent of independence and merging of the Khasi states with Indian Union there have been very important changes in Khasi and Jaintia economy. These changes have introduced the Khasis into an active commercial economy which was brought about various changes in the social life of the Khasis and Jaintia Hills. The most important feature of this change is the development of private ownership of land. Today we get a picture of predominantly private ownership of land. The variations at present between rich and poor are considerable in a Khasi community in comparison with that of Garos.

Some chieftains have sold out or disposed of Raj lands without reference to the traditional Durbars. Natural resources are being exploited by the Syiems without the sanction of the traditional authorities and treated them as private ownership since independence.

The land tenures have caused much confusion. Traditional customs and usages defy codification and myths have been created to hide today the ground reality of emergence of private ownership of land and forests—two prime resources of any community, based on agriculture.

In Jaintia Hills, since British annexation, clearly and positively private ownership of land, forest and natural resources has been recognised and revenue administration organised as well. Patta system is now prevalent in land transactions. Direction is clear in the field of social and economic progress for the rise of early capitalism in place of feudal confusion elsewhere.

The British penetration and gradual occupation of the Garo Hills nearly 150 years back was due to protect the British territory of Bengal districts of Rangpur and Mymensing and also the district of Goalpara in the West. In due course of time, the prospect of almost untapped mineral resources like coal and limestone and the availability of cheap short stapple cotton for Manchester mills made such an occupation permanent. As in Cherrapunjee area of Khasi Hills English Company was there even before such a permanent occupation. As a result the isolation of the Garos from money economy was slowly breaking. The markets established on the borders of Garo Hills by the Zamindars of Bengal and Goalpara monetised the economy and the barter system with the coming of the British finally broken down. The Zamindars of Bengal gradually became owners of large tracks of land and hills of Garo Hills, which in the post colonial period with the abolition of zamindari system became B-Mahal land. This land forms about 20 percent of Garo Hills and has been cadastrally surveyed. There are also few hundred hectares of land in isolated pockets known as Khas land now managed by the District Council and surprisingly it is not cadasterally surveyed.

The rest of settlement in the Garo Hills are divided into a large number of well defined areas, *a'khing* land under the occupation and ownership of a large number of matrilineal clans *(machong)* managed by a small group of close matri-relations *(machari)* in consultation and with advice of a *Nokma* who is the custodian and manager of the *akhing* land on behalf of his wife.

The legal authority over land resources rests with the owner—lineage held by the principal male *(Nokma)* of the household on behalf of his wife. Sale, mortgage or transfer of any part of the *akhing* land (clan land) could be made by the *Nokma* in the name of his wife who is the titular head of the *akhing* with the consent of the clan elders. Since the coming of the Autonomous District Council, the council has been issuing patta (document of title of such settlements) on the recommendation of the *Nokma* concerned. Bank gives loan on the strength of such patta on the surety of certain authorities. *Akhing* land is well defined land area and an exclusive property of a lineage clan. But private land ownership of the *Akhing land* emerged gradually, with the introduction of money-economy and more so in post-colonial period with coming of the Autonomous District Council in Garo Hills. During the British period, the boundaries of the *Akhing* were made and it also recorded the rights and geneological trees of the *Nokmas*. It became ultimate reference to the rights to *Akhing* land and the beginning of the emergence of private property in the Garo Hills. In the pre-colonial days, the system of transfer of land through sale was present at the level of *a'Khing*. Even in shifting cultivation a family retains an implicit right over a plot of land allotted to it earlier by the *Nokma*. Even if a family leaves village, it retains the right over the orchards and trees planted by it. Every household has its usufruct right over *akhing* land and sale, mortgage or transfer of any part of it could be made with the support of *Nokma* and the clan elders and on such recommendation Pattas could be had from the Garo Hills Autonomous District Council.

The joint ownership of the *Akhing* land worked well in precolonial days. With the British occupation of Garo Hills, the traditional egalitarian Garo society received rude shocks. In place of barter economy, money economy penetrated deep with growth of large number of markets at the border villages of Garo Hills. A tier of over rights was established over the hills by the new rulers and house-tax was also introduced. Mohols were created for exploitation of natural resources of the hills. Money-economy created a new political power which passed to the hand of wealthy traders. Plots in *Akhing* land became disposable commodity. Private ownership right were created.

In the post-colonial period the Autonomous District Council was established in Garo Hills which inherited the land and land revenue administration. The over right in the hills was claimed by it and it assumed the role of issuing of Pattas which sealed the transition to private ownership of land.

From the community ownership of land, the control and direction of *akhing land* increasingly passed out to Autonomous District Council which is now empowered to encourage permanent cultivation in place of shifting cultivation by way of terracing of the hill slopes and by setting up of horticulture plantations. Private ownership of land grew out of wet cultivation and horticulture. There is a built-in incongruity between wet-cultivation and community ownership of land in the present day societal setup. The application of Assam Land and Revenue Regulation, 1966 is definitely indicative of emergence of private ownership in land in Garo Hills. Cadastral survey is in operation for almost thirty years. The terraced cultivation plots vation plots are now settled permanently.

A neo-rich rural stratum grew up in the hills and landless labour force is indicative of emergence of private ownership in place of community partnership in land based activities. A new socio-economic money-based relations have developed all over the tribal world in North-East India.

CHAPTER 17

Agrarian Structure and Land Relations in Meghalaya

❑ S.K. AGNIHOTRI

In order to understand agrarian structure and land relations in Meghalaya, it is desirable that the legal position regarding land administration is first examined. Apart from this, an overview of the customary land tenure system in the state is also needed to appreciate agrarian problems in their proper perspective.

The constitution has given power to the state legislature to make laws on land that is to say, rights in or over land, land tenures including the relation of landlord and tenant, and the collection of rents, transfer and allienation of agricultural land, land improvement and agricultural loans; colonisation. The state legislature can make laws even on those matters relating to land which have been allotted to the district council by provisions of the sixth schedule. However, the power of a district council in the administration of land in an autonomous district is extremely limited.[1]

The district councils in Meghalaya have passed the following Acts on land matters.

The United Khasi-Jaintia Hills Autonomous District Council[2]

(a) The United Khasi-Jaintia Hills District (Transfer of Land) Act, 1953.

(b) The United Khasi-Jaintia Hills District (Revenue Assessment) Regulation, 1953.

(c) The United Khasi-Jaintia Hills District (Land Revenue) Regulation, 1953.

The Jaintia Hills Autonomous District Council[3]

(a) The Jowai Autonomous District (Management and Control over Land and Assessment and Collection of Revenue) Regulation, 1969.

The Garo Hills Autonomous District Council[4]

(a) The Garo Hills District (Revenue Assessment) Regulation, 1953.

(b) The Garo Hills Regulation, 1953.

(c) The Garo Hills Grazing Regulation, 1953.

(d) The Garo Hills District (Jhum) Regulation, 1954.

(e) The Garo Hills Autonomous District (Land and Revenue) Regulation 1954.

(f) The Garo Hills District (Transfer of Land), Act, 1955.

(g) The Garo Hills District (Awil Fees) Act, 1960.

None of these enactments of the district councils deal with the basic land system prevailing in their area. The United Khasi and Jaintia Hills District (Transfer of Land) Act, 1953 was declared as ultra vires in Sitimon Sawain V Mandhwaj Bhandari AIR 1968 A & N. The decision will a'so apply to the Garo Hills District (Transfer of Land) Act, 1955.

In addition, the state government have passed the following Acts on land matters.[5]

(a) The Meghalaya Transfer of Land (Regulation) Act, 1971.

(b) The Gauripur (Gholla) Zamindar's Annuity Rights Abolition and Extinguishment Act, 1979.

(c) The Meghalaya Land Survey and Records Preparation Act, 1980.

(d) The Meghalaya Removal of Restrictions on Use and Enjoyment of Land Act, 1980.

Inspite of these enactments passed by the district councils and the state legislature, the matter relating to rights of people over the land they occupy and how to acquire them still remains vague.

Land Tenure System

The Khasi Hills[6]

The land tenure system in the Khasi hills is in an indeterminate state. As per customary land tenure system of the Khasis, land has always belonged and is still held to belong to the people and not to the rulers or the government. There are two main classes of land, *ri raid* and *ri kynti*. There is no system of land revenue according to the ancient customs and usages.[7]

The raid Lands

The ri raid lands are lands set apart for the cummunity over which no person has proprietory, heritable and transferable right excepting the right of use and occupancy. Such right reverts to the community when a person ceases to occupy or use the land for a period of three years consecutively. Heritable and transferable rights over *ri raid* lands accrue only when the occupant has made permanent improvement on the land. But even these rights lapse if the person completely abandons the land over such a period as the *raid durbar* (community assembly) deems long enough. The management and control of these lands is completely within the jurisdiction of the community concerned.

There is no system of payment of land revenue. If any payment is to be made, it is for the improvements made or services rendered. A member can not claim more land than what he can actually occupy or actively make use of. He cannot bar any person from occupying or using any vacant plot of land by claiming that it is within his occupation or has otherwise acquired it unless he has incontrovertible evidence of his actual occupation or use of the land. If a person vacates or does not make use of the land under his occupation for three consecutive years, the land reverts to community, village, *raid* or *elaka* (area) as the case may be. The use and occupation of *ri-raid* land is of purely temporary nature, for example for seasonal cultivation. However a person acquires heritable and transferable rights on *ri-raid* land if he has made permanent improvement on it by way of construction of a permanent building or buildings or cultivation of permanent crops and plants like fruit trees or converting it into wet paddy cultivation, fish ponds etc. But even in cases of this nature, a person loses the right automatically if he leaves the house or if he abandons a grove or garden or permanent cultivation etc. for a period over three years.

Any Khasi who is not a member of the village or of the *raid* or of the *elaka* cannot occupy *ri raid* land of that village or of *raid* or of *elaka*. He has no right of use or occupancy unless he submits himself to the jurisdiction of the village, *raid* or elaka and is accepted and recognised as one of it. The traditional system of administration of the *raid* lands is reported to be no longer observed. Indiscriminate issuing of *pattas* by village and *raid* authorities and *systems* has resulted in the loss of land to the real tillers of soil and in considerable litigation. People from outside the village or *raid* get the land allotted in their name by means of *pattas* issued to them either by the village headman or the head of the *raid* or even the chief of the *elaka* who may be influenced to issue pattas to such people. Such people basically belong to two categories. People living in the urban areas, who come to know in advance about the governments programme of acquisition of land for certain public purposes, get allotment and *patta* from the concerned authority.

Pattas are also being issued to Nepali graziers by the local chiefs of varying hierarchies on receipt of fees etc. The losers are the villagers who depend for their livelihood on the product of the land.[8] Ultimately they leave their village in search of arable lands elsewhere. Indiscriminate and unauthorised issue of leases or *pattas* by village headman or *sirdars* of the *raid* or *syiems* or heads of *elaka* both to Khasis and non-Khasis has created a difficult situation as these are against the customary law. To overcome the situation, it is necessary that a law is enacted to specify the basic principles on the procedure and manner of the management and control of *raid* lands by village *durbars* and the *elaka durbars*, the form and content of the documents to be issued to land holders and the persons or authorities competent to issue them.

The Ri Kynti Lands

These lands were set apart at the time of founding of the *elaka* (specific habitation) for certain clans upon whom were bestowed the proprietary, heritable and transferable rights over such lands. These also include any part of *ri raid* land which at later times were bestowed upon a person or a family or clan for certain yeoman's service rendered to the *elaka*. The same rights devolve on a Khasi owner to whom such lands are disposed of by the original owner by way of sale or transfer on receipt of full consideration.

According to the Khasi customary land system, the *ri kynti* owners cannot part with their land in any manner to a non Khasi without the permission of the *durbar hima.*

The *ri kynti* lands are of two categories-ancestral and self-acquired. The *durbar kur* has control over the former, the person acquiring the latter has full control over it. But the self-acquired property becomes ancestral when it passes to the children of the person who acquired it.

The management and control of *ri kynti* lands are in the hands of the owners themselves. The state has no control whatsoever over such lands and except the settlement of dispute between the claimants if brought to the *durbar* of the village, of the *raid* or of the *elaka.* Each clan has its own way of management and control of the *ri kynti* lands of the clan, or, if it has been divided between the branches of the clan, that branch has its own way and if the branch has divided its share between the different families then family has its own way. The management and control however always remains in the hands of the male adults of the *kurs.*

The *ri kynti* land belonging to a clan which has not been divided and is known as *Ri Kur* is under the management and control of the male members of the clan. The male members are generally the eldest maternal uncles, one representing each branch constituting a clan.. Where there is no maternal uncle, the eldest brother represents the branch or family in the *durbar kur.* Normally, it is the eldest maternal uncle who acts as head of the *durbar kur* of these uncles.

The *durbar kur* apportions land among the members and also manages and controls the disposal of *ri kynti* land in case of an emergency. Women can also attend and give their views when consulted.

After the advent of the British, the Khasi *ri kynti* land owners started issuing periodic leases or *pattas* to Khasis to whom they have disposed of land on payment of full value at the time of sale or transfer. Earlier it used to be invariably an outright sale. This practice still prevails in most of the rural areas. However in Shillong and its urban fringes the *patta* imposes conditions restricting the purchaser in many ways. The consent and approval of original owners is given only on payment of a *salami* or a key money which is a percentage of the total sale price of the property. Sometimes annual land revenue is charged. At present there is no control on *ri kynti* owners to issue *pattas*. In fact they make their own conditions without the sanction of any legal or constitutional authority and these conditions differ from one clan to another or even from one family to another in the same clan. This has caused hardship, and difficulties to the landless Khasis who are at complete mercy of the land owners.

The imposition of annual land revenue by *ri kynti* owners on land whose full value had been realised at the time of sale is against customary law, and so also is the imposition of other conditions restricting the heritable and transferable rights of a Khasi purchaser. It is, therefore, desirable to systematise and codify the customs and usages governing the administration of *ri kynti* lands. However, since the practice of the levy of annual land revenue has been in vogue for nearly a century in some parts of Khasi hills including Shillong, any law which may be enacted should take into account this fact.

The *ri kynti* owner does, however, have the sanction of custom to levy rent from a person who takes land on lease for seasonal cultivation. However, he cannot charge any tax. This practice has also sometimes been misutilised by the *ri kynti* land owner by collecting thirty or forty percent of the produce of land if taken in kind or an equivalent in cash. This has affected agrarian system as landless farmers taking land on lease for short periods cannot make improvement on land because at the end of the term of their lease the land reverts to the owner and the expenditure made by the lease on improvements become infructuous to him. It is, therefore, impossible for him to make any improvement of permanent or semi permanent nature and so the yield is always low keeping him barely at subsistence level. In order to rectify the situation, it is desirable that necessary laws are framed to secure the position of the cultivators by codifying the land tenure system in the Khasi Hills. This is all the more necessary as the owners themselves cannot make required improvements because they have more lands than they can manage. This has resulted in setback in agricultural production. It is however recommended that the law take into account the rate of rent leviable in view of the custom prevailing for a long time. It is also recommended that sale deeds be executed and registered.

Preparation of a record of rights is also necessary from the sociological point of view. The khasis no longer depend on agriculture as the sole means of their livelihood. They are following many trades and professions. Further, the cohesion of the clan centering round the land is fast disintegrating. In the family the important position of *u kni* (maternal uncle) and the near equal high position of *ka khatduh* (youngest daughter) are on the decline due to modernisation. The system of inheritance is also important as it has considerable impact on the land tenure system.

The Government Lands

After the occupation of the Khasi hills, the British government had its first headquarters at Cherrapunjee. They were given land for construction of a civil sanatorium and a cantonment by the state of Cherra covering that part of land known as *Saitsohpen*. This land was given in 1829 in exchange of British village Pandua located in the Sylhet District (now in Bangladesh). The British government treated *Saitsohpen* as their own territory and issued *pattas* to the lease holders. They also levied land revenue on them. The British government considered a Khasi *syiem* not as a territorial ruler but as a chief whose authority extended only to the citizens of his area.

When the headquarters was shifted to Shillong, the British government purchased and leased land for the establishment of the capital. For this land the *syiem* of Mylliem entered into an agreement with the British government in 1863. The agreement covers the European ward, the Police bazar and the Jail road wards of the Shillong municipality. During the British period these areas were considered as normal areas where the acts and rules of the state government were applicable. It appears that the land was actually taken on lease from the *ri kynti* land owners. In spite of this, the British government treated the land as their own and settled it on lease after levy of land revenue.

The British government followed the same policy with respect to other land which they purchased later in Rilbong and

Kench's Trace. These areas known as administered areas where the *syiems* and the *durbar* still wield certain restricted administrative and judicial powers.

The land formerly known as Lachumiere was compulsorily acquired after independence under the Land Acquisition Act. It is also considered as an administered area. The government have been resettling all these land leased, purchased or acquired under various rules issued from time to time.

There are also government land outside municipal area *e.g.*, land in Wahdienglieng and Lumsohphoh later known as Risa Colony which formed part of the land purchased by the government during the British regime to constitute protected forests around Shillong. These were deforested after independence.

Certain lands were also acquired for defence purposes like Happy Valley and for creating forests like the Riat Khwan forest and Shyrwat forest. These are reserved forests/lands. In the same category Nongkyllem reserve falls in the Ri Bhoi district. The government is exercising complete proprietary rights over these lands including protected or reserved forests.

The government of Meghalaya constituted a land reform commission for Khasi hills in 1973 to enquire into the land tenure system. The commission recommended codification of the laws on land tenure and on inheritance and suggested certain important measures like survey and preparation of maps, preparation of record of rights and extension of the Indian Registration Act, 1905 to the Khasi Hills.

The Jaintia Hills[9]

All lands in the Jaintia hills were measured in 1859. The total area was classified into two categories-land held by the *raja* himself for cultivation through tenants or hired labourers, and land held by various class of officers, namely *dolois* and subordinate village officials, *lyngdohs, pujaris* and also by *chowkidars* and servants of the *raja.* After measurement of the land, no land revenue was actually imposed and instead a house tax of Re. 1 per household was introduced.

Heath, the then sub-divisional officer of the Jaintia hills was directed to enquire into the system of land tenure in 1882. He classified the land into two categories—*hali* or low land and high land. The *hali* lands were terraced and permanently cultivated. The *hali* lands were divided into two classes—*raj hali* lands considered as a private property of the *raja* and private *(buniaj) hali* lands or service tenures. The high lands were considered fit for *jhum* cultivation and consisted of two classes—high lands where the villagers practised *jhum* cultivation and government waste land, *i.e.*, land which nobody claimed.

The government in 1884 declared that the entire Jaintia hills would be treated as its absolute property. Thus, the system of land tenure in the Jaintia hills was put on a different footing from that in the Khasi hills.

Only *raj hali* lands were assessed to land revenue during the British period and these lands were considered the private property of the *raja* who was pensioned off. The cultivators of such lands were considered to be the tenants who paid rent to the *raja*. The British claimed that they stepped into the shoes of the *raja* and hence demanded land revenue in place of rent. The occupants of the *raj hali* lands were treated as land holders and not tenants, In 1989 they were given periodic *pattas* for 10 years which did not confer any permanent, heritable and transferable right of use and occupancy although periodic *patta*-holders in Assam enjoyed such rights. Fresh leases for another 10 years were granted in 1901, after expiry of leases in 1899. In the next settlement made in 1912 the period was raised to 20 years. This period expired in 1932 but was extended to 1942. The next settlement was due in 1952; but by that time the administration of lands in the autonomous district passed on to the district council under the sixth schedule to the constitution of India.

The district council abolished land revenue in the Jaintia hills in December 1980.

The differences in land administration and revenue system of the Khasi hills and Jaintia hills are mainly due to historical reasons. There was house-tax and land revenue in the Jaintia hills; the people in the Khasi hills paid no such tax or revenue.

The district council has replaced the old periodic lease of *raj hali* lands by a new form of lease which is applicable to all *hali* lands. The period of the lease is not mentioned in the *patta* but it is said that the land is settled with the lessee, his heirs and representatives. Thus, the lease or *patta* granted by the district council is a lease in perpetuity. A land holder has a permanent, heritable and transferable right of use and occupancy in his land. There is a provision in the *patta* that the land will be free of revenue.

Earlier, though the villagers practised *jhum* cultivation, the right of a *jhum* cultivator to return to the same plot after a few years was recognised by custom as per report of Health submitted in 1882. Even sales, mortgages and leases had been made of these lands since the advent of the British. The district council has not framed any regulation for the management and control of *jhumming* and as such *jhumming* is practised according to customs which vary from place to place. Private rights are claimed to high lands which are used for betel nut or *pan* cultivation or as an orchard. No *patta* is issued for high lands but a land holding certificate is issued to a private individual who applies for it. He has to prove that he has been in continuous possession of such high land. Thus, a process is going on in the Jaintia hills of converting lands to private property by issuing of *pattas* and certificates.

The Garo Hills[10]

The Garo hills were formed into a district in 1866. It is inhabited predominantly by the Garos. The other original inhabitants are the Rabhas, the Hajongs, the Koches and the Kacharis.[11] The Garo hills may be divided into two parts considering prevailing land system: *(a)* the hilly lands covering 94.25 percent of the total district area where mostly the customary laws govern the land rights; and *(b)* the plain lands covering the remaining 5.75 percent of the total area where the relevant provisions of the Assam Land and Revenue Regulation are applicable.

In hills, the customary laws govern the land tenure system. Lands in the hills portion of the Garo hills mostly belong to one clan or the other. The deputy commissioner of the Garo hills got the *A'khing* boundaries demarcated and surveyed in early twenties. The *A'khing* lands with their boundaries and the names of the *nokmas* were entered into a register which is being maintained by the deputy commissioner even now and kept up-to date. *A'khing* land belongs to the clan[12] but the head of the clan who is a female is the real nokma. She is the owner of the *A'khing* land in a limited sense as she is the recognised authority for disposing of or allotting the land to the clan members for cultivation. In all important matters, however, such as transfer or alienation of land she has to consult the adult members of the clan. Usually her husband is called *nokma* who has no right over the *A'khing* land and only manages it on her behalf.[13]

Any member of the clan can cultivate portion of *A'khing* land without payment of any fees to the *nokma*. Sometimes, however, a member of different *A'khing* comes to take settlement in a particular *A'khing*. The nokma gives settlement to him if land is available and realises a small amount of fee which is called *A'wil.*[14] The district council passed the Garo Hills District (*A'wil* Fees) Act, 1960 for the regulation, assessment and collection of *A'wil* fees. In this act, *A'wil* fee is described not only as a fee paid by an outsider who is allowed to cultivate *jhum* in a particular *A'khing* but also as fees assessed on timber and all other forest produce in addition to any royality assessed in respect of such timber or other forest produce extracted from the *A'khing* land. Thus, the district council brought forest royalty within *A'wil* fee. The *A'wil* fee are collected by the *laskars*. The *nokma* of the *A'khing* gets 25% of it and 75% goes to the district council to be spent for the collective benefit of the residents of the *A'khing*. However, it has been reported that not all the *nokmas* are getting their share.

The most serious problem in respect of the *A'khing* land is the occupation of land within the *A'khing* by non-tribals. There have been cases of settlement of land within the *A'khing* with a non-tribal which is prohibited by the customary law. In some cases, even *patta* has been granted by the district council with the consent of the *nokma*. The procedure is that any occupant of *A'khing* land can apply, with the consent of the *nokma*, to the district council to survey the land and give him a *patta*. Also, there are Nepali graziers on *A'khing* land paying grazing tax to the district council. The legal position, however, is that no *A'khing* land can be allowed to be occupied or used for grazing by a non-Garo either with permission of the *nokma*, or of the district council or of both.

The district council has made Garo Hills District (jhum) Regulation, 1964. There is a provision in the regulation for introduction of terraced form of cultivation and horticulture.

For proper management of the land tenure system, it is recommended that the district councils make a comprehensive land regulation. The regulation should cover aspects relating to *(a)* rights over land: how rights are acquired and extinguished, *(b)* settlement operation, *(c)* issue of certificate and demarcation of land, *(d)* preparation of record of rights, *(e)* registration of occupation, etc.

Land Reforms

Till date no land reforms legislation has been enacted by the state government for abolition of intermediary rights, introduction of tenancy reforms and fixation of ceiling of land holdings to make the tiller of the soil owner of it. There are intermediary rights in all the seven districts. In Garo hills there are a large number of *jotedari* leases under which *jotedari* sublet their lands to the tillers of the soil and realise rent from them. In Khasi hills, the *ri-kynti* land owners are leasing their lands so also the permanent occupants of *ri-raid* lands. Similarly, in Jaintia hills the owners of private *hali* lands and private high lands are sub-letting their lands. The incidence of leasing of lands was noted during agricultural census 1976-77. It covered an area of 13080 hectares in 8561 holdings. There is no fixed tenure, fair rent or freedom from ejection. Enactment of legislation to regulate rent and ejection is an immediate necessity.

For introduction of ceiling on land holdings, there has to be a reliable record of land holdings. There are no such records in Khasi hills (except in Shillong) and in the valley of the upper reaches in Garo hills and Jaintia hills. There are proper records in the plains *mauzas* of Garo hills and some records in respect of *rajhali* lands and private *hali* lands in Jaintia hills. After the creation of the state in 1971, an urgent need was felt to have the land in the state surveyed and records of rights prepared. This was considered of prime importance in order to get loans and assistance from financial institutions. In the absence of land records, the financial institutions and government organisations found it extremely difficult to accept claims to title over land and to advance loans on the security of such land. The government of Meghalaya therefore passed the Meghalaya Land Survey and Records Preparation Act, 1980. The act was amended in 1991 to include district councils within the purview of the act. It was decided to implement the scheme jointly by the district councils and the state government. The district councils were to propagate the merits of the cadastral survey to the people and decide areas, villages and towns for undertaking the survey. The state government will provide funds and technical expertise for the survey. In fact survey operation was initiated in the state during the sixth plan period. The progress of survey has, however been negligible. The people are wary and apprehensive of the scheme. They feel that survey may lead to a dilution of the customary laws and ultimately to the imposition of land revenue in the state. The process needs to be accelerated as implementation of land-reforms measures cannot be undertaken without dependable record of rights. Das[15] has, however, identified 971 holdings with an area of 13493 hectares on the basis of agricultural census, 1976-77 which could be brought under land ceiling taking a view that these holdings have an area of more than 10 hectares.

Development and Regulatory Measures

The government both at the state and national levels have taken certain measures to remedy the situation. Some of the important measures are as follows:

(a) The state government have passed the Meghalaya Transfer of Land (Regulation) Act, 1971 prohibiting transfer of land to a non-tribal either from a tribal or from a non-tribal without previous sanction of the competent authority. The law has inhibited industrial growth because a company is a legal entity and not a tribal; hence cannot acquire land for the establishment of an industrial enterprise. This is inhibiting both tribal and the non-tribal entrepreneurs in establishing industrial units including agro-processing industries. The act however, has helped in non-alienation of land to non-tribals.

(b) The state government have enacted the Meghalaya Land Survey and Record Preparation Act, 1980. The number of cadastrally surveyed villages is very small. The progress has been inadequate due to possible apprehension in the minds of the people that it might violate customary laws and traditions and the government may impose land revenue and tax their land. Even the district councils have not extended cooperation in the matter.

(c) The state government have established a unit for undertaking codification of the customary land tenure system. The progress has, however, been negligible.

(*d*) The state government are implementing a *jhum* control scheme under the state plan and central sector scheme on control of shifting cultivation. Even though there has been some progress in the implementation of these schemes, the progress has not been up to the mark due to various constraints *viz.* land tenure system, cropping pattern, low technological absorption capacity etc.

(*e*) The state government have constituted a state land use broad to serve as a policy planning, coordinating and monitoring agency for issues concerning the health and scientific management of state land resources.

(*f*) The national land use and conservation board set up in the ministry of agriculture has decided to prepare a perspective plan for the north eastern zone for the conservation, management and development of the land resources within the zone with a view to having optimal utilisation of the land resources.

The current agrarian relations in Meghalaya are a product of various techno-economic and social cross currents which have arisen in the wake of the pressures of policies and programmes of the successive five year plans.

Till very recently the Khasi, the Jaintia and the Garo societies were ekeing out their existence under conditions comparable to the primitive state of an economy.

The basic tenets of the traditional land laws of the Khasis, the Jaintias and the Garos centre around shifting cultivation in which land-man relationship is primarily based on three principles—(*a*) allocative principle *i.e.*, the village or clan chief is vested with powers to make minor dispositions of land among members from time to time for *jhum* cultivation; (*b*) the allottee has usufructuary rights; and (*c*) the allottee has to cultivate with the family labour endowments. The size of disposition of land among the families is normally in proportion to the labour endowment of the family, making the per capita labour output ratio to be equal across the families and leading to economic equality and socio-economic equilibrium. There are naturally, no landlords and landless labourers in such a situation; there is no land scarcity also. The British intervention in the social and economic affairs was marginal that is, it left the bulk of the pre-existing land-man relationships unaffected in the state.

Thus, at the time of independence the state inherited more or less, the centuries old land-man relationship woven around shifting cultivation or *jhum*.

The fifth five year plan document of the government of Meghalaya had estimated the population dependent on *jhum* as 3.5 lakh. However, there are no reliable estimates and the above estimate was based on a sample study conducted by the Agro-Economic Research Centre, Jorhat. In the meantime the field observers had noticed a decrease in population dependent upon *jhum*. Thus, to obtain a reliable data on the *jhummia* population the Registrar General of India was requested to include this as a special study. According to their data (1981) there were 51,666 households (24.65 percent) out of the total of 2,09,618 rural households which were dependent upon *jhum*. Since, the model operational *jhum* field size is 1.0 hectare, the total annual area under *jhum* in 1981 was estimated at 51,666 hectares.[16] In 1980-81, the estimated net sown area was 1,92,945 hectares of which 26.77 percent was probably under *jhum*. In other words, 24.65 percent of the rural households were cultivating 26.77 percent of the net sown area. As per field reports, the incidence of *jhum* has been further declining and correspondingly the settled cultivation is steadily rising.

This transformation of the agricultural scenario can be viewed as a progress but its impact on land-man relationship is retrograde in the sense that individuals are acquiring permanent interest in the occupancy of a plot of land which in its turn is imputing monetary value to land.[17] The land is being transferred between individuals through out-right sale but mostly through the medium of credit mechanism which is working in favour of money-lenders thus dispossessing the actual tiller of the soil. This is also causing the conversion of owner-farmers into tenant-farmers who have to take land on rent at rates ranging from 20-50% of the produce of the land. This change is further deteriorating the financial condition of the farmers, pulling them deeper into debt thereby creating the classical situation of an Indian farmer who is born in debt, lives in debt, and dies in debt. Thus, within a period of around 50 years, the farmers in Meghalaya have been converted from *jhummia* into bonded settled farmers—from the bondage of poverty of one kind to that of another kind.

The modernisation process has eroded the traditional land laws by giving rise to *de facto* property rights over land in contrast to the usufructuary rights only which are the *de jure* rights under the traditional land laws.[18]

Even hill slopes have been demarcated by individuals who are exercising proprietory rights with or without cultivating them against the established norms of usufructuary rights. The custodians of the customary laws have become so weak or are themselves so enmeshed in deviant behaviour that they cannot do anything about it. In other words, the modernisation process has introduced factors which have made shifting cultivation and all its socio-politico mechanism untenable and is substituting it with peasant economy.

The government of Meghalayas is aware of the structural changes in the land-man relationship and its inegalitarian consequences on the society and deleterious effects on environment. It has enacted some laws and regulations to control effects of normlessness in land management but unfortunately the socio-politico ethos has not yet permitted their implementation and in the meantime the incidence of concealed tenancy, share cropping, absentee landlordism is continuing to rise, particularly with respect to valley bottom land. A review and systemic study of the land is required in the state.

In conclusion it may be stated that:

(a) shifting cultivation has already been replaced to a great extent;

(b) the egalitarian structure of the tribal society is dissolving;

(c) the traditional land laws have no *de facto* validity on ground;

(d) the district council is planted to mediate between the modern and traditional politico-administrative structure;

(e) the state government has the constitutional powers to enact laws to regulate land-man relationship;

(f) neither the district councils nor the state government have the social sanction or willingness to intervene in giving direction to land-man relationship;

(g) agriculture operations are being conducted as per traditional system and considerable innovative efforts are necessary to improve the situation.

References

1. A.I.R., 1972, S.C. 787.
2. Acts, Rules and Regulations of the United Khasi-Jaintia Hills Autonomous District (1952-1961), Executive Committee, District Council, United Khasi and Jaintia Hills, Shillong, 1962, p. 205.
3. Acts, Rules, Regulations, etc., of the Jaintia Hills Autonomous District Council (1967-1985). The Executive Committee, Jaintia Hills Autonomous District Council, Jowa, 1986, p. 341.
4. The Garo Hills District Council Act, Rules and Regulations as amended up to Dec. 31, 1968, Garo Hills District Council, Tura, p. 241.
5. Phira, J. M., The Meghalaya Land and Revenue Manual, Government of Meghalaya, Shillong, 1989, p. 344.
6. Report of the Land Reforms Commission for Khasi Hills, Government of Meghalaya, Shillong, 1975, p. 276.
7. Gurdon, P.R., The Khasis, Cosmos Publications, Delhi, 1975, pp. 86-91.
8. Dutta, B.B., Dutta, P.S., Land holding pattern among the Khasi-Jaintias-the tradition and the deviation, quoted in Alienation of Tribal Land and Indebtedness, Tribal Research Institute, Assam, 1986, pp. 149-156.
9. Report of the Commission of Inquiry on Autonomous Districts Administration in State of Meghalaya, Government of Meghalaya, Shillong, 1984, pp. 56-61.
10. *Ibid.*, pp. 77-82.
11. Mazumdar, D.N., Problem of Land alienation and indebtedness among the hinduised communities of Western Meghalaya., quoted in the Alienation of Tribal Land and Indebtedness, *op. cit.* pp. 58-66.
12. Sangma, J., Principles of Garo Law, 1973, pp. 22-23.
13. Playfair, A., The Garos, United Publishers, Guwahati, 1975, pp. 73-74.
14. Dev, B.J., and Lahiri, D.K., 'Land Disputes among the Garos-interaction of Custom and Law', in The Garo Customary Law (ed)., S.K. Chattopadhyay and M.S. Sangma, Directorate of Arts and Culture, Meghalaya, Shillong, 1989, pp. 91-96.
15. Das, J.N., A Study of the Land System of Meghalaya, LBS. Guwahati, 1990, pp. 168-169.
16. Tayeng, J., Census of India, 1981, Series-14, Meghalaya, Paper 1 of 1983, Special Report on Jhum, p. 181.
17. Nongbri, T., The Khasi Land Tenure System; Need for Conceptual Refinement in the Land Relations in North-East India (ed), B.B. Dutta and M.N. Karna, Peoples' Publishing House, 1987, pp. 71-81.
18. Majumdar, D.N., Land and Land Problems in Garo Hills in the Land Relations in North-East India, *ibid.* pp. 157-165.

CHAPTER 18

Land Tenures and Land Use Pattern in Arunachal Pradesh: A Review*

❑ A.C. TALUKDAR

Agriculture is the mainstay of the people of Arunachal Pradesh. It is the vital source of livelihood for them. There are very few tribal people in the state population who are not dependent on agriculture wholly or in part. A great majority of them draw everything they need from land for their living either in exchange of labour or as gifts of nature. The relationship of the people with land in the State is therefore something intimate and emotional. In spite of this, no land legislation exists in the State. The only legal framework concerning the ownership of agricultural land is the Jhum Land Regulation, 1947. The State is also not yet cadastrally surveyed and there is no land record to determine the ownership of land.[1]

The Agricultural Department of the State has however generated certain data through its agricultural census carried out every five years since 1970-71. The present study which attempts to review the existing land tenure and land use system in the State and examines the ways of possible land reforms in the State is based on such data and the author's observation of the situation for last 25 years.

* Revised version of the paper presented in 'Worshop on Land Reforms, Agends for North-East, ISCD, Guwahati (3-5 April '95). Sponsored by LBS Academy of Administration, Mussoorie.

Ownership Pattern

In absence of any ownership or tenancy legislation in the State and also lack of any land records, the ownership of land is governed by the customs and traditions of the various tribes. The Jhum Land Regulation, 1947 mentioned earlier, only recognises the ownership to a piece of Jhum Land, once an area is operated by someone and in Jhum system such operation essentially happens to be by the community. The individual ownership of land and the right to use it is therefore regulated by traditional and customary laws of the people. Although they differ from tribe to tribe or sometimes even from clan to clan in their details; a study of these traditional laws of land ownership reveals that there are three types of land ownership—*(i)* Clan or community ownership, *(ii)* Private ownership, and *(iii)* Mixed type of ownership.[2] The community ownership is the most common type of ownership and is the result of Jhum system of cultivation which warrants frequent collective efforts. This is however more theoretical in nature as every community land is divided among the individual family and the right of a family to operate the same plot again and again is well recognised. The private holding is common for all permanent cultivation plots and is held by a person or a family with all the rights of inheritance or transfer. The third type is found in areas where there is both Jhum cultivation and permanent cultivation. Here Jhum plots are held by individual families within the framework of community ownership and the permanent plots are held individually. Besides, in certain areas there are some lands, mainly forest lands which are owned by the whole community. Any member of the village may use these lands for hunting or fishing purposes or even for gathering materials for construction purposes. In any case, however, women are not allowed to own land.

In recent years it is observed that these traditional patterns of ownership are fast changing and giving place to private ownership of land in all areas, owing to a number of factors. The most important of them is the development of permanent cultivation, due mainly to government efforts. In 1971 only 28006 hectares of land out of a total cultivable land of 489011 hectares were under settled cultivation against 46,1005 hectares of Jhum cultivation. In 1985-86 the respective figures are 76,759, 34,4234 and 26,7495—a 274%

increase in the area under settled cultivation.[3] The second important factor is inter-migration of people and emergence of several multi-clan villages. With the passage of time single clan villages have developed a tendency to. grow into multi-clan villages with new settlers coming from other villages for various reasons. These new settlers acquire land mainly through transfers, allotment or purchases, which becomes their private holdings. There are also other factors like growth of semi-urban centres with better income opportunities and better educational, medical or transport facilities attracting heavy influx of people from distant villages. This encourages the neighbouring villages to turn into multi-clan villages through migration. Thus, cross migration, which is an accepted fact in almost all areas of Arunachal, has led to a strong tendency towards private holdings. It is true that often a newly arrived person is first allowed to settle in the village with the permission of the village council which allots him a plot of land. Sometimes he is allowed to clear a plot of virgin land for cultivation. But with the passage of time his right over the plot is recognised and the land becomes his own private land.

Another recent phenomenon in ownership pattern in land is frequent transfer of land. In the entire stretch of foothill areas where most of the permanent wet rice cultivation plots are located, there are now frequent cases of sale and leasing out of land although these transactions are not registered or recorded. The seller or the buyer hardly takes anybody's permission for such transfers. Even in interior villages where Jhum lands were allowed to be used by co-villagers by the owner when it is not used by him, is increasingly being rented out on share-cropping basis or on lease on payment of cash. Occasional selling of such plots is also not entirely unknown. Thus although there is no land record as such, private ownership type of land tenure system is gradually emerging in Arunachal Pradesh. The following table (Table 1) gives an idea of land holding pattern in Arunachal Pradesh.

A look at the table reveals certain trends :

(a) Individual holdings are increasing over the years and this increase is mainly due to increase in the number of small and marginal holdings.

(b) More than 50% holdings are small holdings of the size of 1 hectare to 4 hectares.

(c) Size of average holding is gradually decreasing.

(d) No. of large holdings are decreasing both in numbers as well as in percentage of total holdings.

Table 1

NO. OF LAND HOLDINGS ACCORDING TO SIZE

Size of Holdings	*Nos. of Holdings*				
	1970-71	*1976-77*	*1980-81*	*1985-86*	*1990-91*
Marginal (below 1.00 hect.)	6060 (7.67)	6442 (9.69)	12936 (16.53)	14781 (17.18)	16500 (17.38)
Small (1.00 to 4.00 hect.)	29920 (37.88)	30367 (45.67)	38392 (48.89)	43056 (50.05)	48500 (51.05)
Medium (4.00 to 10.00 hect.)	28750 (36.40)	18169 (27.32)	22073 (28.10)	23237 (27.00)	25800 (27.15)
Large (10.00 hect and above)	14260 (18.05)	11521 (17.32)	5091 (06.48)	4964 (05.77)	4200 (04.42)
Total	78990 (100.00)	66499 (100.00)	78542 (100.00)	86038 (100.00)	95000 (100.00)
Size of average holdings	6.19 hect.	5.95 hect.	4.27 hect.	4.00 hect.	3.62 hect.

Source: Agriculture Department, Arunachal Pradesh.
Figures in bracket indicate %.

They are mainly due to the changes described in the previous pages and the process of increasingly individualisation of holdings. Transfer by sale or lease a recent phenomenon is also responsible for this trend.

Land Use Pattern

Most parts of land in Arunachal Pradesh are steep hills, deep terrains and thick forests. About 62% of the land is covered by forest, supposed to be the biggest endowment of nature. The rest of the land is put to different uses. About 34% of land is shown as unreported areas, which probably includes private lands reserved for hunting and fishing and residential areas. Only 4% of land is presently available for agricultural purposes which comes to some 3,400 squâre kms.

According to the Agricultural Census carried out by the State, the total cultivable land increased from 28006 hectares in 1970-71 to 76,759 hectares in 1985-86 in respect of settled cultivation and decreased from 46,1005 hectares to 26,7495 hectares in respect of jhum land. Still in 1985-86 about 78% of the total cultivable land were Jhum land while the rest were under permanent cultivation. Table 2 gives the details of total arable lands in the State and the Jhum-settled ratio of cultivable land during the period from 1970-71 to 1990-91. It also shows the proportion of fallow land in Jhum areas. Needless to say that Jhum-settled ratio of the land under cultivation is very important to understand the real nature of land-use pattern in Arunachal Pradesh and for any talk of probable land reforms in the State.

Table 2

TABLE SHOWING TOTAL AREA UNDER CULTIVATION REPORTED IN DIFFERENT AGRICULTURAL CENSUSES

Particulars	*In Hectares*				
	1970-71	*1976-77*	*1980-81*	*1985-86*	*1990-91*
1. Total area operated	489011	395526	335732	344254	344000
(a) Settled	28006 (5.73)	40013 (10.11)	52012 (15.49)	76759 (22.30)	n.a.
(b) Jhum (total)	461005 (94.27)	355513 (89.89)	283720 (84.51)	267495 (77.70)	n.a.
(i) Net area shown	27220	71901	66220	72555	n.a.
(ii) Fallow land	169352	130004	80380	49008	n.a.
(iii) Culturable waste land	148698	84540	47595	44426	n.a.
(iv) Other uncultivated land (other than fallow land)	19164	49850	34888	28655	n.a.
(v) Land not available for cultivation	36571	19218	54637	48129	n.a.

Source: Agriculture Department, Arunachal Pradesh.
Figures in bracket indicate %.

It is evident from the above table that domination of Jhuming in the agricultural scene continues to be overwhelming till today.

It also shows how a large portion of Jhum land remains unused in any given time (77.60% in average) although it declined from 81.08% in 1970-71 to 72.88% in 1985-86. This may be due to the fact that some Jhum land has been converted into permanent cultivation land and in certain areas some Jhum land has been diverted to horticultural crops. Some tribes use the fallow land for grazing purposes. For example in Adi areas there is a practice of gathering all mithuns to a fallow Jhum area and fence around the area to confine the mithuns there during farming season, so that the mithuns cannot cause any damage to standing crops in operated area. They call it "Lura". Traditional practice of forest use was also more environment friendly. Trees were cut or materials were drawn from the common forest only under tacit permission of the community. Even fishing and hunting were regulated to some extent. Private forest (called Morang or Ada morang—among the Adis) was very judiciously used. All these have undergone a change now. Need for more and more land for Jhum and lucrative timber business have led to wanton destruction of forest in recent years.

Possible Land Reforms

Agriculture, the mainstay of life in Arunachal Pradesh is yet to develop into a remunerative economic pursuit. Jhum or shifting cultivation which is a very labour consuming and uneconomic practice still dominates the agricultural scene. Borthakur reports that in 1980-81 out of 2,69,542 main workers of Arunachal Pradesh 211160 were cultivators, 16945 cultivators were less than 14 years of age and 11,180 were more than 60 years old.[5] These figures show how intensely Jhum cultivation demands labour participation irrespective of age. Besides, Jhum cultivation engages one plot of land for cultivation and locks several others as fallow land as seen from Table 2. It is just opposite to the concept of multiple cropping which is a must for improved productivity.

It is widely felt, therefore, than land use pattern must change to relieve these helpless people from this situation and to make room for increased productivity of land.

So far as distribution of land among different holding categories is concerned, certain unhealthy trends are noticed. In 1980-81, 30% of individual holders (holding size 40 to 50 hectares) owned 3.07% of land, while 4.89% of marginal farmers possessed only 29% of total arable land. In the last few years the situation must have worsened, certain sections of the new rich have shown a tendency to purchase more and more land specially wet rice cultivable lands in the foothill areas.[6] Besides, in certain areas like the Apatani areas of Lower Subansiri district, landless people have considerably increased. Another problem that may soon arise is the fragmentation of land holdings. The 1970-71 agricultural report warned that with the increase of area under permanent cultivation the problems of fragmented holdings in scattered parcels may come to the fore.[7] In subsequent censuses this tendency is already established. For, while the number of marginal holders (below 1 hect.) has increased by 272.27% from 1970-71 to 1990-91, the number of large holders (10 hect. and above) has decreased by 29.45 percent during the same period. However, the said census report hopes that this trend can be effectively checked if there is a proper system of land ownership and land records.

(a) Any land reform measure in the State therefore must start with a cadastral survey of the State, and introduction of proper land records. As I said in the beginning, all data currently available are collected through agricultural census only. But they do not give us an exact picture of the situation. Often they are results of only sample surveys. But Arunachal situation is so heterogeneous that one can hardly rely on sample surveys. Secondly, it is mainly based on the information of the respondents who can hardly give an accurate information of an area under his possession.

Similarly the importance of land record can hardly be over emphasised for a correct assessment of the situation.

(b) Land ownership laws should be introduced in the state without further delay. At present, women who are the main actors in agricultural practices in Arunachal Pradesh, are not allowed to own land, and hence they hardly participate in government programmes directed to wean them away from Jhum cultivation or the introduce improved means of cultivation. Change in land ownership laws is likely to change this scenario for favourable results. Besides, the inheritance laws should be uniform in all areas. For in Apatani areas where only the eldest son is allowed to inherit land, it led to a rise in number of landless people.

(c) Land transfer and land transactions which are already an accepted fact of life should be officially recognised with suitable legislation providing for their registration. This will help in getting information of land-holdings in the state.

(d) Jhumlands suitable for conversion into settled cultivation land should be surveyed and identified and its owners should be encouraged to convert them into settled cultivation land. Official recognition of private holdings and transfer of land will greatly help this process.

(e) Efforts should be made to find alternative use of Jhum land. In Arunachal Pradesh people are practising shifting cultivation not by choice but because of compulsions of nature. Therefore, it will not be possible to convert a large section of the Jhumland into settled cultivation land. So only an alternative efficient and scientific use of the land will be able to alleviate the situation and also may make available large areas of land for cultivation. A present horticulture is tried as an alternative use. But due to its long gestation period and lack of proper market, the marginal and small farmers cannot take advantage of it. An alternative choice may be vegetable gardening and production of spices.

(f) On the legislation front, the Jhum land Regulation, 1947 may be amended to extend recognition to private holdings. The scope of Land Records Department introduced in 1978, the activities of which are presently confined to urban areas only should be extended to rural areas also. This will bring some uniformity in land tenure system without disturbing greatly the traditional system.

(g) Last but not least, we may suggest several measures for land reforms in Arunachal Pradesh, but we must always bear in mind the tribal customary laws. Change must be introduced gradually and with continuity of tradition so that the changes are acceptable to the people and they do not disturb the age old harmony of the society. Certain positive features of the customary laws such as collective ownership of the village community over certain land and the practice of maintaining private forest should be effectively incorporated in any probable land reform measures.

References

1. According to Mr. K.K. Chaudhury, a retired D.F.O. of Arunachal Pradesh, small patches of lands in Seijusa area in East Kameng District and Lekang in Lohit District were cadastrally surveyed with the help of Forest Department for purposes of settlement of ex-servicemen.

   Now-a-days some official land records exist in the Land Record Department of the State regarding urban lands which are allotted to different individuals.

2. See, A.C. Talukdar and A.P. Das, "Exploring Possibilities of Land Reform in Arunachal Pradesh." *Assam Economic Journal,* Vol. VI, No. 1, 1988, p. 75.

3. Arunachal Agriculture in Brief (Series 3) 1980-93, Directorate of Agriculture, Arunachal Pradesh, Naharlagun. p. 4.

4. *Ibid.*

5. J.K. Barthakur, *Census of India: A Portrait of Population,* p. 107.

6. According to Dr. T. Mibang an Adi Intellectual and a teacher in A.U., a Section of the Service holdings and Businessmen having surplus money are trying to acquire more and more land in the State.

7. Agricultural Census, 1970-71, Series 1, Vol.1, State Agricultural Census Commissioner, Naharlagun, p. 2.

CHAPTER 19

Risk, Insurance and Land Reform in Arunachal Pradesh

❑ N.C. ROY
❑ P.K. KURI

Introduction

Risk is a common phenomenon. It affects economic life-albeit in varying extent—at all stages of development. One basic characteristic of risk is that the return yielded by an enterprise is usually related positively with risk. This positive correlation between risk and return indicates that a person desirous of having a higher amount of return must carry a higher magnitude of risk. However, too often it becomes difficult for an individual agent to carry a high amount of risk, he then wants to trade some risk with part of his income. This risk trading tendency of individuals creates the demand for insurance. Two problems, however, stand in the way of emergence of insurance market—one is the moral hazard and the other is the adverse selection (Williamson, 1975).. These two problems are universally present. The solution of these problems requires screening of those who want to be insured and close monitoring of their performance once they have been insured. Screening is concerned with the correct estimation of the magnitude of risk faced by different economic agents demanding insurance coverage and monitoring deals with the collection of information as regards the behaviour of the insured having bearing upon the probability of the event covered by insurance. No doubt the adequate screening can reduce the magnitude of the adverse selection and close monitoring at least partly removes the problem of moral hazard but instituting such a mechanism requires usually heavy investment and this seems to be the main factor restricting the operation of insurance market specially in the rural areas of many development countries. In fact, in rural areas of a typical developing country the market insurance is non-existent and the non-existence of market insurance indicates that a risky venture promising even a very high return may not be undertaken.

The agricultural sector in Arunachal Pradesh exhibits the features that are commonly found in many developing societies. In this State, till recently, a high proportion of cultivable land was communally held; with the advance of permanent cultivation the individual property rights in land have come to be established gradually. At present all permanently cultivated land is individually owned and even major portion of land under shifting cultivation—locally called jhumming—has come under individual ownership.

The general technology of production in agriculture is largely traditional and the productivity of land under permanent cultivation has no doubt increased but the growth of productivity is not very significant. With the establishment of individual property rights in cultivable land specially that under settled cultivation the inequality in the ownership of such land seems to be on the rise.* The inequality in landholdings has increased the amount of risk of the small peasants and the rural landless people. The increasing inequality in the ownership of cultivable land, apart from its risk enhancing effect upon the poor, is likely to produce negative effects upon the growth of agricultural productivity. This paper highlights the nature of risk faced by the peasants in Arunachal Pradesh and the type of mechanism they have evolved to mitigate the effect of different risky events threatening their income and consumption in the absence of market insurance. The next step in the study is to show the extent of extra risk being generated by the increasing inequality in land ownership, and, the rationale of land reform is derived from the possible risk mitigating and productivity enhancing effects of such reformist measures. For convenience, this paper is divided

* The data on landholdings collected by different agricultural census shows a declining trend in inequality of ownership of land. However, the information collected through a village survey by us and some other studies—for example (Das, 1989)—indicate a rising trend in inequality of landholdings and landlessness.

into three sections. In the first section we show the nature of risk and the traditional risk-coping mechanism in rural Arunachal Pradesh. Section-II deals with the development of the rationale for land reform. Finally, we conclude in Section-III.

Section I

The fluctuating nature of agricultural production subjects the peasants to a high magnitude of risk. In rural Arunachal Pradesh, agriculture being the main activity, the variability of agricultural production provides a measure of overall risk suffered by the peasants. During the eighties the production variability as measured by standard deviation of yield of paddy per hectare was as high as 40.15. The detailed information on the area, production and yield of paddy is shown in the Appendix. The risk, in agriculture originates from a number of sources. Broadly the sources can be classified into two: socio-economic milieu and natural environment. The socio-economic factors bearing on the risk include the variability of family labour supply, non-availability of credit, etc. While the natural factors include the variation of rainfall, the attack of pests and insects, etc. Apart from the risk in supply of input affecting production, there is also risk in consumption and this risk is caused by the price variability. Though agriculture in Arunachal Pradesh is practised with a spirit of autarky to meet the family's consumption needs, variable yields of different crops and inability to produce at home some essential items of consumption create the necessity for exchange. The exchange carries with it the usual risk. Thus if the price of the commodity which is in surplus falls in relation to the commodities to be purchased, peasant's consumption is likely to decline. The increasing exchange of commodities in the rural areas of this state has led to an extra dimension of risk being created.

The traditional economy of Arunachal Pradesh has, however, devised different methods to cope with the risk. The risk associated with the variability of family labour supply, in the absence of wage labour, is reduced by creating a system of mutual obligations which meet the labour needs of a family in case of any contingency. Credit need is met through mutual exchange of necessary inputs and commodities. Normally, surplus is used to aid the person who is in deficit. The risk originating from the natural factors is likely to affect all. However, some are affected more than others. For example, a spell of drought may affect the production of those lands whose gradient is higher than that of less steep lands. In such a situation, the least affected peasant may provide his surplus to those who are more affected. This process of transforming the surplus into aid is a type of risk-coping mechanism. The aid giver trades his expected risk with a premium being paid with the current surplus. In covering his current risk through the receipt of aid, the peasant with deficit is providing future insurance to the aid giver.

In general, two methods are used to minimise the risk in the traditional regime. In the first place, a variety of crops are grown to diversify away the risk in production. Crop diversification also tends to reduce the price risk. Secondly, the surplus may be given to a person having deficit or if the amount of surplus is very large, then part of surplus may be exchanged for procurement of valuables whose price is not subject to much variability. In the usual mode of aid through the disposal of surplus, agriculture commodities are treated like fungibles in a mutuum and this tends to shield the parties from any price variability.

One important factor motivating the development of customary risk-coping devices based on mutual insurance is the communal ownership of land (Roy and Kuri, 1995). When land is communally owned and the individual derives the usufruct by virtue of his being a member of the community, the individual does not have the absolute right over the entire produce of the land cultivated. The community seems to have a right over part of the produce mainly the surplus part of it. The right of the community creates the obligation for the individual and this individual obligation takes the shape of the disposal of surplus production in a way which promotes mutual insurance. When a peasant has a surplus he discharges his obligation to the community by giving his surplus to those who are in need of it. Again, when he suffers deficit, he receives the aid from those who received his past surplus. This way the property rights regime which gives the ownership right of land to the community and usufructuary right to the individual generates a system of insurance which enables the community to tide over the risky events. One problem with such a property rights regime is that it can cope with the risk associated with the cultivation using traditional inputs which give rise to low productivity. Since the application of new inputs in many cases involves risk not covered by the customary system of mutual insurance, the incentive of undertaking innovative activity in agriculture remains low. Moreover, the incentive for application of new inputs aimed at the permanent improvement of the land is low when the land is usufructed. So communal ownership is not normally found to facilitate the permanent improvement in the productivity of land and this is responsible for non-existence of substantial net accumulation of capital in a community having such a property rights regime.

The property rights regime undergoes changes with the onset of technological innovation. The innovative technology along with new inputs enhances the productivity of land and this raises the value of land creating the incentive for its individual ownership. The value of land also increases with the emergence of secondary and tertiary sectors.

The establishment of the individual ownership on land having high productivity enables the owners of these lands to accumulate savings which they can use to purchase more land. The emergence of such a property rights regime on land and the development of land market have the effect of producing inequality in land holdings. The available information on ownership of cultivable land in Arunachal Pradesh shows a high degree of inequality.

The magnitude of inequality as estimated by Gini-coefficient is shown in table 1.

Table 1

Year	*Value of Gini-Co-efficient (in %)*
1980-81	51.8
1985-86	48.99
1990-91	46.06

Source : Agricultural Census, Arunachal Pradesh.

The inequality and landlessness are indicative of the gradual insignificance of mutual insurance. The traditional risk-coping mechanism has not been able to prevent the landlessness being created in substantial degrees in a number of communities.

Section II

The emergence of individual property rights in land and the gradual improvement in productivity of land consequent upon the application of new inputs such as HYV seeds, fertilisers, irrigation etc. have made profit the basis of agricultural production. An active land market has developed to facilitate transfer and mortgage of land under permanent cultivation (Dutta *et al.*, 1987). With the rising productivity of land under settled cultivation, the demand for such land has increased (Talukdar, 1995). Those who are holders of good amount of productive land have tended to raise their holdings resulting in inequality (Das, 1995). The poor peasants are either being pushed to the landlessness or where jhum land is available they have been forced to remain confined to the practice of jhumming.

The main effects of the gradual establishment of individual property rights on permanently cultivable land and partly on jhum land are as follows:

1. Emergence of Tenant Cultivation

A new type of contractual arrangement not practised previously in Arunachal Pradesh has come up: this is the leasing of cultivable land either on fixed rent basis or on the basis of sharing of output. The factors which have brought this new type of contractual arrangement are the insufficiency of family labour and non-availability of wage labour. The insufficiency of family labour for cultivation is due to the occupational diversification. This has been entailed by the gradual expansion of secondary and tertiary sectors. The local wage labour being not available, those having good amount of fertile land tend to bring tenants from outside the State. The households which have successfully diversified their sources of earning have boosted the level of their income. Agriculture, however, still remains an important source of income for these diversifiers, this source generating income either in the form of cash when land is cash-rented or in the form of crops when land is cultivated through the arrangement of share-cropping.

2. Landlessness

The establishment of individual property rights in land under settled cultivation has tended to concentrate the ownership of lands leading to the landlessness. Plain land is no doubt scarce in Arunachal Pradesh, so many people have no access to it. One outcome of individual property rights is that some people living in the plains have no land for settled cultivation. Since these people are to depend only on jhumming which has low productivity, they are unlikely to accumulate sufficient savings to purchase the permanently cultivable land. A glaring picture of landlessness is provided by Lower Subansiri district where in some Apatani villages around 30 percent of peasants have been reduced to the status of landlessness (Das, 1989). In some areas having both permanent cultivation and jhumming, the people with no land for settled cultivation are resorting to marginal type of jhum cultivation promising hardly any satisfactory production.

3. Weakening of Traditional Risk-Coping Mechanism

The traditional risk-coping mechanism working through mutual insurance is based on communal ownership of land. The gradual breakdown of this regime and the growth of individual property rights in cultivable land have tended to weaken the basis of mutual insurance. Of course, market insurance has come up and the ability to self-insure has increased with the rise in income. But this has remained limited to the high income group. A farmer practising settled cultivation generating surplus is in a position of self-insure and he can also purchase market insurance. The landless poor can neither self-insure nor can they purchase market-insurance. The weakening of the traditional system of mutual insurance is likely to affect the consumption stream of these people. Though the non-agricultural sectors are expanding, yet these poor people can not take advantage of these expanding opportunities because of their having not been equipped with education and skill necessary for getting employment in these newly emerging sectors. Their poverty also prevents their children from being educated and skilled.

What has emerged from the establishment of individual property rights in land having high productivity is the inequality in land holdings and the inability of many people to have access to such land. The new property rights regime has made land an income-generating asset—a mere ownership of some amount of land provides the owner with a stream of income. The owner also gets the right to sell his land and invest the money so obtained in some other activities promising better returns. Thus, individual property rights in land have not only enhanced the income stream of the owner, it has extended the horizon of his choice.

Since the new ownership regime has been brought about by the growth of land productivity caused by the new inputs originating exogenously, the customary land laws are unlikely to cope with the problems created by these changes. This inability of customary laws creates space for government intervention in the land market. The area of intervention is, however, highly complex. The land available for permanent cultivation is limited. However, landlessness demands modificatory action from the government. The traditional risk-coping mechanism based on mutual insurance being less effective in emerging areas of development, it is unlikely to neutralise the negative effects produced by new technology and institution. On being endowed with private property rights, land has become an important asset capable of providing some security against many a risky event. The reformist measure of the government must take this risk-coping aspect of land so that the rural landless people can get some amount of land. Another point which requires stress is the productivity of land. The available literature on tenant cultivation, though not unambiguous seems to indicate that it may not be in some cases, as effective as owner cultivation.*

In the context of Arunachal Pradesh, the emergence of tenant cultivation does not appear to be a healthy development. Apart from its possible negative productivity effect, tenant cultivation has undesirable social ramifications. So on these grounds also land reform measures can be suggested. Fixation of ceiling on plain land and redistribution of surplus land may be one way to promote agricultural growth and provide security to the people reduced to the status of landlessness. However, Riba (1994) rules out the

* The question of tenancy efficiency has been studied extensively since Adam Smith. Marshall's well-known hypothesis (Marshall, 1920) is that share-cropping is an inefficient mode of contract resulting in sub-optimal production equilibrium. Marshallian position on share-cropping is supported by the findings of a number of scholars (Bardhan & Srinivasan (1971); Adams and Rask, (1968), Boxley (1971). The studies by Cheung (1969), Raid (1976) and Dutta (1986) contradicted the Marshallian position. Newberry and Stiglitz (1979) show that share-cropping does not provide superior risk-sharing. Though the studies of tenancy have developed a large volume of literature, they have failed to make any generalisation on the efficiency of tenancy.

possibility of fixation of land ceiling by the government. According to him if ceiling is at all necessary the government should involve the village councils to achieve the objective.

Section III

Though government intervention is called for to bring about institutional changes suitable for sustained growth of agricultural productivity and provide security to the weaker section of the rural population, the government of Arunachal Pradesh has not yet proceeded much in this respect. A bill on land record and settlement was introduced in the Assembly in 1988 but it could not be enacted because of strong opposition. This is indicative of the fact that the demand for land reform is not yet strong. However, the inequality, landlessness and gradual breakdown of traditional risk-coping mechanism based on mutual insurance appear to form the rationale of undertaking measures aimed at the reduction of negative effects of new property rights regime in land.

Appendix

TIME SERIES DATA ON AREA, PRODUCTION AND YIELD OF PADDY IN ARUNACHAL PRADESH (1980-81 TO 1990-91)

Year	*Area (thousand hectares)*	*Production (thousand tonnes)*	*Yield Kgs./Hectare*
1980-81	83.4	88.2	1,058
1981-82	90.1	94.2	1,046
1982-83	93.5	97.4	1,042
1983-84	101.0	106.0	1,050
1984-85	108.0	117.6	1,088
1985-86	108.0	117.6	1,088
1986-87	116.0	125.1	1,078
1987-88	116.0	125.1	1,078
1988-89	120.6	135.8	1,126
1989-90	121.3	138.8	1,144
1990-91	121.8	142.5	1,170

Mean Yield = 1088 kg/hectare Standard deviation of yield = 40.15
Variance of yield = 1612.02

Source: Basic Statistics of North-Eastern Region, 1992, p. 39.

(We received valuable information from Dr. A.C. Talukdar and Dr. T. Mibang, Professors, Arunachal University. Mr. P. Tado, Mr. R. Taba and Mr. T. Riba, Lecturers, Arunachal University provided us with information on different problems of land reform in the State of Arunachal Pradesh. We express our thankfulness and a deep sense of gratitude to all of them. We had also a thorough discussion with Mr. J. Riba who was appointed by the Government to study the different aspects of land reform in Arunachal Pradesh. We remain grateful to him.)

References

1. Adams, W.D. and Rask, N. (1968): 'Economics of Cost Sharing in Less Developed Countries,' *American Journal of Agricultural Economics*, 50, 935-45.
2. Bardhan, P.K. and Srinivasan, T.N. (1971): 'Cropsharing Tenancy in Agriculture: A Theoretical and Empirical Analysis,' *American Economic Review*, 61, 48-64.
3. Boxley, Robert F. (1971): 'Cost-share Leases Revisited Again,"*American Jounal of Agricultural Economics*, 54, 529-32.
4. Cheung, S.N.S. (1969): 'Private Property Rights and Sharecropping,' *Journal of Political Economy*, 76, 107-22.
5. Das, G. (1995): *Tribes of Arunachal Pradesh in Transition*, New Delhi, Vikas Publishing House.
6. Das, J.N. (1989): *Land System of Arunachal Pradesh*, Guwahati: Law Research Institute, Guwahati High Court.
7. Datta, P.S. *et al.*, (1995): 'Report on Arunachal Pradesh' paper presented at the workshop on Land Reforms' Agend for North-East, Guwahati: April 3-5.
8. Datta, S. (1986): 'Sharecropping as "second-best" form of tenancy in traditional Agriculture', *The Indian Economic Journal*, 30.
9. Govt. of Arunachal Pradesh (1981, '85, '91): Agricultural Censuses of Arunachal Pradesh.
10. Marshall, A. (1920): *Principles of Economics*, London: Macmillian.
11. North-Eastern Council (1992): *'Basic Statistics of North-Eastern Region.*
12. Newberry, D.M.G. and Stiglitz, J.E. (1979): Sharecropping, risk sharing and uncertain labour markets, *Review of Economic Studies*, 44, 585-594.
13. Roy, N.C. and Kuri, P.K. (1995): 'Risk, Land Reform and Agricultural Productivity in Arunachal Pradesh' paper presented at the International Seminar on 'Environment Bio-diversity and sustainable development in North-East India' (NEHU: Aizawl, Mizoram, 26-27 September, 1995).
14. Reid, J.D. Jr. (1976): 'Sharecropping and Agricultural Uncertainty.' *Economic Development and Cultural Change*, 24, 549-76.
15. Riba, J. (1994): 'A Study of Land Tenure and Land Revenue System in Arunachal Pradesh', Report Submitted to the Govt. of Arunachal Pradesh. (unpublished).
16. Talukdar, A.C. (1995): 'Land Tenure and Land Use Pattern in Arunachal Pradesh: A Review. Paper presented at the workshop on 'Land Reforms: Agenda for North-East (Guwahati, April 3-5).
17. Williamson, O.E., (1975): *Markets and Hierarchies: Analysis and Antitrust Implications*, New York: Free Press.

CHAPTER 20

Customary Land Tenure System and Its Change Among the Galos of Arunachal Pradesh

❑ D.K. DUTTA

The Galos, a sub-group of Adi tribe, inhabit the central part of the West Siang District, Arunachal Pradesh. There are forests, hills, rivers and springs with full of natural resources. Galos have been fully depending on the timbers, bamboos, canes, thatches, edible roots, leafy vegetables, fishes and meat for the subsistence since time immemorial. So, after occupying the area as a whole they redistributed the land among themselves clanwise for enjoying the forest products equally. While demarcating the boundaries of the occupied land, some people were not satisfied with the extent of land they owned. Sometimes they encroached upon the land of others which brought ultimately feuds among the clans as well as the adjacent tribes. The elders to avoid the problems of land disputes framed land law to be obeyed, and allowed the heads of the families to occupy land as much as they liked. A folktale of Gallos says that there was a long fight for good and fertile land between the Nibo (Man) and the Robo (spirit) who were brothers. It means that the land disputes had been continuing since old days. However, each head of the families covered sufficient land by clearing the jungles or simply declearing the jurisdiction of land in the village. Some families were not interested to have or declear any extra plot of land except the utilised ones. When any member of a clan approached to other clan for settlement, if the term was good, he was given land on lease. But soon he would get the ownership right and immersed into the same customary law of the village. Later on, when his next generations run their families, they enjoy the inheritance rights as the members of other families in the village do.

Now, in the same way a father distributes the acquired and inherited land among the sons equally whenever he likes to do so. As per the customary law the best plots of land should go to the eldest or the youngest one. If the father desires to give the best one to the middle or the other sons, the eldest or the youngest son may object the matter customarily but can not obstruct if the father gives his own share to the sons he likes. At the death of the father, the eldest brother distributes the inherited land equally among other brothers. If the distribution is not fair, or it becomes the cause of dispute, the deceased fathers' brothers interven if necessary and take the help of local council KEBANG.

Women have no right to inherited the landed property. If married women become widow they get support for the livelihood out of the landed property of their deceased husbands which pass over to the sons or the brothers of the deceased.

When somebody migrated to another place he used to offer his landed property to the relatives or villagers at free of cost. But, today nobody is going to offer the land without cost due to change in materialist outlook.

People have started buying land not only in their own village, but also in other villages. After occupying the land they possess the ownership right *i.e.*, right to sale, right to mortgage, right to give on lease. The sellers or donors take the consent of their relatives for disposing of the land as the nearest kins of the sellers or doners have right to claim the disposed land.

The Galos select residential area at the source of water. Further, they examine the actual location for construction of the houses by reading omen. The persons who want to construct houses put on a few pieces of ginger or onion on the soil of the proposed sites and after three-four days consult with the priest to know whether it suites them or not; if not they change the sites and repeat the process. The place which is not favourable to a person may be good for others. After selecting the sites they can not keep the lands for a longer duration if others demand the same for constructing houses.

The owners of the plots around the residential area have to leave some spaces for expanding the residential area without demanding any cost as and when required. Every body has right to utilise the land of the village residential area. But to utilise a plot of occupied land of others, one has to take permission of the owner to maintain the law and the peace of the village. Otherwise, it is a punishable offence according to the customary law. While constructing a new house now-a-days, the people maintain a distance of average 30-40 feet between the houses to avoid fire accident. In the early days the villagers made the houses close to each other with an intention to help each other if enemy or wild animals attacked but there was risk in case of fire accident. The houses have no boundary fance. The community activities like festival, marry-making function, tournament, etc. are done temporarily in any suitable place which may be under the custody of any occupant who is also a member of the community. In case of permanent utilisation of land people volunterily offer a piece of land for the welfare of the village.

A little deviation in case of occupation of land for construction of house in the village residential area is noticed recently. The individual who first occupied a plot claims compensation for labour charges he had expended for preparation of the plot from the later user.

The people being cultivator possess plots of land meant for cultivation. They practise mainly the shifting cultivation. Tarrace and W.R.C. are of recent origin. When they prepare plots of land and demarcate with big stones, natural spots like spring, hillocks or by planting HUZO tree with the help of co-villagers, automatically the area of the persons concerned become familiar to all the villagers. Besides, the owners sacrifice mithuns or pigs to satisfy the spirits of the newly opened plots and distribute some pieces of meat of the sacrificed animal to the villagers. These villagers become the witness in case of any problem with regard to the plots. Except the witness no other document are placed to prove the ownership of land. Even the village council solves the problems of disputed land in the traditional way. Whenever the disputed parties are not satisfied with the version of the witness the council restores to supernatural power or omen. The priest of the village reads the checken liver to find out the guilty or the innocent one. Now-a-days, the council forwards land case to the next higher authority as some disputants do not believe in the decision of the council either due to lack of faith on the omen or for the provision of appealing at the district court or so.

The land owners allow the interested cultivators to cultivate the land verbally on lease free of cost, but some of them have started taking cash or kind for the same purpose. The land owners become sure about the boundary of the plots before leasing out the land. Some people apply, now-a-days for land possession Certificate from the Administration.

The people extract timbers, bamboos, canes, etc. for their own use from the land of their own jurisdiction without obligation. If one needs more materials, takes the reciprocal helps of others. Some people start buying the forest products in or outside the village from the local sellers to minimise both times and labours needed to fetch from distant forests.

The people not only occupy the land for constructing houses, hunting games, cultivating crops but also occupy rivers, rivulets, springs for fishing, irrigating fields etc. The demarcate certain portion of rivers or spring where no one can catch fish without permission. Otherwise, it is an insult to the owners who takes it seriously and run to the village council for imposing fine.

The land which is actually far from the heart of the village remains as unclaimed or forest land. The villagers can extract the forest products for their personal use but not for commercial purpose. It is noted that unclaimed land is hardly found in the village now-a-days.

People have realised that the selling of forest products from the land of their own jurisdiction has been a new source of income. So individual ownership right is becoming more significant. This is a great change among the Galos in recent years.

The govt. may take steps to record or prepare map of the boundaries of the plots of the individuals as the interest of the people in recording the boundary of owned land as is observed, quite encouraging.

Acknowledgement

I acknowledge my gratitude to Shri Jummo Padu, Darka village, West Siang District alongwith others who helped for preparation of the article.

CHAPTER 21

Land Reforms in the Hill Areas of Assam

❑ B.N. BORDOLOI

Land Reforms As a Concept

The Indian Planning Commission, in the Seventh Five Year Plan document stated that the land reform measures should include the following aspects—*(i)* abolition of intermediary tenure, *(ii)* tenancy refers aimed at security of tenure, regulation of rent and confer-ment of ownership rights on tenants, *(iii)* ceiling on land holdings and distribution of surplus land, *(iv)* consolidation of holdings, and *(v)* compilation and updating of land records.[1]

According to Prof. B.K. Roy Burman, approach to land reform in the tribal areas of North-East India requires critical appreciation of *(a)* concepts of land tenure and land reform, *(b)* method of determination of existing status of rights and obligations in respect of land, *(c)* diverse perceptions about land relations, *(d)* nature of problems arising out of approaches based on diverse perception, and *(e)* emerging perspective.[2]

To make a critical appreciation of any land reforms measures one must be well conversant with the land tenure system—past and present. I also feel that coverage under land reform programmes should also include the land settlement policies which have rather a greater implications on the implementation of the land reform measures. Since the tribal people have a close link with forests, the land reform measures should also take into account the forest policies and how these policies affect the people so far as land matters are concerned.

Resume of the Hill Areas of Assam

The present hill areas of Assam comprise only two districts, *viz.*, Karbi Anglong and the North Cachar Hills. Before discussing the land reform matters in these two hill districts, it is necessary to produce here a resume of the formation of these two districts. During the British days the land revenue administration applied in these areas was not subjected to the type of administration prevalent during that period.

During the pre-independence days the districts of Karbi Anglong and the North Cachar Hills as such had no existence.

A new district, namely, the United Mikir and North Cachar Hills was created formally with some parts of the then Sibsagarh District and the then Nowgong district and the then United Khasi and Jaintia Hills district of undivided Assam on 17th November, 1951.[3]

The new district had two subdivisions—Mikir Hills and North Cachar Hills. The creation of the erstwhile United Mikir and North Cachar Hills district was followed by the establishment of the Mikir (now Karbi Anglong) Hills Autonomous District Council with H.Q. at Diphu on 23rd June, 1952 and the establishment of the North Cachar Hills Autonomous District Council with H.Q. at Haflong on 29th April 1952 under the Sixth Schedule to the Constitution of India.[4]

Subsequently a new civil district was created comprising the North Cachar subdivision of the United Mikir and North Cachar Hills District on 2nd February, 1970. In the year 1982, the name of the Mikir district was changed to Karbi Anglong district.[5]

Land Reform Measures During Pre-Independence Days

As per Govt. of India Act 1935 the North Cachar Hills subdivision of Cachar district and the Mikir Hills Tract in Nowgong and Sibsagarh districts were declared as "Excluded Areas" and "Partially Excluded Areas" respectively.[6]

The main intention of declaring these areas as "Excluded Areas" and "Partially Excluded Areas" along with some other tribal areas of the North-East was to keep them outside the normal administrative reforms. In other words, normal administration was not applied to these areas. The Governor of the Province administered these areas at his discretion which meant that the administration of these areas was the special responsibility of the Governor of Assam.

The main land law of the Province of Assam, that is, the Assam Land and Revenue Regulation, 1886, was not applied to these areas. In the North Cachar Hills subdivision, however, the British Govt. assessed the wet rice cultivation lands in and around Maibang area specially at ordinary rates of revenue prevailing in the plains of Cachar and for the remaining areas House Tax @ Rs. 3/- per house.

Land Reforms in the Hill Areas of Assam in the Post-Independence Period

It has earlier been mentioned that the newly constituted United Mikir and North Cachar Hills district became part of the Sixth Schedule to the Constitution of India. One of the important factors conceptualised in drafting the Sixth Schedule by the Sub-Committee headed by Mr. Gopi Nath Bordoloi was that "Adequate protective measures against exploitation of the people from the plains on account of their superior organisations and experience in business. The hill people are afraid of the fact that if suitable provisions are not made to prevent the plains people from acquiring lands in the hill area, large number of them will settle down and they will not only occupy land belonging to the hill people but will also exploit them in non-agricultural professions like money lending, etc."[7]

Under the provisions of the Sixth Schedule to the Constitution of India legislative powers have been given to the District Councils to administer all matters concerning land and forest management except the State Reserved Forests and to enact suitable laws. As such land reform matters have become a subject of the Karbi Anglong and North Cachar Hills District Councils.

Prior to taking up of the discussion on land reform measures in these two hill districts it would be worthwhile to describe briefly the traditional land tenure systems prevalent among the different tribal communities inhabiting these two districts.

Traditional Land Tenure Systems

Here instead of discussing the traditional land tenure systems prevalent in the hill areas of Assam districtwise we propose to discuss them tribewise. Now let us take up the case of the Karbis first.

Traditional Land Tenure System of the Karbis

All lands where shifting cultivation is done were owned and are still owned by the community. For Jhum land no revenue was paid. Each household is required to pay 'Chang Khajana' @ Rs. 3/- per annum. Land under wet rice cultivation is, however, owned privately. Unlike some of the tribal communities of North-East India, the Karbis do not have clan lands.

The traditional village headman called Sarthe assisted by the members of the village council called Mei-Amei selects the Jhum sites, allots Jhum plots to individual families and also decides as to whether the village is to be shifted to the new Jhum site or not since the villages in the hills by and large do not have fixed boundaries.

On the Jhum plots, however, the families have no permanent heritable rights. A family at the beginning of a new Jhum cycle may or may not return to the same plot of land. For cultivation of Jhum land no land revenue or rent is paid to anybody as per their traditional land tenure system.

It is also worthwhile to mention that in the hill portion of the Karbi Anglong district a revenue village has a separate connotation. A village is called revenue village not because of the fact that land revenue from the inhabitants of the village is collected but because of the fact that house tax is collected by the authority from the households of the village.

Traditional Land Tenure System of the Dimasa Kacharis

The traditional land tenure system prevalent among the Dimasa Kacharis is almost similar to those of the Karbis. So far as the Jhum lands are concerned, the entire village community owns the land within the boundary of a village. Their traditional village council is called Salis and the village headman called Khunang is the chief of the council. This council selects Jhum sites, fixes rotation and distributes Jhum plots to different families of the village. Like the Karbis the Dimasa Kacharis also do not have any clan lands. For cultivating Jhum land neither land revenue nor rent is to be paid to any one. For the privately owned land meant for wet rice cultivation, the cultivators are required to pay land revenue as per provisions of the Assam Land and Revenue Regulation, 1886.

Like the Karbis a Dimasa family may or may not return to the same plot of land at the beginning of a new Jhum cycle. Every family is free to select and cultivate a plot of land suitable to it. The Salis only fixed the area according to the manpower resources and capability of the family concerned. Thus, a family does not have permanent and heritable right on Jhum land.

Traditional Land Tenure System of the Zemei Nagas

The traditional land tenure system among the Zemei Nagas of the North Cachar Hills district is somewhat different from those of the Karbis of the Karbi Anglong district and the Dimasa Kacharis of the North Cachar Hills district.

In each Zemei village there is a traditional landlord or land owner whom they call Kadeopo. The Kadeopo not only owns the village site but also owns most of the hills within the jurisdiction of the village boundary. In the village site for occupation of homestead land by different families, the Kadeopo does not take any revenue or rent. The Jhum lands owned by him are distributed among the families of the village and for cultivation of his Jhum land every family has to pay him rent in kind @ about 5 kg. of paddy per annum irrespective of the area cultivated.[8]

Apart from this the Zemei Nagas have well-demarcated clan lands also. Each of the six Zemei clans has a sizeable area of Jhum land where only the clan members have the right to cultivate. The elderly members of a clan in a meeting allot plots to every family. The families, however, do not have permanent heritable right over the plot of land cultivated by it. In the clan lands also there is no question of payment of any rent or revenue.

The Zemei Nagas also have privately owned land where wet rice is cultivated. For the cultivation of wet rice land, land revenue as per provisions of the Assam Land and Revenue Regulation, 1886 has to be paid to the North Cachar Hills District Council. All the families residing in a Zemei village are required to pay House Tax @ Rs. 3/- per annum.

Traditional Land Tenure System Among the Hmars

Among the Hmars of the North Cachar Hills district while Jhum lands are owned by the entire village community, the lands under settled cultivation are privately owned. In the M.C. Hills the traditional village councils of the Hmars are almost defunct. It is the headman of the village appointed by the North Cachar Hills District Council who manages the village affairs. The village headman in consultation with the elderly male members of the village selects Jhum sites, allots Jhum plots to different families and also decides rotation. Individual families do not have any permanent heritable right on Jhum lands. The land will be under the possession of family only during the year or years of allotment. For cultivation of Jhum land neither rent nor any revenue is paid. The Hmars do not have clan lands. It is also very interesting to note that among the Hmars privatisation of Jhum land has also been taking place. The Hmars are very good horticulturists. They cultivate pineapples in large quantities by terracing hill slopes which were originally Jhum lands. Such terraces are considered to be privately owned with permanent and heritable rights and none would try to occupy such land by force.

Traditional Land Tenure System Among the Kukis

Although in Manipur a Kuki village chief owns all the lands within the boundary of a village and a common Kuki has to pay him rent for use and occupation of his land, it is not so among the Kukis of the North Cachar Hills. Here the Kuki chief of a village is the custodian of the community land and the ownership of land is vested with the people. He, therefore, acts like a democratic chief.

In the North Cachar Hills district the traditional land tenure system among the Kukis is more or less similar to that of the Hmars.

Land Reforms in the Karbi Anglong District

When the British annexed Assam in accordance with the treaty of Yandaboo in 1826, the Mikir Hills region was included in the district of Nowgong. In the year 1881, under the Assam Frontier Tract Regulation a 'Mikir Hills Tract' was formally constituted. In 1893, a part of the 'Tract' was included in the district of Sibsagarh without breaking the integrity of the tract.[9]

The Mikir Hills Tract, therefore, fell partly in Nowgong and partly in Sibsagarh districts. As has been mentioned earlier the Mikir Hills Tract was declared as 'Partially Excluded Area' under the Government of India Act, 1935. Thus, the plains portion of the Mikir Hills Tract which was included in the Nowgong and Sibsagarh districts came under the purview of the Assam Land and Revenue Regulation 1886 and remained so till the creation of the United Mikir and North Cachar Hills district.

Under the Sixth Schedule to the Constitution of India the Karbi Anglong District Council can make laws only in respect of allotment, occupation or use or setting apart of land for agricultural, grazing or residential or non-agricultural purposes or in respect of shifting cultivation.

In 1953 the Karbi Anglong District Council (the erstwhile Mikir Hills District Council) had adopted the Assam Land and Revenue Regulation, 1886 by enacting the Mikir Hills Land and Revenue Regulation Act, 1953 with suitable modifications. The primary purpose of the District Council's adoption of the above Regulation was, however, to assess and collect land revenue.

The land reform measures so far undertaken by the Karbi Anglong District Council can broadly be divided into the following four categories:

1. Control of Jhum and management of forests.
2. Prohibition of transfer of tribal land.
3. Land settlement policies.
4. Survey and settlement operations.

1. Control of Jhum and Management of Forests

For the purpose of control of shifting cultivation as well other matters connected with it, the Mikir Hills District (Jhuming) Regulation, 1954 was enacted by the District Council and it was amended in 1966.

The main purpose of enacting this Regulation is to control Jhum and to dissuade the people from shifting of their villages to the Jhum sites. This Regulation provides for:

(1) Fixation of permanent boundary of each village.

(2) Prohibition of shifting of a village to the new Jhum site.

(3) Prohibition in cutting of forests and doing shifting cultivation within a radius of about one kilometre from the boundary of a village.

(4) Selection of new Jhum sites in consultation with the Sarkari Gaonbura meaning the village headman appointed by the District Council and the local Mauzadar and the distribution of Jhum plots by the Sarkari Gaonbura.

(5) Prohibition of Jhum sites where there are valuable trees.

The Mikir Hills District (Forest) Act, 1957, empowers the District Council to constitute Reserved Forests even if the areas where the Reserved Forests are constituted might fall in the areas where the people are used to Jhuming.

This Act also prohibits trespassing the damaging District Council's Reserved Forests, falling and burning of trees, pasturing cattle, collection of minor forest produces, now called non-wood forest product, etc.

One of the most important provision of the Act is, however, constitution of village forests for the collective benefits of the village community. These collective benefits include collection of minor forest products and pasturing of cattle. But the people have to protect, preserve and improve the village forests in lieu of the benefits extended to them.

2. *Transfer of Land*

In order to protect and promote the interest of the scheduled tribes on land, the Karbi Anglong District Council enacted the Mikir Hills (Transfer of Land) Act, 1959. So far as the land reform measures in the Karbi Anglong district are concerned, this Act is the most important one.

As per provisions of this Act no land within the jurisdiction of the Karbi Anglong District Council shall be sold, mortgaged, leased, bartered, gifted or otherwise transferred by the tribal to a non-tribal or by a non-tribal to another non-tribal except with the previous permission of the Executive Committee of the District Council.

While the Act provides for maintenance of *status quo* in respect of right on land already acquired, provision for ejectment of such persons other than tribals who are in possession of land other than in accordance with the provisions of the Act is also incorporated. But the penalty fixed for an offence is in monetary terms only and it is too nominal.

Although the main purpose of this Act is to prevent transfer and alienation of tribal land, none-the-less, unscrupulous people have found the loopholes in the Act and made the Karbi people inhabiting the plains portion of the Karbi Anglong District to alienate their land temporarily but with a tendency to perpetuate for an indefinite period.

Although there are several devices like Paikas, Khoi Bandhak, Sukti Bandhak, Mena, Adhi etc. nonetheless, the most common as well as the most important is the Paikas system.

What is Paikas System?

It is a system of temporary alienation of tribal land by payment of cash advance injected among the Karbis inhabiting the plains portion of the Karbi Anglong District specially in the Howraghat Tribal Development Block area by the East Bengal (now Bangladesh) refugees who were rehabilitated in these areas after the partition of the country.

Under this system a tribal cultivator takes an advance from a non-tribal cultivator and in lieu of the advance taken he alienates his land temporarily to the non-tribal cultivator for a period of one year or two years. At the end of the specific period the non-tribal cultivator is required to vacate the occupied land. But in reality it does not take place since the tribal cultivator takes another dose of advance from the non-tribal cultivator even before the stipulated period comes to an end. Once a tribal land owner enters into this vicious circle he can hardly get out of it and the temporary alienation of tribal land becomes almost perpetual. The actual owner becomes a mere spectator while the non-tribal tills the land and reaps the harvest year after year as if he were the actual owner of the land. This system has rendered many Karbi families paupers and their condition is worse than that of the landless people.[10]

The author himself had conducted a survey in a few tribal villages inhabited by the Karbis within the jurisdiction of the Howraghat Tribal Development Block in the year 1973. The survey reveals that about 70 percent of the Karbi families had allowed the neighbouring non-tribals to cultivate their land year after year mainly on Paikas system.

It is also pointed out in the survey report that under the provisions of the Mikir Hills District (Transfer of Land) Act, 1959, Paikas cannot be considered illegal since hiring of tribal land by non-tribals has not been prohibited. It can not be regarded as 'Mortgage' also since there is no question of paying back the cash advance taken from the Paikas holder at the end of the stipulated period. The unscrupulous non-tribals, therefore, have taken the full advantages of the loopholes in the provisions of the above Land Transfer Act.

On receipt of the copy of the survey report, the Land Advisory Committee of the Karbi Anglong District Council had become alive to the situation created by the Paikas system. This had resulted in the enactment of the Karbi Anglong District (Land Reforms) Act, 1979. This legislation is, in fact, an important piece so far as the land reforms are concerned.

The most important provisions of this Act are as follows:

(A) Paikas and mortgage are totally banned.

(B) If the cultivator is still found to occupy the land of the settlement holder after the release of the land at the end of the stipulated period, he shall be evicted forthwith.

(C) A settlement holder may resort to Adhi if considered essential.

(D) No restriction is imposed on mortgaging land to financial institutions to obtain agricultural loan.

3. Land Settlement Policies

Land settlement policies are a part and parcel of the entire process of land reforms as well as land management. The Karbi Anglong District Council has formulated a set of land settlement policies with a view to safeguarding the interests of the hill tribes in land. These policies are as follows:

(*a*) In the matter of settlement of land in Karbi Anglong the first preference is given to the *bonafide* scheduled tribes.

(*b*) Second preference in respect of land settlement is given to the scheduled tribes (Hills) coming from the other autonomous district.

(*c*) No settlement of land shall be made with any non-tribal who has come into this district after 15th August, 1947 and all such persons coming after that date and found to occupy land shall be evicted.

(*d*) The District Council may, in special cases relating to the victims of unusual natural calamites such as floods, earthquake, etc. who are already in occupation of land in the district, order settlement of land with the affected non-tribal people on recommendation after due enquiry from the Deputy Commissioner.

(*e*) Waste lands in the district which are suitable for permanent wet paddy cultivation after reclamation are reserved for the people belonging to the scheduled tribes of the district only.

4. Survey and Settlement Operations

Survey and settlement operations in the Karbi Anglong district was started in the year 1975 and they are still going on. In those areas where such operations have already been completed periodic pattas or leases have been issued to the settlement holders for lands under permanent settled cultivation. In case of Jhum land where such operations have been completed only annual pattas or leases are issued to the settlement holders.

Land Reform Measures in the North Cachar Hills District

Compared to the land reform measures undertaken and executed by the Karbi Anglong District Council, such measures adopted and executed by the North Cachar Hills District Council are very few and far between.

In 1953, the N.C. Hills District Council had enacted the North Cachar Hills land and Revenue (Adoption of Assam Land and Revenue Regulation) Act, 1953. Through this enactment only those sections of the Assam Land and Revenue Regulation, 1886 were adopted which are applicable and relevant to the North Cachar Hills. The Law Research Institute, Guwahati, observes that the few sections provide only for recovery of arrears of land revenue and other government dues by attachment and sale of moveable property and nothing more. It is further observed that important procedures like mutation and declaration of the right of landholders are totally left out.[11]

Now let us examine in what respects the North Cachar Hills District council has adopted and executed land reform measures.

1. Control of Jhum and Management of Forests

The North Cachar Hills District Council has neither enacted any laws nor issued any Executive Instructions for the purpose of controlling Jhum and management of forests.

2. Transfer of Tribal Land

The North Cachar Hills District Council has not so far enacted any law prohibiting transfer of tribal land to non-tribals. It had, of course, issued some Executive Instructions only.[12]

The most important aspect of these Executive Instructions are as follows:

So far as the land under periodic lease is concerned a tribal settlement holder can not transfer his land to a non-tribal without prior permission of the District Council authority. In according permission, the District Council authority sees whether the person to whom the land is proposed to be transferred is a permanent resident in the district and secondly whether he has enough land in his possession already even though he is a permanent resident.

3. Land Settlement Policy

According to the Land Settlement Policy Resolution of 1954, the first preference goes to indigenous local tribals in settlement of Government land. The second preference is given to the permanent non-tribal residents of the district who are electors in the District Council constituencies. A tribal belonging to the same community but hailing from another village may also get settlement of land in the village provided the other people of the village where the person is proposed to be given settlement do not object.

4. Survey and Settlement Operations

In this district survey and settlement operations are at the initial stage only.

An Assessment of the Land Reform Measures and Concluding Observations

Land reform measures like the abolition of intermediaries, protection of the rights of the tenants, regulation of rent, confirmation of ownership rights on tenants, ceiling on land holdings and distribution of surplus land, etc. which are applicable to the plains areas of Assam are not applicable to the hill areas where the traditional land tenure system is still prevalent.

Under the traditional land tenure system there are neither intermediaries nor tenants. The Zemei Nagas who cultivate Kadeopo's land on payment of a very nominal annual rent can not be said to be tenants. Similarly there can not arise any question of fixation of ceiling on land holdings and distribution of surplus land to the landless people. Under the traditional system of shifting cultivation every family has a right to cultivate a piece of Jhum land which is a community land and as such there can not be landless people in the true sense of the term.

In the hill areas, however, where extensive shifting cultivation is going on, control of Jhum cultivation as well the protection of Unclassed State Forests is much more important as land reform measure.

The Mikir Hills' District (Jhuming Regulation 1954 and its subsequent amendment in 1966 are, therefore, right steps as land reform measures.

It is very interesting to note that previously the Karbi villages had no fixed boundaries and the villages were very frequently shifted to the new Jhum sites thereby vitiating all attempts on the part of the Government as well as the District Council authority to execute development schemes of important nature in such villages.

Now due to the enforcement of the above Regulation shifting of villages to new Jhum sites in the Karbi Anglong district has been stopped totally. This is really a positive aspect.

Another positive aspect is the selection of new Jhum sites by the people of a village in consultation with the Sarkari Gaonbura and the local Mauzadar.

This has stopped indiscriminate selection of Jhum sites which is detrimental to maintenance and preservation of ecology and environment.

The constitution of District Council Reserved Forests under the Mikir Hills District (Forest) Act, 1957, is another positive step towards land reform. This has resulted in saving some of the forest areas from further destruction.

The creation of the village forests, which is now a part of the new forest policy of the Government of India, under the provisions of the above quoted Act clearly reveals the foresightedness of the Karbi leaders of byegone days. 'Let people grow, protect and preserve their forests for their own benefits' is the motto behind this.

Protection of tribal land from being transferred to non-tribals is a very important aspect of land reform measures in the Karbi Anglong district. However, immediate action is needed in the implementation of the provisions of the Mikir Hills District (Transfer of Land) Act 1959 and the Karbi Anglong District (Land Reforms Act, 1979 specially in respect of temporary transfer like Paikas, mortgage, etc.

In fact the legal provisions have failed to check Paikas. A survey carried out by the author in five Karbi inhabited villages in 1988 within the Howraghat T.D. Block reveals many interesting facts. The survey reveals that Paikas alone accounts for 26.41 per cent of the alienated land. There might be more Paikas incidence in disguised form also.

Prior to the enactment of the Karbi Anglong District (Land Reform) Act, 1979, there were written agreements on stamped papers between the Paikas holder and the settlement holder. But now the Paikas holders do not insist on written documents. The Paikas holders are now introduced as KAMLAS, meaning wage earners working in the fields of the settlement holders and such devices have made it difficult to detect the incidence of Paikas fully unless one uses the participant observation method as a tool for collecting data.

Since Adhi has been legalised by the Karbi Anglong District (Land Reform) Act, 1979, the survey further reveals that Adhi accounts for 66.76 per cent of the land alienated. Thus the remedy suggested is worse than the disease since many cases of Adhi might be in the form of disguised Paikas.[13]

The land settlement policies formulated by the Karbi Anglong District Council have reflected the interest of the indigenous tribal people of the district Nevertheless, influx of people in this district has been going on unabated since any one can go to the interior, clear the jungles and squat and there is none to stop him from doing it or to evict him forthwith.

Survey and settlement operations are going on in this district at a snail's pace and most of the tribal families are yet to get their record of right on the land occupied by them.

During survey and settlement operations Jhum lands above 90^{0} slopes are declared as District Council forests and no settlement is given to the persons occupying such lands. Although this has reduced the area under Jhuming such actions are beneficial for preservation of environment and ecology.

In the North Cachar Hills district there are no acts for the Jhum control and management of forests. Regarding prohibition of transfer of tribal land there are executive instructions only. Non-tribal people constitute less than one third of the total population in this district and, therefore, incidence of alienation of tribal land is not so significant. If the Executive Instructions are followed in letter and spirit, there may not arise any occasion to enact land transfer legislation.

The land settlement policies formulated by the N.C. Hills District Council are quite favourable in protecting the interest of the indigenous tribal people of the district on land.

Non-starting of survey and settlement operations in this district till the other day reflects a negative aspect towards land reform measures.

After assessing the land reform measures in the two hill districts I want to make only one important suggestion and it is like this:

In both the districts there are Land Advisory Committees. But these are more or less lying dormant. The two District Councils should activise them so that they might meet frequently, review the land reform matters among others and suggest practically feasible actions to be undertaken by the District Councils for the benefit of the scheduled tribes (Hills) inhabiting these two districts.

References

1. Seventh Five Year Plan, Planning Commission, Govt. of India, 1985-90, Vol-I, p. 62.
2. Roy Burman, B.K.: "Issues in Land Reforms in N.E. Tribal India," Published in Mainstream, August 1 and 8, 1987.
3. Bordoloi, B.N.: District Handbook, United Mikir and North Cachar Hills, 1972, p. 1.
4. *Ibid.*, pp. 46 and 50.
5. Notification No. HAD. 140/78/108-A, dated 31.5.82, Govt. of Assam.
6. Govt. of India (Excluded and Partially Excluded Areas) Order 1936 in persuance of Govt. of India Act. 1935.
7. Bordoloi, B.N.: "Tribal Development Plans and Programmes in the Sixth Schedule Areas with Special Reference to Management of Land—A Critical Appraisal", published in the Bulletin, Assam Institute of Research for Tribals and Scheduled Castes, Vol-I, No. VII, 1990.
8. Bordoloi, B.N.: "The Land Ownership and Cycle-Migration among the Zemei Nagas", published in North East India—A Sociological Study, edited by S.M. Dubey, 1977, pp. 406 and 407.
9. A Study of the Land System of North-Eastern Region, Vol-I, Assam, Law Research Institute, Guwahati, 1982.
10. Bordoloi, B.N.: Transfer and Alienation of Tribal Land in Assam, Guwahati, 1991, p. 216 and 217.
11. *Op. cit.*, at Sl. 9.
12. Memo No. GA/REV/5/14/62/21. dated 6.7.62, issued by the North Cachar Hills District Council.
13. *Op. cit.*, at Sl. 10, p. 261.

CHAPTER 22

Aspects of a Land-Scarce Semi-Primitive Economy : Traces of Capitalist Farming in Mizoram

❑ K.K. UPADHYAYA

The note aims at delineating some traces of capitalist farming in the hill state of Mizoram even as the predominant form of farming is shifting cultivation engaging about every second family in the state.

The signs are unmistakable. Thus a recent study of two villages Hortoki and Tuipuibari II (Upadhyaya, 1991) showed that 10 of the 100 sample farms used irrigation waters, had some flat land. Their paid-out labour ratio was in the range of 57-81 percent and they used fertilizers and chemicals. In Hortoki a planter had been netting upwards of Rs. 40,000 consistently for several years.

These farms, constituting 10 per cent of sample population, would not stand out from the rest really and there may not be evidence of "polarisation", but it may be fairly said that signs of emergence of "capitalist mode of production" in agriculture in Mizoram are manifest and reveal themselves even in off-centre spaces like Hortoki and Tuipuibari-I. If the land is narrow yet it is about as narrow as in West Bengal or Bihar, short of caste subordination of workers, the army of landless labourers, high concentration of land ownership and usury.

The reported study confirmed a phenomenon generally recognized about Mizoram farming. The government employees, people with close links with politicians as also the politicians themselves were found to have a stake in farming : like the deprived sections of the population they were free to turn the forests but they also had "garden passes" *(huan pass)* to enable them to develop settled farming and plantation cropping.

The emergence of commercialization of agriculture in the two villages of Mizoram is far from sporadic. Another study of a village near the capital down of Aizawl and on the national Highway 54 (Upadhyaya, 1989) confirms the trend.

Even as both Arunachal Pradesh and Mizoram are predominantly tribal, while the former would appear to be still primitive, the latter definitely describes a semi-primitive economy where the change in the property relationships has been phenomenal since independence in 1947.

Land has traditionally been held communally in Mizoram at the level of village overseered by the village chief who could not deny land to any resident whose only liability was to pay the usual taxes and be loyal to the chief. Where a chief was too arrogant there would be exodus of population to other villages, so he would lose tax revenue. This inalienable right of the "citizens" of the "village state" was acknowledged when on abolition of chiefship in 1955 compensation was paid not on the land in the village but on the number of households there. The territory is now strewn with hundreds of private gardens for settled farming, animal husbandry and plantation crops. As one drives along any stretch of the three thousand odd km of road network of Mizoram state, one sights the signs for the private gardens—their acquisition and their sizes depending purely on political connections of the holders. Similarly. Land Settlement Certificates are issuable to any desirous Mizo for house-site against a negligible fee. But the most extensive privatization of land has been done under the New Land Use Policy of the Government of Mizoram since 1984 under which to each family which offers to shun shifting cultivation about 4 hectares of land is assigned without any consideration and, in fact, with a subsidy of about Rs. 30,000 in a phased way to sustain itself during the period of 2-4 years over which it hopes to make his new settled farming and plantation self-sustaining. The idea here is to rope in all the farming families as fast as practicable with about 10,000 families having already been allotted about 20,000 hectares of land by 1990-91.

In urban areas which now accommodate about 50 per cent of the population of Mizoram (having a phenomenal rate of urbanization because of regrouping of villages, growth of office economy and high public outlay) house-sites held at vantage positions through Land Settlement Certificates obtained earlier are the prize possessions. The transfer values of these are comparable to those in towns of similar sizes elsewhere in the country even as the transfer is limited to natives.

The change in respect of labour market also has been remarkable, again occasioned largely by state. Till the legislation on abolition of chief's rights under Lushai Hills (Acquisition of Chief's Rights) Act, 1955, slavery was legal and the chief could demand forced labour from his subjects as help on his own farms or for upkeep of roads, ponds and springs of the village or on deployment on village security. In fact, part of such labour was made available to district administration (in central places like Aizawl) as coolies for development and maintenance of social overheads.

With plentiful availability of government and other jobs against cash payment the traditional practice of framework in lieu of food and drinks or labour on barter has also ceased. Now, cash payment of farm labour, without any ties either of loan or lease of some cultivable land, is the rule with no exceptions.

A fall-out of such changes in land and labour market would be expected in women's rights. The bride in Mizoram would traditionally hold no property except the marriage gifts she brought with her to her husband's house where she would be considered an "outsider" till the couple broke loose from the larger family and started a nuclear family of its own, and even as a housewife she would have no claim on family property or children who belong to the "patriarch" in the patrilineal set-up. A woman was remarriageable and separation was easy, but her status was clearly low with men having right to keep concubines if they could afford to (Nunthara, 1984 and Vanlawma, 1972). But now the situation has changed beyond recognition with women jealously guarding their property rights in real estate, buildings and business and swamping both the offices and shops. However, when they separate they often do not keep the children with them.

References

1. S.N. Mishra (1982): Arunachal's Tribal Economic Formations and Their Dissolution, Economic and Political Weekly.
2. C. Nunthara (1984): Background Paper on the Mizos, Seminar on Development Strategies in Historical Perspective in North-East India, North Eastern Hill University, Shillong.
3. K.K.Upadhyaya (1989): Semi-Primitive Economy of an Indian Village, Mittal Publications, New Delhi.
4. K.K.Upadhyaya (1986): Development Problems and Prospects of Mizoram, Inter-India Publications, New Delhi.
5. K.K.Upadhyaya (1991): Size-Productivity Relation and Capitalist Development in Agriculture with Theoretical Underpinnings, The Indian Journal of Economics, (Vol. LXIX, no. 275).
6. R. Vanlawma (1972): My Country and I. Zoram Printing Press, Aizawl.

CHAPTER 23

Role of Primary Agricultural Cooperatives in Rural Credit

(With Reference to Manipur State)

❑ KH. SOMORENDRO SINGH

Introduction

The Agricultural Cooperatives of our country were launched with a view to relieving the agriculturists from the clutches of money–lenders and to providing the required credit in time at low rates of interest. Agricultural Credit Cooperatives play important role in rejuvenating rural economy. Indeed, credit is the life blood and key input for overall development. The most important source of institutional credit for rural development is agricultural credit cooperatives. This sector thus has been playing a vital role in the process of the integrated rural development. Manipur witnessed a new trend in 1976-77. Traditional types of Primary Agricultural Cooperatives and Farmers Service Societies were reorganised into bigger societies known as Gram Panchayat Level Multi Purpose Cooperative Societies Ltd. (GPLMPCS) in the valley areas and the large size agricultural multipurpose cooperative societies (LAMPS) in the hill areas when the State Government adopted the recommen–dation of the National Commission on Agricultural and Bawa Committee (1976-77) with a view to making them economically viable units.

Objectives

The following are the main objectives of the proposed study:

(i) To compare the position of target and achievement of credit distributed by the Agricultural Cooperatives in North-Eastern Region.

(ii) To identify the role and present position of Primary Agricultural Cooperatives.

(iii) To trace out the emerging problems.

(iv) To recommend the suitable remedial measures.

Methodology

To appraise the role of Primary Agricultural Cooperatives, the data were collected from the publication of the Government of India, Department of Agricultural and Cooperation, Annual reports published by Govt. of Manipur, Registrar of Cooperative Societies. Other published materials from various sources related to the topic also made part of the data for the preparation of this paper. To study these aspects the Manipur State Cooperative Bank has been selected. This bank is working at the Apex level in the State.

Need for Institutional Credit

The Agricultural Credit in the North-Eastern Region is largely arranged and made available by the unorganised money market consisting of moneylenders, landlords, merchants and relatives. Besides, a larger section of the region remains non-monetised and non-banked.

Many studies have revealed that more than 70% of the agriculturists borrow from the unorganised money-market. As such the development of institutional credit has become a very important condition for agricultural planning and rural development.

The objectives of the institutional credit are to make a breakthrough in the vicious circle of poverty, rack-renting and usury and to stimulate the farmers to boost agricultural productivity. The ultimate aim of the entire system of primary agricultural cooperatives is to help the people living in rural areas to improve their standard of living.

North-Eastern Region—A Comparative View

North-Eastern Region consists of Assam, Tripura, Meghalaya, Manipur, Mizoram, Nagaland and Arunachal Pradesh. In the planning era, the states in the Region have been recognising the Cooperatives as an important sector for the development of their states and specific roles to them have been assigned and are being continued to assign. If we compare the position of target and achievement of short term, medium term and long term loans distributed by Agricultural Cooperatives in different states of North Eastern Region in relation to 8th plan target, we find Manipur occupying the highest position in Short Term Credit. Assam occupied highest in medium term and long term credits. The details are shown in the given tables--

Table 1

TARGET AND ACHIEVEMENT OF SHORT TERM LOANS DISTRIBUTED BY COOPERATIVES IN NORTH EASTERN REGION

(Rs. in crores)

Sl. No.	*Name of the State*	*8th plan 1992-97 Target*	*1991-92 Achive-ments*	*1992-93*		*1993-94*	
				Target	*Achieve-ments*	*Propos-ed by State Govt.*	*Targets Recom-mended by W. Group*
1.	Assam	10.00	2.70	8.00	3.00	8.00	8.00
2.	Arunachal Pradesh	0.25	0.10*	0.13	0.13	0.13	0.13**
3.	Manipur	15.00	9.00*	11.00	11.00	11.00	11.00**
4.	Meghalaya	2.50	0.61	0.50	1.50	1.75	1.75
5.	Mizoram	2.50	1.00*	1.50	1.50	1.50	1.50**
6.	Nagaland	6.00	3.50	4.00	4.00	5.00	5.00
7.	Tripura	3.00	1.75	3.00	3.00	3.50	3.50
	Total	39.25	18.66	29.13	24.13	30.88	30.88

Notes: * — Agreed outlay for 1991-92.
** — Agreed outlay for 1992-93.

Source: Cooperative Movement in India—A Statistical Profile 1993—Government of India, Department of Agriculture and Cooperation.

The table 3 indicate that the cooperative credit, in the 8th Plan which flowed to the highest targets of Rs. 39.25 crores in short term, Rs. 19.50 crores in medium term and Rs. 11.25 crores in long term respectively in the north-eastern states. It recognised that Agricultural cooperatives have occupied a strategic place in cooperative credit structure in North-Eastern States. Through the State Cooperative Banks, the Reserve Bank provides finance to the Agriculturists. The State Cooperative Banks (Apex Banks) mobilise financial resources from the public and borrow from the money market, making funds available to the Primary Agricultural Cooperatives. Finally, the Primary Agricultural Credit Cooperatives (PACS) played active role in lending business.

Table 2

TARGET AND ACHIEVEMENTS OF MEDIUM TERM LOANS DISTRIBUTED BY COOPERATIVES IN NORTH-EASTERN STATES

(Rs. in crores)

Sl. No.	*Name of the State*	*8th Plan 1992-97*	*1991-92 Achive-ments*	*1992-93 Target*	*1992-93 Achieve-ments*	*1993-94 Propos-ed by State Govt.*	*Recom-mended by W. Group*
1.	Assam	6.00	5.00	6.00	1.50	6.00	6.00
2.	Arunachal Pradesh	0.25	0.12*	0.15	0.15	0.15	0.15**
3.	Manipur	3.00	1.50*	2.00	2.00	2.00	2.00**
4.	Meghalaya	2.00	0.61	1.25	1.25	1.25	1.25
5.	Mizoram	2.00	1.00*	1.50	1.50	1.50	1.50**
6.	Nagaland	1.25	1.00	1.25	1.25	2.00	2.00
7.	Tripura	5.00	3.87	3.00	3.00	4.00	4.00
	Total	19.50	13.10	15.15	10.65	16.90	16.90

Notes: * — Agreed outlay for 1991-92.

** — Agreed outlay for 1992-93.

Source: Cooperative Movement in India, Government of India, (1993).

The 8th Five Year Plan pointed out that the strategy for cooperative credit development would be as follows--

(*i*) Building up the cooperative movement as a self-managed, self-regulated and self-reliant institutional set up by giving more autonomy to cooperatives and by democratising the movement;

(ii) Enhancing the capabilities of cooperatives for enabling to play a significant role in improving the productivity of the economy and in creating employment opportunities for the people living in rural areas for service of weaker sections, and

(iii) Development and training of cooperative functionaries in professional management, etc.

Table 3

TARGET AND ACHIEVEMENTS OF LONG TERM LOANS DISTRIBUTED BY COOPERATIVES IN NORTH-EASTERN STATES

(Rs. in crores)

Sl. No.	*Name of the State*	*8th plan 1992-97 Target*	*1991-92 Achivements*	*1992-93*		*1993-94*	
				Target	*Achievements*	*Proposed by State Govt.*	*Recommended by W. Group*
1.	Assam	5.00	7.00	7.00	2.50	7.00	7.00
2.	Arunachal Pradesh	—	—	—	—	—	—
3.	Manipur	2.00	1.00*	1.25	1.25	1.25	1.25**
4.	Meghalaya	0.75	0.17	0.50	0.50	0.50	0.50
5.	Mizoram	—	—	—	—	—	—
6.	Nagaland	1.50	1.00	1.00	1.00	1.00	1.00
7.	Tripura	2.00	0.83	1.50	1.50	1.50	1.50
	Total	11.25	10.00	11.25	6.75	11.25	11.25

Notes: * — Agreed outlay for 1991-92.
** — Agreed outlay for 1992-93.

Source: Cooperative Movement in India—A Statistical Profile 1993—Government of India, Department of Agriculture and Cooperation.

Efforts have been made during the last Five Year Plans to expand the various programmes and also to diversify the activities. However, many steps still remained behind their potentialities for the development of cooperative institutions.

Primary Agricultural Credit Societies

At the grass root level Primary Agricultural Credit Societies are the foundation of the cooperative system which has been built up in the country to serve the rural farmers. This unit epitomizes the vitality and service potential of the Cooperative movement in the country. Since the adoption of these GPLMPCS and LAMPS in the state their numbers have been increasing over the years. At present there are 194 Cooperatives; 130 are the GPLMPCS and remaining 64 are LAMPS. Apart from the credit facilities to its members the PACS also undertake various other activities. Fertilizer business is the next biggest business after crop loan business since it can boost up crop productivity and earn more income by the farmers. These agricultural cooperatives also play a major role in the mechanisation of Agriculture in the State. There are 77 Agro-Service centres run by the PACS, of these 58 are in the valley areas (GPLMPCS) and remaining 19 are in the hill areas (LAMPS). These centres are one of the best services rendered by the PACS to its members as well as to the general public. Each Agro-service centres consist of atleast one tractor, two power tillers and two or five pump sets provided by the centres themselves. In the field of agriculture, the PACS are playing an important role for the development of the state to keep pace with the modern method of cultivation in the state. Total number of district wise Agricultural Cooperatives which gave credit to the farmers in the state as on 31st March, 1994 is given below—

Sl. No.	*No. of Agricultural Cooperatives*		*Name of the District Valley/Hill*
1.	130 GPLMPCS	—	Valley areas of Imphal, Thoubal, Senapati and Bishenpur Districts.
2.	64 LAMPS	—	Hill areas of Churachandpur, Ukhrul, Senapati, Chandel and Tamenglong Districts.

Note: *(i)* GPLMPCS—Gram Panchayat Level Multipurpose Cooperative Society Ltd.

(ii) LAMPS—Large size Agricultural Multipurpose Cooperative Society Ltd.

Various agencies have been explored for the greater flow of the credit to the farmers.

At village level : At the grass root level the Primary agricultural credit societies act as a very important point of delivery.

At the higher level : At the higher level the State Coop. Banks are formed working for the agricultural credit.

They have designed not only for short term crop loans but also for medium term and long term loans. In fact, the Agricultural Cooperatives have to work in order to increase the periodical production, but also for creating assets in the long run.

Present Position of Agricultural Cooperative Societies in Manipur

Present position of agricultural cooperatives regarding the number of societies, village covered, membership, paid up share capital, percentage of recovery to demand and average of membership per society are given in Table No. 4.

Table 4

PROGRESS OF PRIMARY AGRICULTURAL COOPERATIVES IN MANIPUR

Sl.No.	*Particulars*		*As on 31-3-1994*
1.	No. of societies	—	194
2.	Percentage of village covered per society	—	11
3.	Membership	—	1,27,901 lakhs
4.	Paid up share capital	—	461.46 lakhs
5.	Working capital	—	2,215.00 lakhs
6.	Percentage of recovery to demand	—	7.8
7.	Average of membership per society	—	659.00

Total number of membership of Primary Agricultural Cooperatives during the year 1991-92 was found 121368 lakhs. It has increased spontaneously upto 121901 lakhs during the present year 1994-95. Increase in membership is mainly due to the comming up of new societies. Share capital collected from the members constituted the primary source of the paid-up share capital of the GPLMPCS and LAMPS. Besides, Government contribution also form a major source of fund. Paid-up share capital of these societies also increased from Rs. 456.83 lakhs (1991-92) to Rs. 461.46 lakhs (1994-95). At the end of the year 1994-95, average of membership per society is found 659. The existing 194 agricultural credit societies are giving direct economic benefits to the members as employment opportunities and indirectly benefitting 4.15 lakhs people in the State.

The Manipur State Cooperative Bank

At the State level, the Manipur State Cooperative Bank has been working as the regional authority in terms of credit planning and distribution. It also controls the allocation of credit in the rural sector. Being the Apex Bank in the State of the Cooperative structure, the Bank has got its own policies and commitments to be executed with the financial assistance of many financing agencies, *viz.*, NABARD, SIDBI, Govt. of India, Govt. of Manipur etc. depending on the nature of its scheme and period.

The Cooperative Agricultural Credit in Manipur is of comparatively recent origin. However, it made a real beginning only in 1956 with the establishment of the Manipur State Cooperative Bank Ltd. An Apex Bank in the State of Manipur with its net work of eight (8) branches in all important towns of every district, has been extending short term, medium term and long term credit facilities to the farmers through its adopted GPLMPCS and LAMPS to the extent of Rs. 2,176.30 lakhs as on 31st March, 1995. Area wise details of loans advanced as on 31st March, 1995 are given in Table 5.

Table 5

STATEMENT SHOWING POSITION OF LOANS ADVANCED IN MANIPUR AS ON 31-3-1995

(Rs. in lakhs)

Sl. No.	*Name of the District Valley/Hill Areas*	*Types of Loans*			*Total*	*% of Recovery*
		ST	*MT*	*LT*		
1.	***Valley Areas***					
	(a) Imphal Dist.	482.75	517.17	115.99	1115.90	11%
	(b) Thoubal Dist.	230.33	63.60	55.93	349.86	5.7%
	(c) Bishenpur Dist.	196.46	71.50	21.27	289.24	5.8%
					1754.99	

Sl. No.	Name of the District Valley/Hill Areas	Types of Loans ST	MT	LT	Total	% of Recovery
2.	*Hill Areas*					
	(a) Churachandpur Dist.	70.93	—	9.51	80.44	5.8%
	(b) Ukhrul Dist.	87.71	—	4.70	92.41	1.1%
	(c) Senapati Dist.	207.92	40.62	—	248.54	0.8%
	Total	1276.10	692.89	207.40	2176.39	7.8%

Source: Manipur State Cooperative Bank Ltd.

It is clear from Table No. 5 that Rs. 1754.99 lakhs have been advanced in the valley areas and Rs. 421.39 lakhs in Hill areas as credit facilities to the farmers of this State. Since their inception GPLMPCS and LAMPS have been advancing various types of loans to the farmers in their respective areas to meet the credit need of the members. Short term loans are provided for carrying out seasonal agricultural crops, medium term and long term loans are provided for purchasing agricultural implements like tractor, power tillers, pump sets, bullock carts, etc. However, during the years 1993-95, the PACSs could not advance any sort of loans to the members since the banks were not in a position to fulfill their credit need in various sectors. This is because, almost all the PACSs were in heavy overdues position. Their recovery percentage as on 31-3-95 is just 7.8 percent. This has created a major problem and the financing banks have not been able to recycle the credit flows. It is also found that the conditions of the Bank has not been developing upto the expected level despite several measures to unkeep the level of the Apex Bank of the State which can be seen from figures placed below--

The Bank had experienced many ups and downs in its working due to crisis at the top level of management. Slow growth rate is also due to lack of states patronage. And choking of refinance channel and accumulated losses are due to high overdues, lack of professionalisation at the top, poor liquidity position of the bank arising from poor recovery of loans, lack of supervision, monitoring and also political interference on many levels of working of the Bank.

Table 6

PRESENT WORKING POSITION OF MANIPUR STATE COOPERATIVE BANK

(Rs. in lakhs)

Sl. No.	*Year*	*Deposit*	*Advances*	*Profit & Loss A/C*
1.	1989-90	(–) 1.69%	(–) 24.58%	(+) 15.81
2.	1990-91	6.67%	(–) 5.11%	(–) 15.82
3.	1991-92	19.68%	43.58%	(–) 19.60
4.	1992-93	9.28%	12.14%	(–) 64.34
5.	1993-94	(–) 27.53%	(–) 1.23%	(–) 147.65

Source: The Manipur State Cooperative Bank Ltd.

The Table 7 shows the amount of loan disbursed and percentage of overdues during the plan period in Manipur.

Table 7

LOAN DISBURSED BY AGRICULTURAL COOPERATIVES DURING PLAN PERIOD AND PERCENTAGE OF OVER-DUES TO OUTSTANDING LOAN

Sl. No.	*Plan Period*	*Total Amount of Loan Disbursed*	*Percentage of Overdue to Outstanding*
1.	3rd Plan period (1961-62 to 1965-66)	Rs. 58.46 lakhs	NIL
2.	Annual Plan (1966-67 to 1968-69)	Rs. 104.02 lakhs	57.82%
3.	4th Plan (1969-70 to 1973-74)	Rs. 217.08 lakhs	67.59%
4.	5th Plan (1974-75 to 1978-79)	Rs. 558.43 lakhs	45.23%
5.	6th Plan (1980-81 to 1984-85)	Rs. 308.34 lakhs	94.06%
6.	7th Plan (1985-86 to 1989-90)	Rs. 1935.38 lakhs	37.64%
7.	8th Plan (1990-91 to 1994-95)	Rs. 1488.80 lakhs	65.35%

Source: The Manipur State Cooperative Bank Ltd.

Certain Problems

In the north-eastern states, the Cooperative Credit Structure continues to be extremely weak. Even in the enactment of cooperative Laws in these States as well as in the approach papers of their Planning Board, the State Policy on Cooperative is not clearly spelt out. Though quantitative growth is visible, the qualitative aspect of development is a missing link as is a matter of great concern.

The mounting overdues, the poor progress of linking of credits with marketing are simply visible. The insignificant member participations, increase dependence on the State, poor level of planning and ineffective monitoring systems are eating into the vitals of the cooperative growth. Moreover, weak Human Resource Management is also one of the main reasons. The Agricultural Credit Review Committee of Reserve Bank of India, (1989) has also highlighted the comparative backwardness of the Region in the Agricultural Credit Front of the country as a whole.

Further, non-collection of additional shares, lack of arrangement of activities for internal resources mobilisations, non-maintenance of land records and production plan of individual members are the main weakness of these societies. Again, timely repayment of loan is not the sole criteria for making a society as living being. Annual general body meetings are not held in time. Also, Annual Budget is not prepared in time, attendance of cooperative education class is very poor. If we want to see a living viable PACS each of the above activities are to be activated without delay.

Need for Action Programme

The better functioning of Agricultural Cooperatives at the grass root level and cooperative Banks at the Apex level largely depend on dedicated leadership coupled with the real spirit of cooperation and the vital factors like effective management, proper distribution of funds, high morale of employees, etc. The Government should also come out with a well-defined state policy on cooperation based on National Cooperative Policy. The success of cooperatives considerably depends upon the degree of support and coordination they get from the Government and other related organisations.

Despite some weaknesses in the cooperative credit system, it can be said that there is no alternative to the cooperatives in rural credit system. Therefore, strengthening and streamlining of cooperative institutions is the need of the hour. Due consideration should be given by the planners, because it is really a very important part of the National planning. It has to be dynamic and professional with committed cooperative leadership at all levels, only a democratic and efficient management can face the challenge facing it.

All development agencies, which exist to assist the development of cooperatives in the North-Eastern Region like NABARD, IDBI, NCDC, NAFED, TRIFED and NCCF should suitably reorient and amend their approach and pattern of assistance and support in order to overcome organisational, financial and managerial weakness which have hindered balanced and rapid development of cooperatives in the Region.

References

1. Singh, Kh.S.: Rural Credit and Role of Cooperatives, Bai Bhaba, ICM, Bhubaneshwar, 1993, p. 55.
2. Singh, Kh.S.: Rural Credit with special reference to the role of Primary Level Agricultural Cooperatives in Manipur during Plan period (unpublished, Ph.D. Thesis).
3. Choubey, B.N.: "Institutional Finance for Agricultural Development", p. 28.
4. Subramanian, M.: "Restructuring Cooperative Movement", IASSI Quarterly, Vol. 98, No. 4, April-June, 1991, p. 28.
5. Wali, M.K.: "How Credit Cooperatives Fail to Reach the Poor", Cooperatives News Digest, Vol. 31, No. 8, August, 1980, p. 139.
6. Mamoria, C.B.: Rural Credit and Agricultural Cooperation in India, p. 146.
7. Mathur, B.S.: Cooperation in India, 1988, p. 89.
8. Reserve Bank of India, All India Rural Credit Survey Committee (Vol. II), 1954.
9. Reserve Bank of India—A Review of Agricultural Credit Survey in India (1989).
10. The Maharashtra Cooperative Quarterly, Vol. LXXVI/No. 1, July, 1992.
11. Goswami, U. (1991): "Business Development Planning in India"—The Manipur Cooperatives, Vol. XXVIII, No. 105.
12. Shah, J.V. (1990): "Importance of Primary Cooperatives"—The Cooperators, Vol. XXVIII, No. 10.
13. Government of Manipur (Report)—Annual Administratives Report, (1990-91), (1991-92), (1992-93) and (1993-94).
14. Background paper of State Level Cooperative Seminars on Agricultural Credit Cooperatives Societies, 1995, Government of Manipur, p. 2, and p. 23.

CHAPTER 24

A Review on Agricultural Cooperative Finance in Manipur

❑ S.K. VERMA

The primary sector of the economy is the pre-dominant sector in Manipur. However, it is necessary to develop this sector to see how the shifting and slope cultivations could be stabilised so as to keep the people involved in the regional economy. For this, the development of Agriculture cooperatives is the best way to change the life of the people of this region. With this backdrop attempt is made in this paper to discuss agricultural cooperative finance in Manipur.

Cooperative Movement in Manipur

In Manipur, the formal cooperative movement has started since the year 1947 with the adoption of the cooperative societies Act, 1912 as the Manipur State Cooperative Societies Act, 1947 and a number of consumer cooperative societies came into existence.

Although the movement has started since 1947 its growth was not spectacular. During the year, 1955-56 with the launching of the 2nd Five Year Plan and with the adoption of the Assam Cooperative Societies Act in Manipur cooperative movement in the State took massive spurt. The Manipur State Cooperative Bank came into existance. Thus, in Manipur the real movement was started in the field of Agricultural credit as a bulwork against the malpractices of village money lenders and for improvement in the standard of living of the cultivators who form 80 per cent of the total population. In Manipur the Agricultural Credit Societies were started in the forms of M.P.C.S. (Multipurpose Cooperative

Societies), then came the large size Agricultural Credit Cooperative Societies and service societies during the year 1954-55 and 1959-60 respectively. The following tables bring out the highlights of Cooperative movement in last forty years in Manipur.

Table 1

DEVELOPMENT OF INDICATORS OF COOPERATIVE SOCIETIES IN MANIPUR

	1950-51	*1960-61*	*1970-71*	*1980-81*	*1990-91*
1. Societies (Nos.)	350	629	1028	2921	3770
2. Membership (No. in lakhs)	0:21	0.39	1.00	2.95	3.66
3. Share Capital (Rs. in crores)	0.42	0.19	0.58	7.90	47.34
4. Working Capital (Rs. in crores)	0.51	0.63	1.24	9.51	352.12

Source: Administrative Report of Cooperative Department, Manipur.

During last forty years the number of societies increased to 3770 by the end of 1990-91 from 350 in 1950-51. The membership of the societies has gone up by eighteen fold with 112 fold increase in share capital and 690 fold increase in working capital.

Table 2

DISTRIBUTION OF COOPERATIVE SOCIETIES IN MANIPUR AS ON 31-3-1991

Type of Societies	*Numbers*	*Membership Numbers*	*Paidup Shares (Rs. 000)*	*Working Capital (Rs. 000)*
1. Non-Agricultural	08	15,988	26,433	2,49,217
2. Thrift and Credit	125	5,633	217	568
3. Agricultural Credit	714	1,82,945	4,027	46,633
4. Non-Credit				
(*a*) Non-Industrial	1668	64,055	10,634	42,212
(*b*) Industrial	1760	97,683	6,037	13,493
Total	4275	3,66,304	47,348	3,52,123

Source: Annual Administrative Report, 1991-92, Deptt. of Cooperation, Government of Manipur.

The emphasis on cooperative sector has been laid in various plan policies of Central and State Governments. The State Government's Cooperative policies encouraged the people of the State to go for more and more societies in various sectors over the period of time. The growth of the membership, paid-up-capital and working capital of various sectors can be seen from table 2.

The Non-Agricultural Credit Societies were dominated by banks whereas Agricultural Credit Societies were dominated by GPLMPCS (Gram Panchayat Level Multipurpose Cooperative Societies), LAMPCS (Large Size Agricultural Multipurpose Cooperative Societies), small size cooperative societies. The maximum number of beneficiaries through membership were found in Agricultural Credit Societies.

Agricultural Credit

Cooperative Credit movement has had a long history of development dating back to 1904 while establishing credit cooperatives great stress was laid on them for combating rural indebtedness and for making credit cheap in rural areas. In the seventies, the concept of cooperatives has changed from "Catering Credit" to "developing project". Thus, the cooperative credit movement aims at improving the socio-economic status of the rural people and incorporating the principle of "equity". It is a pre-condition for the involvement of people in the process of development.

Improving the weaker farmers by purveying credit is the objective of Indian Planning. The special role of the credit cooperatives is to provide rural credit for achieving the three B's *viz.* better farming, better business and better living.

The PACS played a crucial role with the assistance of marketing cooperatives in supplying farm inputs namely improved seeds, fertilizers, pesticides, and insecticides, implements, etc. and disbursed about Rs. 2,423 crores by the end of 1989-90. Further, they marketed agricultural and consumer commodities worth about Rs. 5,929 crores in 1991 in rural areas. The short term and medium term credit advanced by them recorded an increase from 22 crores in 1950-51 to Rs. 5,493 crores in 1991. All in all, the cooperative credit movement had made sound progress in the field of agricultural credit.

Agriculture Credit in Manipur

So far the number of Primary Agricultural Credit Societies in Manipur stands at 721. Since its inception the PACS have been catering the short term and medium term agricultural credit needs of the agriculturists. But in the year 1976 Manipur had passed its own cooperative societies act with the recommendation of the National Commission on Agriculture and the Bawa Committee. The organisational setup of the credit society has changed and accordingly 52 Large Size Agricultural Multipurpose Societies (LAMPS) in the hills and 95 Gram Panchayat Level Multipurpose Cooperative Societies in the valley were organised. Before the reorganisation of PACS, the only financing bank was Manipur State Cooperative Bank Ltd. But now some commercial banks *viz.*, UBI, SBI, United Commercial Bank, Vijaya Bank, Allahabad Bank, Punjab and Sindh Bank are also financing such societies.

Credit structure in Manipur, unlike in other states of India is of two tier system. The M.S.C.B. is at the State level and Primary Agriculture Credit Societies at the village level.

State Cooperative Bank

Manipur State Cooperative Bank Ltd. being the Apex Bank in the State of the Cooperative structure has got its own priorities and commitments to be executed with the financial assistance of many financing agencies *viz.*, NABARD, SIDBI, Govt. of India, Govt. of Manipur etc. basing on the nature of its scheme and period. Besides, its jurisdiction covers the entire Manipur. Its network of 8 (eight)

Table 3

Sl.No.	*Heads*		*(Rs. in lakhs) As on 24-3-95*
1.	Share Capital contribution	—	239.04
2.	Reserves	—	87.82
3.	Deposits	—	704.31
4.	Advances	—	1976.69
5.	Borrowings	—	1485.85
6.	Profit and Loss	—	(—) 286.65

Source: Administrative Deptt. of MSCB, 1995

branches in all the important towns of every district has been serving the credit needs of the people for the last many years with dual functions of Central Cooperative Bank and Apex Cooperative Bank. At present, the working of the MSCB is given in Table 3.

However, the condition of Apex Bank has not been developing upto the expected level despite several measures to upkeep the level of Apex Bank of the State which can be seen from the figures placed below--

Deposit Year	*Growth Rate* (Rs. in lakhs)	*Advances Year*	*Growth Rate* (Rs. in lakhs)
1989-90	(—) 1.69%	1989-90	(—) 24.58%
1990-91	6.67%	1990-91	(—) 5.11%
1991-92	19.68%	1991-92	43.58%
1992-93	9.28%	1992-93	12.14%
1993-94	(—) 27.53%	1993-94	(—) 1.23%
Remarks :	(—) Growth is due to lack of state patronage		Choking of refinance Channel is due to high overdue

MSCB had suffered loss during the year 1991-92, 1992-93, 1993-94 continuously of Rs. 19.60, Rs. 64.34 and Rs. 147.65 lakhs respectively. During the year 1992-93 the Manipur State Cooperative Bank Ltd. had disbursed short term loan of Rs. 2. 85 crores to 1,21,368 members through the 116 GPLMPCS & 61 Lamps. Recently, the Govt. of India has formulated an effective Direct Action Programme specially for sick units and insisted upon them to get signed an agreement among financial agencies, State Govt. and the institution in the form of MOU (Memorendum of Understanding) to attain viability within a specific period of 5 (five) years.

The MSCB Ltd. has already prepared the same and got it signed on 27-9-1994. Accordingly, it has started its functions as per the terms of the agreement. A cell at the Head Office for monitoring of the activities has already been set up.

Imphal Urban Cooperative Bank Ltd.

Imphal Urban Cooperative Bank was the first Urban Bank in the North-Eastern India to get licence from the Reserve Bank of India under the Banking Regulation Act, 1949.

As on 31st March, 1993, there were 52,037 depositors and 2,590 beneficiaries enjoying credit facilities under various schemes. Out of the total advances 81% was for priority sector and out of this 25% was for the weaker section of the society.

At present, it practises only two kinds of loaning system *viz.*, short term and medium term patterns; the long term financing is yet to be implemented. The bank has been providing ST and MT loans for agriculture and non-agricultural purposes. Under short term loan, cash credits and guarantee operations constitute major share in the financial assistance provided to its members. The MT loan to agriculture is limited only to poultry and sericulture. Table 4 shows the trend of credit to agricultural sector.

Table 4

(Rs. in lakhs)

Sector	*1988*	*1989*	*1990*	*1991*	*1992*	*1993*
Agriculture Credit	0.78	0.81	38.02	4.34	34.92	37.38
(short term)	(100%)	(4%)	(4775%)	(456%)	(4377%)	(4792%)

Note: Figures in brackets indicate the index growth rates taking 1988 as base year.

Source: Imphal Urban Coop. Bank Ltd., Annual Report, 1993-94.

The medium term loan (MTL) to poultry, sericulture and pisciculture is very negligible. In the year 1989 the bank finance amounted to Rs. 0.06 lakhs in the year 1990. Rs. 0.010 lakhs in 1991. In 1993, the bank finance amounted to Rs. 0.06 lakhs only. These figures show that the Bank has no interest to provide medium term credit to agricultural sector.

Credit from Different Agencies

The institutional credit continued to play an important role in increasing agricultural production and increasing the standard of living by helping the rural community. It helps broaden the income generating base of the producers. Agricultural Credit in Manipur is given in Table 5.

From the Table 5, it is clear that the non-institutional agencies dominate the agricultural credit scene but it reveals that the institutional agency's share in total agricultural credit has gone-up. After the nationalization of 20 commercial banks, the advances of commercial banks are on the increase. Hence, in recent years there has been a considerable increase in the share of institutional credit both from cooperative as well as commercial and regional rural banks. The trend predicts the success of the cooperation.

Table 5

INSTITUTIONAL AGRICULTURAL CREDIT

(Figures in %)

Sources of Credit	*1951-52*	*1961-62*	*1971-72*	*1981-82*	*1991-92*
(a) Institutional source, (Govt.)	3.3	2.6	7.1	8.2	8.9
(b) Cooperatives	3.1	15.5	22.0	24.8	25.7
(c) Commercial Banks/RRB	0.9	0.6	2.4	3.7	4.1
	7.3	18.7	31.5	36.7	38.7
Non-Institutional Sources					
Landlords, Money lenders, trade and commission agents, relatives and others	92.7	81.3	68.5	63.3	61.3
	100.00	100.00	100.00	100.00	100.00

Causes of the Failure of Agriculture Crops

Causes of the failure are as follows--

(1) Organisational problem;
(2) Lack of sincerity of members;
(3) Inability to hold general body meeting;
(4) Lack of professionalisation;
(5) Government intervention;
(6) Low business turnover;
(7) Poor deposit mobilisation;
(8) Lack of dedicated leadership;
(9) Lack of cooperative education and training;
(10) Defective lending policy;
(11) Low recovery of loan; and
(12) Political interference.

Conclusion

In the sphere of agricultural credit, the major policy has been its progressive institutionalisation in order to support the agriculture and rural development programme and to ensure adequate flow of funds to assist the weaker sections and less developed areas. The basic objective is to provide sufficient credit support for agricultural production programmes so as to enable the farmers to adopt modern technology and improved farm practices for augmenting production and productivity which will increase farm income and employment opportunities in rural areas. The primary agricultural credit societies (PACS) are the sheet anchor on which the entire cooperative structure rests. They not only provide term credit, but also undertake marketing of agricultural inputs and distribution of consumer articles.

References

1. Horam, M.: North-East India—A Profile, New Delhi, Cosmo Publication, 1990.
2. Gill, M.S.: Agriculture Cooperatives, New Delhi, Vikas Publication, 1983.
3. Jakhar, B.R.: New Horizon in Agriculture in India, New Delhi, The Coop. Times, 1993.
4. Sah, A.K.: Management for Agricultural Cooperatives, New Delhi, Sterling Publishers, 1993.
5. Samiuddin, Rahman, M.: Cooperative Sector in India, New Delhi, S. Chand & Co., 1983.
6. Thakur Pankaj, Profile of a Development Strategy for India's North-East, Guwahati, Span Publication.
7. Verma, S.K.: Role of BISCOMAUN for the distribution of Agricultural Inputs in Bihar, A Ph.D. Thesis of Magadh University, Bodh-Gaya, 1989.
8. *Ibid.,* Rural Development through Cooperative, Kurukshetra, November, 1994.
9. *Ibid.,* Professionalisation of Cooperative Management "NEEDED", YAON, A Institute of Cooperative Management, Magazine, 1993-94.
10. Government of Manipur; Annual Administrative Report, Department of Cooperation, 1991, 1992.
11. Manipur State Cooperative Bank, Annual Report, 1992-93.
12. Imphal Urban Cooperative Bank Ltd., Annual Report, 1993-94.
13. Annual Report of Manipur State Cooperative Union, 1992-93.
14. Background paper on State level seminar on Agriculture Credit Cooperatives, Deptt. of Cooperation, Govt. of Manipur, 1995.

Part IV

ENVIRONMENTAL REFLECTIONS

CHAPTER 25

Scientific Basis of Traditional Wet Rice Cultivation by North-East Indian Hill Tribes

❑ **P.S. RAMAKRISHNAN**

Introduction

Half of the world population is engaged in agriculture, the vast majority being in the tropics and the sub-tropics. Their agricultural practices are diverse, ranging from a variety of shifting agriculture systems (Ramakrishnan, 1984), fallow systems (Gangwar and Ramakrishnan, 1987), home gardens (Maikhuri and Ramakrishnan, 1990a) and sedentary systems such as wet rice cultivation (Ramakrishnan, 1984; Kumar and Ramakrishnan, 1990).

Small farmers in the wet tropics largely do rice cultivation to obtain their basic needs, because rice, like sugarcane, maize and others have a high calorific value (Finck, 1970). These traditional systems based on technology developed over many generations (Schultz, 1964) are often energy efficient, at the same time providing high economic returns to the farmer, as shown through many studies done by us in north-eastern India (Ramakrishnan, 1984, 1987, 1988, 1992). It is in this context that there is a renewed interest in these traditional agroecosystems. Though shifting agriculture (locally called jhum) is the predominant landuse system in the north-eastern hill region of India (Ramakrishnan, 1992), the tribals here have other important agroecosystem types. Home gardens and wet rice cultivation are two other landuse systems. The present paper looks at some of the traditional wet rice cultivation practices of the tribals of north-eastern India.

This study also examines possible redevelopment strategies of wet rice cultivation so that it would meet certain basic criteria for sustainability, namely, that : *(i)* it should be possible to maintain them without major input of energy from outside the region, *(ii)* it should be compatible with environmental quality on short and long term basis, *(iii)* it should have the flexibility to meet not only present needs of the society but also the long-term demands through adaptive innovations, and *(iv)* finally it should ensure equity with justice.

Rice Agroecosystem

General Description

Like jhum, valley agriculture is practised through out the hill terrain, both at low and high elevations of north-eastern region of India. It is a sedentary form of wet rice *(Oryza sativa)* cultivation and is a complementary system to jhum. It is done wherever the terrain permits, on flat lands between hill slopes (toky and Ramakrishnan, 1981a). However, small terraces may also be built by some tribal communities all around the flat valley land extending into the foot of the hill slopes. This results in a saucer-shaped structure in which rice plots are organized. Obviously, this cropping system is restricted due to topography. The soil in valley lands is fertile due to nutrient wash-out from the hill slopes and therefore does not need added fertilizers. The main advantage is that the land gives sustained yield year after year, unlike the Jhum system that is under cropping only once in a few years of fallow interval depending upon the Jhum cycle.

At lower elevations of Meghalaya, for example, often two crops are planted annually by the Garos on the same land (Toky and Ramakrishnan, 1981a; Maikhuri and Ramakrishnan, 1990a), though others such as the Mikirs and the immigrant Nepalis raise only one crop. Seedlings are generally raised in nursery beds in the month of March, transplanted at the beginning of April and the crop harvested by the end of July or early August. If a second crop is raised soon after the first, the land is again prepared and harvesting completed by October-November. The land is subsequently fallowed between November and March.

At mid-and high elevations of Meghalaya, the land is well prepared before sowing the seeds by broadcasting after the first few showers in June (Mishra and Ramakrishnan, 1981; Patnaik and Ramakrishnan, 1989). Harvesting is done in November, after which the land is fallowed until the following May or June. Only one crop is raised per year.

Table 1

ENGERY (MJ HA^{-1} YR^{-1}) AND ECONOMIC (RS HA^{-1} YR^{-1}) OUTPUT/INPUT RATIOS OF VALLEY LAND AGROECOSYSTEM OF THE GAROS AT BURNIHAT IN MEGHALAYA (FROM TOKY AND RAMAKRISHNAN, 1981, 1982)

Valley Land Agroecosystem	*Input*	*Output*	*Output/Input Ratio*
1st crop	1502(2602)	25639(2820)	17.1(1.1)
2nd crop	1341(2241)	24957(2745)	18.6(1.2)
Both crops	2843(4843)	50596(5565)	17.8(1.1)

In parentheses are monetary values.

Table 2

ENERGY INPUTS (MJ HA^{-1} YR^{-1}) IN RAISING TWO CROPS UNDER VALLEY LAND AGROECOSYSTEM OF THE GAROS AT BURNIHAT IN MEGHALAYA (FROM TOKY AND RAMAKRISHNAN, 1982)

Agricultural Operation	*Energy Input (MJ ha^{-1} yr^{-1})*
Labour input (total)	2813
Field preparation	1564
Nursery preparation	62
Seedling transplantation	49
Irrigation	64
Weeding	537
Harvesting	137
Transportation	53
Threshing	134
Shelling	213
Seed input	30
Total input into the system	2843

In all these areas, the operations of weeding, transplanting, harvesting and threshing are done manually by both male and female members of the family. Only male members prepare the field. The average size of land under wet rice cultivation for a family of five members consisting of two adults and three children is about 0.5 to 1 ha (Toky and Ramakrishnan, 1981); larger families may have land area upto 2 ha (Maikhuri and Ramakrishnan, 1990a). Not more than 10 to 15 percent of the cultivated area would be under this landuse.

Analysis of Low Elevation Wet Rice Agroecosystems of the Garos at Burnihat in Meghalaya

In a study of the valley land agroecosystem of the Garos at Burnihat at lower elevations of Meghalaya (Toky and Ramakrishnan, 1981), 3710 kg $ha^{-1} yr^{-1}$ of rice yield was shown as output per hectare, with an overall energy efficiency (output/input ratio) of about 18 (Table 1). This is double the reported average efficiency value of about 9, for traditional rice cultivation in the Indian plains (Mitchell, 1979). From an energy efficiency point of view, these traditional systems, therefore, are better than most western agricultural systems, which yield only 1 or 2 units of food energy per unit of energy input (Spedding, 1975; leach, 1976; Spedding and Walsingham, 1976; Pimental and Pimental, 1979). The energy efficiency of 18 for the valley system is much lower than that for jhum under a 10-year cycle in the same area (Toky and Ramakrishnan, 1982). This is partly due to lower energy output from a monoculture of rice compared with that obtained through a mixture of crops grown under jhum. The higher labour cost for land preparation and weeding in the valley system is also partly responsible for the lower energy efficiency (Table 2).

The monetary output from the valley system at Burnihat is comparable to one mixed cropping under a 30-year jhum cycle at this site (table 1; Toky and Ramakrishnan, 1981). However, the net gain here was 1/4 of that under jhum under a 30-year cycle.

Comparative Analysis of Low Elevation Wet Rice Land Agro-Ecosystems of Different Tribes Coexisting at Lailad in Meghalaya

In a comparative analysis of a cluster of villages at Lailad (296m altitude) in Meghalaya, valley land agroecosystems as practised by the Garos, the Mikirs and the Nepalis were analysed for their ecologic and economic efficiencies (Maikhuri and Ramakrishnan, 1990a). In these valley systems, unlike the one discussed above for the Garos of Burnihat, some organic manure (386-1137 kg ha^{-1}) is applied by the different tribes. At lower elevations of Meghalaya, the Nepalis and the Mikirs take only one crop during the monsoon, whereas the Garos make more effective use of the land by taking two crops, one during the monsoon and another during the winter. Nepalis in this region, take only one crop in a year, perhaps because of their pre-occupation with a well organized cattle husbandry system for milking. It may be noted here that traditionally tribal communities of north-eastern India do not maintain cattle and this animal husbandry practice wherever found is a recent introduction into the region by the immigrant communities.

The Garos with two croppings in a year had a higher energy input for each cropping under valley agriculture compared with other tribes; the Nepalis expended least energy (Table 3). With the Nepalis obtaining higher yield from one cropping compared with the total from two croppings of the Garos, the former had higher energy and economic efficiencies (output/input ratio) for their system. The Napalis who traditionally do sedentary agriculture, are not only better organized but the returns are equal to that from jhum under a 20-year cycle of the Garos in the region (Maikhuri and Ramakrishnan, 1990a).

Comparative Analysis of Low Elevation Wet Rice Agro-Ecosystems of Different Tribes Co-existing at Balijan in Arunachal Pradesh

Wet Rice Cultivation

At Balijan in Arunachal Pradesh, the local Nishi tribe coexists with the immigrant tribals of the nearby plains of Assam and Bangladesh, such as the Karbis, the Kacharis and the Chakmas. The Nishis, the Chakmas and the Karbis alone do valley cultivation, the former raising one crop of rice annually, the latter raising two crops (Maikhuri and Ramakrishnan, 1990b). Organic manure use in minimal (123-170 kg ha^{-1}). The first cropping of rice is done by transplanting seedings between July-November. The second cropping done by the Karbis alone is a mixture of rice and maize raised between February-June, but the seeds are broadcast. Bullock power is used for ploughing.

Table 3

ENGERY INPUT AND OUTPUT (MJ HA^{-1} YR^{-1}) UNDER VALLEY CULTIVATION AMONG DIFFERENT TRIBAL AND NON-TRIBAL COMMUNITIES AT LAILAD IN MEGHALAYA. VALUES IN PARENTHESES ARE FOR MONETARY INPUT/OUTPUT PATTERN (RS HA^{-1} YR^{-1}) ±S.E. (FROM MAIKHURI AND RAMAKRISHNAN, 1990A)

Production Measures	*Garos*			*Nepalis*
	1st crop	*2nd crop*	*Total*	
Input Total				
Energy	6382	5219	11601	3479
Monetary	1400±68	988±36	2388±123	1316±58
Output Total				
Energy	27656	14282	41938	43172
Monetary	2556±52	1320±18	3876±72	4460±122
Output/input ratio				
Energy	4.3	2.7	3.6	12.4
Monetary	1.8	1.3	1.6	3.4

The Nishis and the Chakmas had similar yield patterns for their valley agroecosystem (therefore, the values for valley cropping as done by the Nishis alone are given here (Table 4). With labour as the chief input, the energy yield under the valley system was equal to the yield under a 5-year jhum cycle as done by the Nishis, but the total of two croppings done by the Karbis exceeded they yield under a 10-year jhum cycle of the Nishis (Maikhuri and Ramakrishnan, 1990b).

From a monetary view point, one cropping under valley as done by the Nishis and the Chakmas was comparable to the output under a 10-year jhum cycle of the Nishis, whereas two croppings of the Karbis yielded more than that under a 60-year jhum cycle (Maikhuri and Ramakrishnan, 1990b). Thus wide variations in yield patterns are evident from these comparative studies.

Mustard Cultivation

Mustard *(Brassica campestris)* is cultivated by the Nishis and the Karbis between October and February on flatlands, as monoculture. Initially, the weedly growth is slashed and ploughed in and the seeds are broadcast. Labour is the only input. Mustard seeds are used for oil extraction, for cooking; otherwise the economic yield from the system is minimal (Table 4), but with a reasonably high energy efficiency. Karbis often raise mustard on much smaller plots, as part of the kitchen garden, but the returns are lower than that under larger flatland.

Table 4

ENGERY OUTPUT/INPUT (MJ HA^{-1} YR^{-1}) UNDER VALLEY COMPARED WITH MUSTARD CULTIVATION DONE BY THE NISHIS AND THE KARBIS OF BALIJAN IN ARUNACHAL PRADESH. VALUES IN PARENTHESES ARE FOR MONETARY OUTPUT/INPUT PATTERN (RS HA^{-1} YR^{-1}) ±S.E. (FROM MAIKHURI AND RAMAKRISHNAN, 1990B).

Production Measure	*Valley Cultivation*		*Mustard Cultivation*	
	1st crop (*Nishis & Karbis*)	*2nd crop* (*Karbis*)	*Flatland* (*Nishis & Karbis*)	*Kitchen garden* (*Karbis*)
Input Total				
Energy	2286	2458	720	450
Monetary	1583±72	1154±52	1070±40	558±81
Output Total				
Energy	37491	12791	10237	4535
Monetary	4940±169	2351±101	2017±40	1042±48
Output/Input				
Energy	16.4	5.2	14.2	9.9
Monetary	3.1	2.0	1.9	1.9

Nishis take only one crop from valley land.

Comparative Analysis of Wet Rice Agro-Ecosystems of the Khasis and the Nepalis at Mid-Elevations at Nayabunglow in Meghalaya

The local tribe, the Khasis and the immigrant Nepalis living at Nayabunglow practise valley cultivation of wet rice (Patnaik and Ramakrishnan, 1989). The Napalis are basically cattle farmers. As these imigrants are not permitted to own land in rural areas, for agriculture, they hire the valley land from the Khasi landlords of the near by Shillong town.

Both the Khasis and the Nepalis take only one crop of rice annually. Some inorganic fertilizer at the rate of 102 kg ha^{-1} is added to the soil by both communities. Ploughing and land preparation is done during the months of May and June using bullocks. The Khasis hire bullocks for the land preparation. Other operations such as transplanting, weeding, harvesting, threshing, etc. are done manually by both male and female members of the family. Both the Khasis and the Nepalis give land revenue as rent to the Khasi owner of the land in the city. There is considerable interaction between the Khasis and the Nepalis in managing their valley land agroecosystem. Consequently the output from valley cultivation of the Nepalis is close to that of the Khasis, but with a slightly higher efficiency for the former because of reduced labour input (Table 5).

Table 5

ENGERY (MJ HA^{-1} YR^{-1}) AND MONETARY (RS. HA^{-1} YR^{-1}) EFFICIENCY OF VALLEY LAND AGROECOSYSTEM OF THE KHASIS AND THE NAPALIS AT NAYABUNGLOW IN MEGHALAYA (FROM PATNAIK AND RAMAKRISHNAN, 1989)

	Khasis		*Nepalis*	
	Energy	*Monetary*	*Engery*	*Monetary*
Input Total	4903	4257	4623	2890
Human Labour	678	3150	427	1897
Bullock Power	491	533	307	333
Seed	193	300	317	300
Inorganic Fertilizer	3541	274	3718	360
Output Total	47795	6334[a]	50825	6460[b]
Output/Input Ratio	9.8	1.5	11	2.2

[a] Rs. 5501 was from grains and Rs. 833 from rice straw.

[b] Rs. 5460 was from grains and Rs. 1000 from rice straw.

Wet Rice Cultivation by the Apatanis of Arunachal Pradesh

The Apatanis with a highly developed valley cultivation of rice perfected over centuries has often been suggested to be one of the relatively advanced tribal societies in the north-eastern region of India (Furer-Haimendorf, 1962, 1985). Wet rice land agro–ecosystems of the Apatanis, like those of other tribes, discussed earlier whose chief land use is jhum (Ramakrishnan, 1984), is also dependent upon nutrient wash-out from the hill slopes. With crop harvest, considerable quantities of nutrients are lost through economic yield (Rosswall and Paustian, 1984; Swamy and Ramakrishnan, 1988) and must be replaced for sustainable land use. Recycling crop residues (Jones, 1976) and use of organic wastes of the village for sustaining soil fertility, as done by the Apatanis is an effective way of restoring soil fertility.

Table 6

SOIL NUTRIENT STATUS (MEAN ± S.E.) IN (0.7 CM DEPTH) RICE AGROECOSYSTEMS OF APATANIS AT HARI IN ARUNACHAL PRADESH (KUMAR AND RAMAKRISHNAN, 1990)

Elements	*With in the Village*	*Outside the Village*
C (%)	2.3±0.2	1.4±0.09
N (%)	0.3±0.02	0.2±0.02
P (mg $100g^{-1}$)	0.1±0.01	0.1±0.01
K (mg $100g^{-1}$)	25.0±1.2	15.0±0.8
Ca (mg $100g^{-1}$)	112.5±9.4	67.5±3.2
Mg (mg $100g^{-1}$)	32.5±1	27.5±0.8

Irrigation farming such as wet cultivation of rice require communal work to maintain it, and to improve the water delivery system (Ruthenberg, 1971). In the absence of a disciplined schedule and scale of water distribution among the beneficiaries, very often economic returns could decline drastically. The Apatanis with cooperative effort under the overall supervision of the village headman, have also optimized water use along with nutrient use in their rice field. Therefore, an understanding of the valley land agroecosystem function of the Apatanis becomes significant.

Cropping and Yield Patterns

Hari is an Apatani village in Arunachal Pradesh at an altitude of 1570 m. and has 418 families and total population of 2021. The average size of a family is about five, living in a large bamboo hut of 15x4 m. floor area. Wet rice cultivation is their only agricultural land use.

Apatanis, at Hari, make effective use of their irrigated land by planting early and late ripening varieties of rice. Early variety is sown farther away from the village where disturbance by animals and poorer irrigation facilities could be major constraints (Kumar and Ramakrishnan, 1990). Lower nutrient status on plots farther away from the village is another consideration. Thus rice plots closer to the village are nutritionally richer than those farther away (Table 6). Closer to the village, where conditions are more favourable, late variety is preferred. Fish culture done here synchronises well with late ripening rice variety. Further, rice is supplemented with *Eleusine coracana* cultivated on elevated partition bunds between the rice plots. The early variety of rice had higher density but with reduced basal area compared to the late variety (Table 7). Economic yield per plant and per unit area of the early variety was significantly lower compared to the late variety. The yield per hectare of *Eleusine coracana* grown on partition bunds of rice plots was higher in plots with early variety than in those with the late variety. Fish production done only along with late-variety rice was substantial.

Table 7

DENSITY, BASAL AREA AND MEAN ECONOMIC YIELD (DRY WEIGHT ± S.E.) OF RICE AGROECOSYSTEM OF APATANIS AT HARI IN ARUNACHAL PRADESH. VALUES IN PARENTHESES ARE FOR *ELEUSINE CORACANA* (FROM KUMAR AND RAMAKRISHNAN, 1990)

	Agroecosystem[1]	
	Rice (Late Variety)[2]	*Rice (Early Variety)*
Density (plant m^{-1})	32(112)	48(104)
Basal area (cm^2 m^{-1})	400(25.7)	216(23.9)
Mean economic yield g $plant^{-1}$	12.7±0.4	7.2±0.3
	(2.8±0.1)	(2.4±0.1)
kg ha^{-1}	4064±141	3456±163
	(102.5±3)	(129.5±5)

Values in parentheses are for Eleusine coracana

1. Average bund area ha^{-1} rice plot was 519 m^2 and 327 m^2 for early and late varieties, respectively.
2. Fish production was 48 kg ha^{-1}

Table 8

ENERGY (MJ HA^{-1} YR^{-1}) AND MONETARY (RS HA^{-1} YR^{-1}) (IN PARENTHESES) INPUT-OUTPUT PATTERNS OF RICE AGROECOSYSTEM OF APATANIS AT HARI IN ARUNACHAL PRADESH (FROM KUMAR AND RAMAKRISHNAN, 1990)

Production Measures	*Rice agroecosystem*			
	Late Variety		*Early Variety*	
Input total				
Rice	846.5	(2481)	904.5	(2677)
Rice + millet	870.2	(2551)	946.0	(2798)
Rice + millet + fish	906.6	(2753)	—	—
Labour				
Rice	713	(2163)	769	(2337)
Millet	23	(67)	40	(116)
Fish	36	(102)	—	—
Organic manure seed	125	(250)	125	(250)
Rice	8.5	(68)	10.5	(90)
Millet	0.7	(3)	1.5	(5)
Fish	0.4	(100)	—	—
Output total				
Rice	66284	(8941)	56367	(7603)
Rice + millet	67956	(9102)	58480	(7817)
Rice + millet + fish	68182	(10062)	—	—
Energy efficiency				
Output/input ratio				
Rice	78.3	(3.60)	62.3	(2.84)
Rice + millet	78.1	(3.57)	61.8	(2.79)
Rice + millet + fish	75.2	(3.65)	—	—
Energy output/labour hour				
Rice	35.6		27.6	
Rice + millet	35.4		27.4	
Rice + millet + fish	34.1	—	—	—

With human labour as the major input (both men and women participating), the Apatanis obtain a high energy output (Table 8).

Labour input for rice/rice+millet where early variety of rice is grown was higher than for the late variety of rice. The Apatanis do not use draft animal power. The output from the system and the net return to the farmer was higher under late variety grown alone or with millet/fish, than under early variety of rice. The economic and energy efficiencies, and output per unit labour hour were also higher under the agroecosystem with the late variety of rice.

The exceptionally high energy efficiency of this valley land agroecosystem (60 to 80 units per unit energy input) is markedly different from the values discussed for other rice systems discussed earlier for other tribes in this region, with an output/input ratio of 4-18 (Mishra and Ramakrishnan, 1981; Toky and Ramakrishnan, 1982; Maikhuri and Ramakrishnan, 1990a). The high energy efficiency shown here also contrasts with that recorded for jhum in north-east India, which does not exceed 50. It is far superior to the traditional wet cultivation of rice of the Indian plains with an efficiency value of just about 9 (Mitchell, 1979) and that done elsewhere in the Philippines (Nguu and Palis, 1977). With 27-35 MJ units of energy output per labour hour, this system compares favourably with similar systems of China (32.8 MJ) (Dazhong and Pimentel, 1984) and more modern agriculture of industrialized societies (Leach, 1976), such as the United Kingdom, with an output of 40 MJ units. In the present context, it is significant that human labour is a free input being largely obtained from within the family itself, and for specific tasks alone through cooperative efforts.

With a highly developed wet rice cultivation, the Apatani economy is largely based upon agriculture alone (Kumar and Ramakrishnan, 1990). Widening plots by digging adjacent higher ground down to an irrigable level seems to be successful responses to population increase and new market opportunities (Brookfield and Padoch, 1994). The net per capita monetary return through agriculture is high. As much as 40 percent of the rice produced is sold to the economically weaker neighbouring tribes such as the Nishis and the hill Miris. However, the agroecosystem of the Apatanis could be improved through appropriate crop rotation and productive utilization of the land during the winter season. Inspite of these possibilities, the Apatani village ecosystem is a good example of economic self-sufficiency of a traditional agricultural society that practises ecologically sound sedentary agriculture in the north-eastern hill region of India.

Conclusion

The variety of rice agroecosystem types that one finds in north-eastern hill areas of India is indicative of the range that exists in the north-eastern India. Many of them represent under-utilization of land and are inefficient. Traditional wet land cultivators of rice such as the local Apatanis of Arunachal Pradesh and the immigrant Nepalis provide examples of a high degree of ecologic and economic efficiency for this system. However, valley land cultivation is constrained by the availability of water for cultivation during the relatively dry winter months. Where tribes like the Garos at Lailad take two crops in a year, they essentially restrict their activity to the monsoon period.

A few possibilities exist for redeveloping this system so that the farmer is able to obtain better returns : *(a)* mere transfer of technology from one tribe to another could be helpful. The Apatani system of farming is one of the most evolved and highly organized system of wet cultivation of rice, *(b)* introduction of early maturing and improved varieties of rice would help in obtaining two or even three harvests in a year, *(c)* water is a major constraint outside the monsoon period. Rain water harvesting and storage in tanks offers immense possibilities for irrigation. The run-off water from hill slops could be collected in 70 to 80 m^3 tanks lined with heavy duty polythene sheets. They are cheap, easy to maintain and have a life span of 20-25 years (Kothyari, *et al.* 1991). By harvesting surface run-off water of the rainy season and by diverting sub-surface seepage water through cheep rainwater harvesting tanks (Kothyari *et al.,* 1991), we were able to link it with a variety of ecosystem rehabilitation efforts, which elicited enthusiastic community participation. This is only just the beginning towards an understanding Indian agroecosystem types and for their redevelopment on a sustainable basis.

References

1. Brookfield, H. and Padock, C., 1994: Appreciating agrobiodiversity: A look at the dynamism and diversity of indigenous farming practices. Environment, 36: 6—11, 37—45.

2. Dazhong, W. and Pimental, D., 1984: Energy Inputs in Agricultural Systems of China. *Agric. Ecosys. Environ.* 11: 29—35.

3. Finck A., 1970: Moglichkeiten de Nahrungs Production in London, *Ernahrungs Umschau,* 2: 47-52.

4. Furer—Haimendorf, C. Von, 1962: The Apatanis and their Neighbours, London, Furer—Haimendorf, C. Von 1985: *Tribals of India : The Struggle for Survival.* Oxford Univ. Press,. Delhi, 342 pp.

5. Gangwar, A.K. and Ramakrishnan, P.S., 1987: Cropping and yield patterns under different land use systems of the Khasis at higher elevations of Meghalaya in north-eastern India. *Int. J. Ecol. Environ. Sci.* 13: 73-86.

6. Kothyari, B.P., Rao, K.S., Saxena, K.G., Kumar, T. and Ramakrishnan, P.S., 1991: Institutional approaches in development and transfer of water harvest technology in the Himalaya. In: Advances in Water Resource technology. ed. G Taskiris, pp. 678. A. Balkema, Rotterdam, The Netherlands.

7. Kumar, A. and Ramakrishnan, P.S., 1990: Energy flow through an Apatani village ecosystem of Arunachal Pradesh in north-east India. Human Ecology, (in press).

8. Leach, G., 1976: *Energy and Food Production.*, IPC Science and Technology Press, Guildford. 137 pp.

9. Maikhuri, R.K. and Ramakrishnan, P.S., 1990a: Ecological analysis of a cluster of villages emphasizing land use of different tribes in Meghalaya in north-east India, *Agric. Ecosys. Environ.* 31: 17-37.

10. Maikhuri, R.K. and Ramakrishnan, P.S., 1990b: Comparative analysis of the village ecosystem function of different tribes living in the same area in Arunachal Pradesh in north-eastern India, *Agric. Systems*, 35: (in press)

11. Mishra, B.K. and Ramakrishnan, P.S., 1981: The economic yield and energy efficiency of hill agro-ecosystems at higher elevations of Meghalaya in north-eastern India, *Acta ecologica-Eecol. Applic.* 2: 369-389.

12. Mitchell, R., 1979: *An Analysis of Indian Agroecosystem.* Interprint, New Delhi. 180 pp. Nguu, N.V. and Palis, R.K. 1977: Energy input and output of a modern and traditional cultivation system in lowland rice culture, Philippines *J. Biol.* 6: 1-8.

13. Patnaik, S. and Ramakrishnan, P.S., 1989: Comparative study of Energy flow through village ecosystems of two co-existing communities (the Khasis and the Nepalies) of Meghalaya in north-east India. *Agric Systems*, 30 : 245-267.

14. Pimental, D. and Pimental, M., 1979: *Food Energy and Society*, Edward Arnold, London. 165 pp.

15. Ramakrishnan, P.S., 1984: The Science behind rotational bush fallow agriculture system (Jhum), *Proc. Indian Acad. Sci. (Plant Sci.).* 93: 397-400.

16. Ramakrishnan, P.S., 1987: Energy flow and shifting cultivation. In : Kumar, V. & D.K. Ahuja, (Eds.), *Rural Energy Planning for the Indian Himalaya*, Wiley Eastern, New Delhi, pp. 247-276.

17. Ramakrishnan, P.S., 1988: Forest farmer and ecosystem redevelopment in the Asian Humid tropics. In: S. Adisoemarto (Ed.), *Ecodevelopment Process for Degraded Land Resources in Southest Asia.* UNESCO—MAB (Indonesia), Jakarta, Indonesia, pp. 103-118.

18. Ramakrishnan, P.S., 1992: *Shifting Agriculture and Sustainable Development: An Interdisciplinary Study from North-Eastern India,* MAB Book Ser., UNESCO, Paris & Parthenon Publishing Group, Carnforth, Lancs., U.K. 424 pp. (republished, Wiley Eastern, New Delhi, India, 1993).

19. Rosswall, T. and Panstian, K., 1984: Cycling of nitrogen in modern agricultural systems. *Plant and Soil,* 76 : 3-21.

20. Ruthenberg, H., 1971: *Farming System in the Tropics*, Clarendon Press, Oxford, U.K., 366 pp.

21. Schultz. T.W., 1964: *Transforming Traditional Agriculture.* Yale Univ. Press, New Haven, Conn. 212 pp.

22. Spedding, C.R.W., 1975: *The Biology of Agricultural Systems,* Academic Press, London.

23. Spedding, C.R.W. and Walsingham, J.M., 1976: The production and use of energy in agriculture, *J. Agric. Econ.* 27 : 19-30.

24. Swamy, P.S. and Ramakrishnan, P.S., 1988: Nutrient budget under slash and burn agriculture (jhum) with different weeding regimes in north-eastern India. *Acta Oecologica-Oecol. Applic.* 9 : 85-102.

25. Toky, O.P. and Ramakrishnan, P.S., 1981: Cropping and yields in agricultural systems of the north-eastern hill region of India, *Agro-Ecosystems,* 7: 11-25.

26. Toky. O.P. and Ramakrishnan, P.S., 1982: A comparative study of the energy budget of hill agro-ecosystems with emphasis on the slash and burn system (jhum) at lower elevations of north-eastern India *Agric. Systems,* 9: 143-154.

CHAPTER 26

Watershed Management in Hills

❑ K.K. SATAPATHY

Introduction

The North-Eastern Hill Region consists mainly of mountain ranges (rising from few meters to 5000 meters above msl). The area is dominated by three land forms, *viz.*, *(i)* greater Himalayas, *(ii)* strong disected high lands, and *(iii)* low lying riverine plains. The topography and climate of the region is conducive to accelarate soil erosion and the management of excess runoff is recognised as a major problem. High rainfall and steep hilly topography, large scale deforestation along with various biotic interferences have caused severe soil erosion posing a serious threat to the environment. According to an estimate, around 17.00 million ha of North-Eastern region (including Sikkim and North Bengal) is affected with soil erosion problem due to shifting cultivation, land slides, torrents and gullies, siltation of reservoirs and stream beds and so on. This paper describes the ill-effects of the continuous non-scientific agricultural land used and discuss some models based on watershed based farming system developed as a remedial measure for controlling the degradation and for better land and water management in the hills.

Erosion Risk Assessment

Quantitative facts on soil erosion hazards from soil erosion studies indicate that except forest land use, none of the land uses are safe and lead to land degradation process (Table 1). Micro plot studies on bare fallow slope of 0, 15, 30, 45, 60, 75 and 100 percent revealed that soil loss and runoff vary from 13.15 to 21.54 t ha^{-1} yr^{1} and 18.49 to 26.82 percent of rainfall respectively (Singh, 1985). Awasti (1984) reported 17.80 to 205.6 t ha^{-1} yr^{-1} soil loss from 65 percent slope (bare fallow). In hills, development of new sites for building construction, development of roads and area under kitchen gardening are major sources of soil erosion. In a case study Singh and Singh (1985) reported 16.8 t ha^{-1} yr^{-1} soil loss from 6.9 ha hilly watershed under homestead land use (Singh *et al.*, 1984). The hydrographic surveys of the Umiam reservoir (Meghalaya) conducted during January, 1990, revealed a sediment deposition of 11703 ac. ft. during the last 25 years, giving an annual rate of sedimentation of 26.05 ha. m per 100 sq. km. of catchment area (Anonymous, 1990). Shifting cultivation is currently ~~being~~ practised by 4.92 lakh farm families of this region in an area of 3.8 m. ha of slopy land. Biotic

Table 1

SOIL EROSION HAZARDS CULTIVATED WITH VARIOUS LANDUSE PRACTICES

Land Use System/Practices	*Experimental Plot Size*	*Soil Loss (t/ha/yr)*	*Average Annual Rainfall (mm)*
Shifting cultivation	Small	30.2-170.2	1600
Shifting cultivation	Field	5.1-83.3	1600
Tuber crops on raised bed (un)	Medium	40.0-50.0	1800
Pineapple cultivation along the slope (first 2 years)	Small	24.0-62.6	1600
Homestead areas	Field	16.8	1600
Mixed crop of maize and rice	Small	19.7-21.0	1600
Rice crop on slope	Small	32.9-45.0	1600
Bare fallow	Small	83.8	1600
Cropping systems	Medium	51.0-83.8	1600
Grass cover (Planted)	Medium	10.83	1600
Natural bamboo forest	Field	0.04-0.52	1600

Note: Area of small, medium and field size plots were in ranges of 2-5, 16.40 and 69,000m^2 respectively.

interferences in jungle cutting, burning, clearing and dibbing of seeds, account for a considerable amount of loss of soil material. The soil erosion from hill slopes (60-70 percent) under first year, second year and abandoned jhum was estimated to be 147,170 and 30 t ha^{-1} yr^{-1} respectively (Singh, 1981). It is estimated that 181 million tonnes of soil is lost every year from this region due to this defective system of farming (Prasad *et al.*, 1981). Owing to increase in the pressure on land, the jhum cycle has reduced to 4-5 years in Meghalaya, 5-17 years in Mizoram and Tripura, 6-15 years in Nagaland and Manipur and 1-17 years in Arunachal Pradesh, giving practically no chance for natural regeneration of soil fertility.

Watershed Approach

Owing to deforestation, shifting cultivation and agricultural encroachments into the marginal lands on steep slopes, land use pattern of hilly terrain has undergone serious changes resulting in intense ecological degradation. Under such conditions, land use activities and conservation measures should be planned and executed within the framework and limitation of environment, ecological and social conditions prevailing in the area. Most of these factors are related to the nature of the drainage basin and the extent to which important activities are coordinated with unit comprising has been physical-biological micro-units as well as socio-economic political micro-units for planning and management of natural resources. Watershed management requires concurrent accomplishment of many tasks among which are proper planning of land use practices as well as adoption of soil and water conservation measures which in long run will enhance the prospect of self reliance in terms of food, fibre and energy. In undulating hilly terrain where intensive agriculture is planned the size of watershed selected is small. Hilly micro-watershed responds more effectively to various engineering, biological and cultural treatments designed to maximise production. Also as water is the best index of watershed management, it provides an excellent monitoring mechanism for evaluation of the impact of the programme at the outlet in the lower reaches. A workable size of the watershed can be decided in accordance with the aim and objectives of the particular project as well as the size of the stream or river for which it forms a catchment.

Integrated Land-use Plan

Changes of land use pattern affect water and soil regime of any watershed. These changes, if properly planned, could be beneficial. Mountain areas are basically suitable for agroforestry system planned on watershed basis. This watershed based mixed landuse system with subsidiary source of income through livestock rearing provides for appropriate farming system on steep hill slopes. Watershed based landuse is recommended for the hills on the following considerations : ensuring adequate protection of land against soil erosion, maximum retention of rainfall within the area, storage of runoff water for pisciculture and irrigation, etc. Integrated landuse plan on hilly slopes should include agriculture, horticulture, silvipasture, forestry and combination of these systems. Studies on alternative farming systems to shifting cultivation indicate that agriculture with bench terrace in the lower portion of the hilly watersheds can provide stable alternative to shifting agriculture system. Crops such as paddy, maize, millet, soybean, groundnut, linseed, topioca, collocasia, pea, mustard, etc. have been grown successfully under rainfed bench terraces with 100-300 cropping intensity. Terrace risers occupying 10-15 percent area have been utilised successfully to growing fodder crops at 100-1000 m altitude. Horticultural landuses also can be practised on slopes upto 100 percent having soil depth of 1 m. Bunds, half moon terraces and grassed water ways are required for land development for horticultural crops. Simple soil conservation measures in the form of contour bunds have been found adequate for range lands to produce quantity and quality of fodder materials for intensive livestock farming. Several pasture species—native, cultivated and silvipasture—have been identified for improved livestock management needs in different lands depending on fertility status and altitude in the area. The above concept based on research findings is presented in Table 2.

Terracing Steep Slopes

Arable agriculture in the sloping land leads to very serious erosion. In many areas the slopes being cultivated must be terraced and the terrace outlets must discharge into protected waterways, which may require simple structure for reducing the velocity of flow. Mere terracing without any change in the local system of farming is

DETAILS OF VARIOUS FARMING SYSTEMS TO REPLACE JHUMING

Sl. No.	*Landuse*	*Hillslope*	*Minimum Soil Depth Requirement*	*Soil Conservation Measures*	*Expected Rainfall Retetiom (%)*	*Soil Loss (t/ha)*	*Cropping Pattern* (Production Potential g/ha in Brackets)*	*Livestock* Rearing Potentiality (ha/unit)*	*Mandays Requireed*
1.	Agriculture	Upto 50%	1m	*(i)* Contour bunding .0.5 to 1m interval (to be converted to bench terraces subsequent) *(ii)* Grassed waterway *(iii)* Bench terracing in foot hills	90	2	rice (16.72), maize (5.25), millet (16.44), Soybean (5.25), arhar (13.39), conseava (83.40), Maize+Soybean (21.04+2.42) Maize+arhar (17.26+13.51) maize+ginger, (17.56+39.10) fodder on terrace risers forest species on hill tops.	1.18	400
2.	Horticulture	Up to 100%	1m	*(i)* Contour bunds at 2m interval *(ii)* half moon terrace at the fruit plant locations	90	1	Assam lemon (11,300, 12,000, 37,200 fruits/ha during third, fourth, fifth year of planting)	N.E.	108
3.	Livestock based farming systems	Up to 100%	5m	*(i)* Contour bunds (1m interval)	90	2	Leguminous, nonleguminous annual, perennial, shurbs and trees.	5	335
4.	Agri-horti-silvipastoral landuse	Up to 100%	1m	*(i)* Contour bunds *(ii)* Bench terrace *(iii)* Half moon terrace *(iv)* Grass wayerways	90	Negligible	*(i)* All crops under agriculture horticulture landuse *(ii)* Fodder type indigenous trees at hill tops	1.18	190

Not estimated : *One livestock unit equals 1 buffalo, 1.25 cattle, 5.0 pigs, 10.0 goats.

Source : Singh *et.al.* (1987).

unlikely to lead to a long term solution to soil loss and fleed damage. Bench levelling of paddy lands results in reduction of surface area for cultivation under bunds, risers and channels. In N.E.H. Region, bench terrace cultivation exist in slopes upto 100 percent having terrace width as low as 3 m because steep slopes normally do not permit terraces of more width. Level beds with vertical interval of about 1 m along with 15 sq.m cross section shoulder bunds and 1/2:1 batter slopes for terrace risers was found satisfactory for movement on these slopes for performing various agricultural operations (Prasad *et al.,* 1987). Experience in ICAR also indicates that contour bunds on slopes get converted into bench terrace lands within 4 to 8 years depending on the crops cultivated. These bunds on steep slopes are created by way of excavating parabolic channels (0.3 m top and 0.2 m deep) on contours and keeping the dug out soil in the form of a bund at lower edge of the channel. These bunds require care and maintenance during the first two years. The experience in ICAR also shows that vegetative barriers alone will not serve the purpose on steep slopes. The vertical intervals of these bunds may vary from 0.5 to 5.0 metres depending on land-use and soil depth. Half moon terraces with level beds having 1 to 1.5 m diameter cut into half moon shape on hill slopes and are used for planting the saplings of fruit and fodder trees in agroforestry landuse. The cost of land development on different soil and water conservation works, namely contour bunds, bench terraces, half moon terraces and grassed water ways in the same farm (30% slope) with the use of manual labour worked out to be 135, 400, 150 and 50 mandays respectively (Prasad *et al.,* 1987). The water way is an integral part of terracing. In most cases, natural depression without shaping and protection is not safe to accommodate extra runoff concentrated by terracing. Channel shaping, grass planting and construction of suitable structures are the different components of water ways installation. Nearly 90 percent soil and water conservation measures can be undertaken by utilising natural resources.

Indigenous Water Management Systems

A variety of typical water management techniques based on local skill and resources are prevalent in the region. Some of these practices, mostly confined to the places of their origin, are as follows:

(a) ***Zabo System:*** Zabo system of farming is practised by the Chakhachang tribe of Kikruma village in the Phek District of Nagaland. The system is a combination of agriculture, forestry and animal husbandry with well founded conservation base for soil erosion control, water resource development and water management as well as protection of environment (fig.1). The rain water is collected from the catchment of protected hill tops of above 100% slopes in a pond with seepage control. Silt retention tanks are constructed at several points before the runoff water enters into the pond. The cultivation fully depends on the amount of water stored in the pond. (Sonewal *et al.,* 1989; Sharma *et al.,* 1990).

(b) ***Drip Irrigation using Bamboo :*** This system is practised by the farmers in Jaintia Hills District of Meghalaya to irrigate arecanut and betelvine grown on steep slopes with bouldry soils. In this system small hill streams from upper reaches are diverted into bamboo fitted about 1 to 2 m above the ground surface with the support of bamboo stands. The water, brought to the field by these channels gravitationally and distributed through secondary, tertiary or more branches of pipe line (fig.2) with a typical water diversion system at the joint of each branch, ultimately drips to the individual plants enabling the system to deliver 15 to 25 litres water per minute at the terminal of these branches (Singh *et al.,* 1981; Rai, 1981).

(c) ***Water Management Practices of Apatani Valley :*** This unique land use and water management technique is adopted by Apatani tribe in the Subansiri District of Arunachal Pradesh to irrigate gently sloping lands at the foot hills by diverting hill streams from upper reaches. Earth, boulders, brush wood dams are used for diversion works. The stream water brought through the main channel is diverted to a net work of subchannels to act as irrigation-cum-drainage channels; lay-out of fields and channels are made is such a way that the entire plateau functions as a water course. Bamboo and wooden log pipes of various sizes are used as prefabricated water management structures for use as conduits for water inlets and outlets, waste weirs and energy dissipators. (Singh *et al.,* 1981; Rai, 1981).

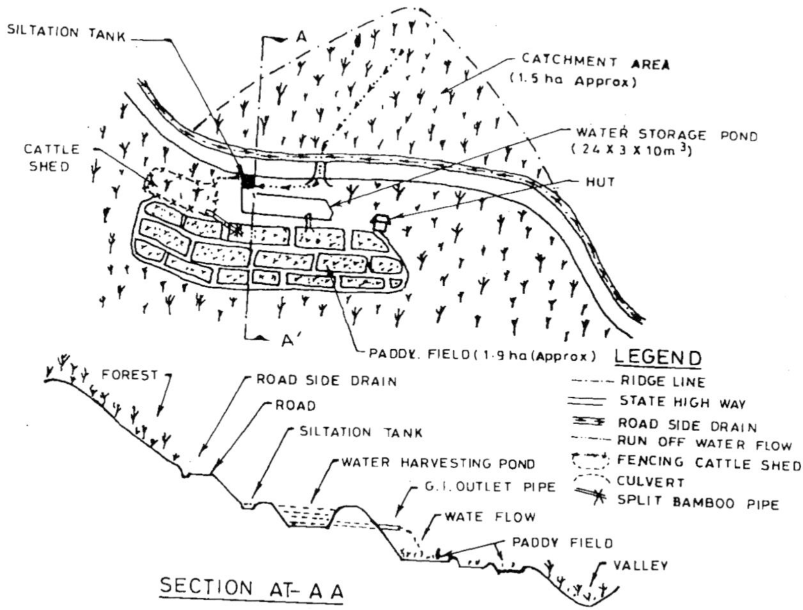

Fig. 1 : Land Management System under Zabo Farming System.

Source : **Sonowal *et.al.*, 1989.**

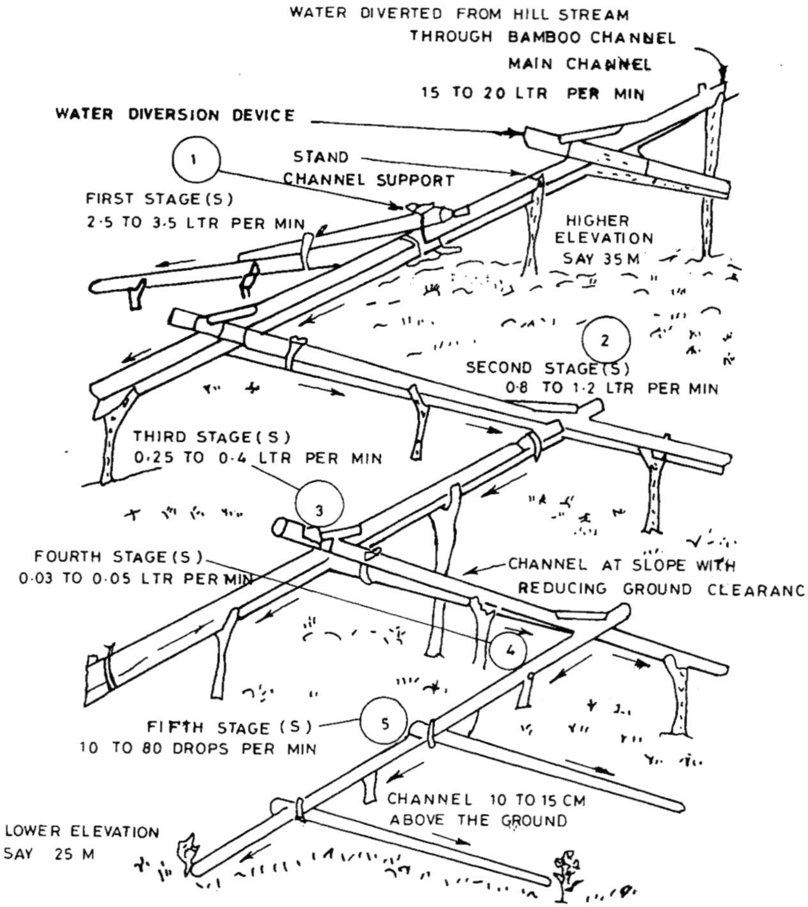

Fig. 2 : Water Distribution and Application in Drip Irrigation using Bamboo.
***Source* : Singh 1981.**

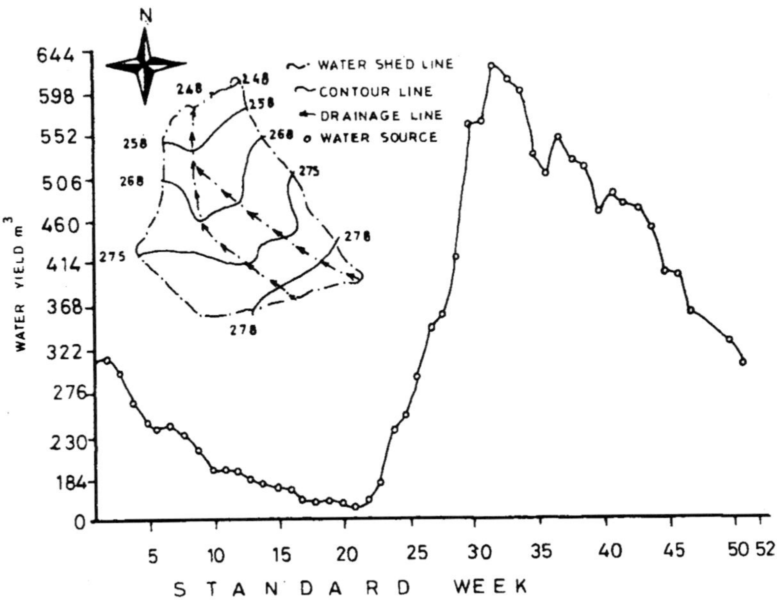

Fig. 3 : Water Yield Behaviour of Spring Located at KVK Farm Tura (Av. 1982 to 1988).

Source : **Yadav, 1988.**

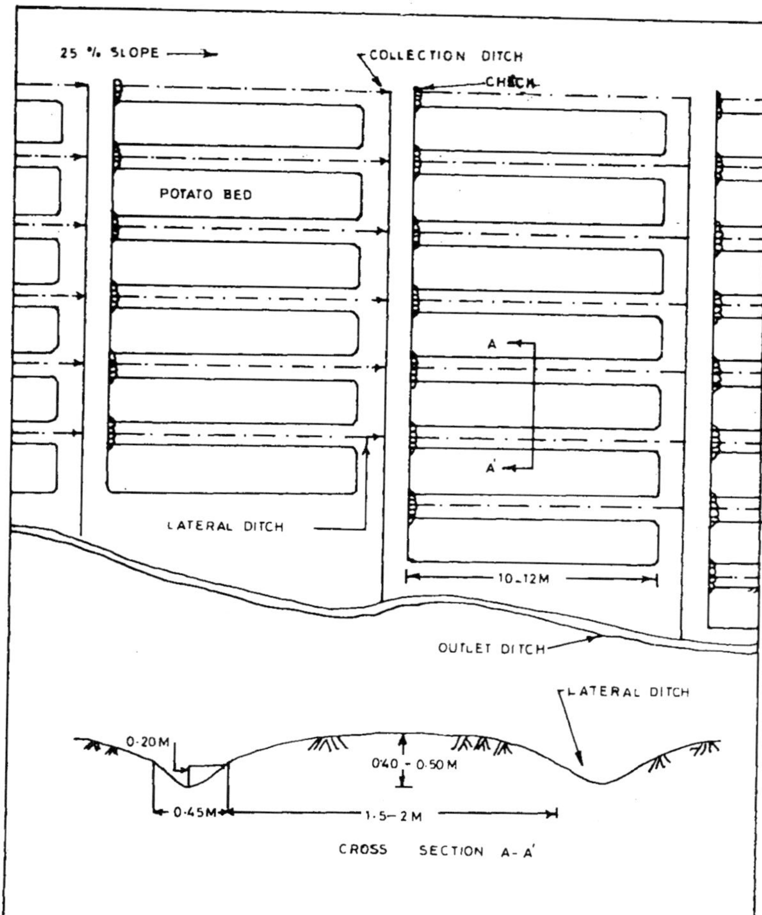

Fig. 4 : Surface Drainage System.
Source : **Sharma, 1983.**

Table 3
Details of irrigation System and Economic Benefits

Sl.No.	Particulars	River Site (New Seithikhima Village)		Tank Site (Naharbari Village)Puranbazar	
		Details	Monetary Value (Rs.)	Details	Monetary Value (Rs.)
1.	Pump Units	Two 10 H.P. pumpsets mounted on carts	36000.00	One 10 H.P pump (installed in a pump house)	18,000.00
2.	Discharge capacity of the pump (lps)	50 lps each	—	50 lps	—
3.	Area covered reclaimed (ha)	24. ha		10 ha	
4.	Crops grown earlier	Waste land covered with scrub jungles and grasses	—	Paddy (Kharff)	—
5.	Crops grown after introducing irrigation	Paddy (pre-kharif and kharif) Pea, patato	—	Paddy (Pre-kharif kharif)	—
6.	Family benefitted	40	—	20	—
7.	Average land holding ha/families	1.45	—	1.2	—
8.	Total cost		44,000.00	—	75,650.00
9.	Cost per ha of area		1,833.33		7,665.00
10.	Water distribution system	Kutcha channel	—	Bricklined channel	
11.	Value of crop production before irrigation	—	—	22 g/ha (kharif paddy)	3,124.00
12.	Value of crop produced per ha after irrigation introduction	Paddy-Paddy	14,200.00		
		Paddy-Patato	47,100.00	Paddy	10,508.00
		Paddy-Wheat	13,380.00	Paddy	
		Paddy-Pea	12,700.00		

(d) ***Stream Flow Lift Irrigation :*** The traditional method of irrigation in hills consists of harnessing the hill streams during monsoon by constructing temporary check dams on stream bed for diversion and conveyance of water through earthen channels. Boulder, timber and earthen dame are built across the stream to raise the level of water for diversion. There is a tradition of such irrigation works done by village/community as a whole to carry water from streams over long distances. Water lift system is essential in the vast tracts which can not otherwise be served by the diversion works. The lift irrigation potential in the region, however, remains largely unexplored. Vast flat lands along the sides of rivers remain under natural fellow with wild bushes. Damaging land use practices (mainly shifting cultivation), extensive felling of trees and friable soils in the hills coupled with high rainfall produce heavy flow loaded with soil particles, pebbles, debris which proceeding through steep mountain courses and soft rock formations come down to the foot hills with enormous force disturbing the existing channel configuration and raising river beds. The rivers are highly meandering type, cutting away lands upto 200-300 metres in one season; washing away the irrigation installations during the flash floods is the common feature. The portable water lift system with pump and engine installed on tyre wheeled bullock cart-cum-trolly was found feasible for river situations where the site and water courses change every year. The result of ORP on lift irrigation (Table-3) demonstrated that large areas of plane and gently sloping lands can be brought under irrigation by installation of high discharge low head pumpsets at the appropriate locations after ascertaining the flow characteristics of the stream at the selected sites. Also, large scale adoption of conservation farming practices supported by bench terraces and allied structures in the hills has also brought into being favourable condition for lifting irrigation water to the terrace located at comparatively higher elevations.

(e) ***Water Harvesting Structures :*** Watershed based farming system in the hilly micro watershed under various land uses *viz.* agriculture, horticulture, forestry and mixed land use coupled with different soil conservation measure such as bench terraces, contour bunds, half moon terraces, grassed waterways and so on are recognised as the most effective means to check land degradation in the hilly tract with potential to retain 80-100% of annual rainfall in *situ* contributing immen–sely towards water development and recharge of streams. Construction of small water harvesting structures (fig.3) in the lower reaches of these micro watersheds to store runoff and intercepted baseflow for utilising the stored water for fish production or the recycle back for life saving irrigation provides ample scope for water resource development at a relatively low cost. Rolling topography of hills and gorges in the tract facilitates the construction of water harvesting structure mainly comprising earthen embankments and spill ways—with high storage and earth work ratio. However, soil in the entire region barring few places, has extremely low water holding capacity and seepage losses are very high. Such ponds therefore, sometime require lining against seepage losses, or otherwise, storage becomes seasonal.

Storage characteristics of two water harvesting ponds with watershed area of 11 and 15 ha and maximum storage capacity of 1.4 and 1.9 ha. m. located at ICAR Farm, Barapani indicate that the contribution to the water storage to the seasonal pond was 14.47—22.4% for direct rain, 0.57—2.3% as runoff and 79.3—84.96% as surface flow. The water yield of well managed watershed was practically silt free. Optimum proportion of watershed and reservoir impounded areas, large flood spill ways, liberal free boards are of vital importance for water harvesting structures in the area. Essentially community owned enterprises are suitable organisational setup. These need to be developed for the effective execution and management of the water harvesting projects with active participation of beneficiary farmers.

(*f*) ***Hill Springs :*** The rugged hilly terrain supports large number of springs—perennial as well as ephemeral—with yields varying from a few litres to tens of cubic metres per hour giving rise to numerous streams and rivulets, the discharge being the highest during monsoons which gets reduced during autumn and reaches at their lowest in summer. These natural springs are the main sources of water supply to bulk of the tribal population living in the hills and hill tops. Six such springs having water yield potential of 0.99 to 7.72 ha.m. per year are being currently pooled for water supply at ICAR Complex at Barapani. Construction of suitably lined storage tanks of adequate size with proper protection measures for possible pollution by human and animals is essential for effective utilisation of these water resources.

(g) ***Drainage of Valley Lands :*** Net or high water table conditions occur near the base of the hill subjected to seepage from high land. The wet area exist because of abrupt changes in topography bringing the land surface near to or in contact with water table surface. Deep open drains are constructed across the slope for the purpose of intercepting surface as well as ground water flow and conveying the same to a safe outlet. An age old practice of growing spring potato through indigenous surface drainage system (fig. 4) has made it possible to harvest two crops in a year from upland valleys in Meghalaya. (Sharma, 1983)

References

1. Anonymous (1976): Development of suitable planting techniques of pineapple in hill slopes. Annual report, ICAR Research Complex for NEH Region, Shillong. pp 122.
2. Anonymous (1985): Report of the working group on development of North-Eastern Region, North-Eastern Council, Shillong. pp 83-84.
3. Anonymous (1987): Basic statistics of North-Eastern Region, North-Eastern Council Secretariat, Shillong.
4. Anonymous (1990): Report on hydrographic surveys and sedimentation studies, Umiam Barapani Reservior project, Meghalaya.
5. Awasthi, R.P. and Prasad, R.N. (1988): Efficient cropping system for rainfed terraces in North-Eastern Region of India as an alternative to shifting cultivation. Status paper presented in National Symposium on efficient cropping system zone of India held at the University of Agricultural Sciences, Bangalore 7-10 January, 1988.
6, Borah, B.C. (1990): Economics of flood eco-system. Paper presented in the seminar on constraints of Agricultural development in North-East India held in Shillong 2rd—3rd July 1990.
7. Borthakur, D.N., Singh, A., Awasthi, R.P., Ghosh, S.P., Prasad, R.N., Sahu, S.D., Varma, Arun, Sachan, J.N., Viswadhar, Datta, H.H., Sharma, B.S. and Samanta, R.K. (1983): Shifting cultivation in North-Eastern Region, Shillong, Meghalaya, India.
8. Borthakur, D.N (1985): Problems of floods in North-East and significance of watershed management. Proceeding of training courses in water harvesting

structures and propagation of its technology in NEH Region. ICAR Research Complex for NEH Region, Shillong.

9. Borthakur, M. (1990): Weather and climate of North-East India. North-Eastern Geographer 18 (2&2): 20-27.

10. Dasgupta, K.R. (1985): Need of Agricultural Resource planning in the North-Eastern Region with a view to Boosting Agricultural Production Social Research 3(3-4) 13-22.

11. Hazarika, R.N. (1988): Operation for the long term management of water resources in the Brahmaputra Basin—A new approach. Souvenir 2rd water resource day celebration organising Committee May 1988.

12. Narain, J. (1990): Hydrology and water potential in the North-East India Region. Lecture note for 1st orientation course on water and land management held at Tezpur, Assam during 16-26 May, 1990.

13. Prasad, R.N., Singh, A., Varma, Arun (1986): Problems of hill lands and their management in North-Eastern India, Indian Journal of Soil Conservation 14(3):66-72.

14. Prasad, R.N. (1985): Degradation of soil and water resources and crop production in NEH Region 1(1):1-8.

15. Prasad, R.N., Singh, A. and Verma, Arun (1987): Application of research findings for management of land and water resources in Eastern Himalayas Region, Bulletin ICAR Research Complex, Shillong. 1-50.

16. Prasad, R.N., Pati Ram, Borooah, R.C. and Munna Ram (1981): Soil fertility and management in NEH Region, Research Bulletin-9.

17. Rai, R.N. (1981): Water Management in North-Eastern Region. Research Bulletin No. 14 ICAR Research Complex for NEH Region, pp. 15-18.

18. Rai, R.N. and Singh, A. (1986): Effect of hill slope on runoff, soil loss, nutrient loss, and rice yield Jl. of Soil Conservation 14(2):1-6.

19. Satapathy, K.K. (1983): Lift irrigation in hills: Some Research experiences. Indian Jl. of hill farming 1-A:37-41.

20. Satapathy, K.K. (1988): Rainfall analysis for crop planning at Dimapur, *Nat symp. Environ.* Pr. Hill Dev. 15-17 Feb. 1988 (Sikkim Sci. Society): 120-125.

21. Satapathy, K.K., Sharma, U.C. and Prasad, R.N. (1990): Water resource development in North-Eastern Region : Prospects and constraints. Proceeding of the workshop on "Research needs on land and water management for enchancing agricultural production in Eastern Region" held at Bhubaneswar during 4-5-October, 1990.

22. Sharma, K.D. (1983): Indigenous surface drainage system in Meghalaya—A case study. AICRP on water management, ICAR Research Complex for NEH Region, Shillong.

23. Sharma, K.D.(1987): Estimating soil erosion hazard through rainfall analysis in the N.E. India. *Jl. Agric. Engg.* 24(1):55-64.

24. Sharma, N.(1982): A broad appraisal of the exploitable water resources and projected water needs of the Brahmaputra basin. India's North-East, A

multifacted view edited by Pankaj Thakur, Prakash Publishing House, Tinsukia.

25. Sharma, U.C., Satapathy, K.K., and Prasad, R.N.(1990): Research Needs on Land and Water Management for enhancing Agricultural production in Nagaland. Proceeding of the Workshop on "Research needs on land and water management for enhancing agricultural production in eastern region" held at Bhubaneswar.

26. Sheng, T.C. (1990): Soil conservation for small farmers in the humid tropics, FAO Soil bulletin (60).

27. Sheng, T.C. (1990): Water management field manual: Watershed survey planning, FAO Conservation guide 13/6/90.

28. Sheng, A., Singh, M.D. (1981): Soil erosion hazards in North-Eastern Hill Region, Research bulletin No. 10. ICAR Research Complex for NEH Region. pp. 20-22.

29. Singh, A., Singh, M.D. (1988): Effects of various stages of shifting cultivation on soil erosion from steep slopes, Indian Forester 106 (2):115-121.

30. Singh, A. (1987): Water Resources development in hills—some experiences talk delivered on 2rd. Nov. 1987 in round discussion on "Our Water Resources" organised by the Institution of Engineers (India) at Kalyani, West Bengal State Centre.

31. Singh, A. and Verma, A. (1988): Land and water management in hills. *Indian Jl.* of hill farming 1-A (2):1-9.

32. Singh, M.D. (1985): Rainfall and soil relationships on varying degree of slope. M.E. Dissertation, Deptt. of Civil Engineering Assam Engineering College, Assam Gauhati.

33. Singh, A. and Singh, M.D. (1984): A case study on farm stead development in hill relation to soil and water conservation from steep hill slopes, *Indian Forester* 106 (2) 115-121.

34. Singh, A. and Prasad, R.N. (1987): Alternative to sifting cultivation, ICAR, New Delhi.

35. Sonowal, D.K., Tripathi, A.K. and Kirekha, V. (1989): Zobo—An indigenous farming system of Nagaland. Indian *Jl. Hill Farming* 2 (1):1-8.

CHAPTER 27

Sustainable Development in Agriculture and Need of Forestry Planning in Arunachal Pradesh

❑ AMITAVA MITRA

The concept "Sustainable Development in Agriculture" has become popular since 1988 when a Technical Advisory Committee of the World Commission on Environment and Development was appointed by the United Nations to look into various aspects of the agricultural sector for developing a programme of sustainable development in agriculture. The Commission Visualised the sustainable agriculture as "The successful management of resources to satisfy the changing human needs while maintaining or enhancing the quality of environment and conserving natural resources". The concept "Sustainable Development" in Agriculture is closely connected with development of forestry in a hilly state like Arunachal Pradesh where around 61.5 percent of total geographical area is covered under forests (around 82 percent of geographical area based on satellite imagery). Forests may be regarded as capital stocks yielding two distinct flows of goods fundamentally different in nature—a flow of private goods such as fuel woods, timber, house-building materials, other minor forest produce, etc. and a flow of public goods like maintenance of environment, causation of rainfall, prevention of soil erosion, control of floods, etc. However, there is a conflict between these two types of goods. In other words, given the quantum of forests, the greater the extraction of private goods in the form of timber, firewood, etc., the less will be the availability of public goods in the form of environmental benefits. So, a compromise has to be brought between the demand for private goods and that for public goods from the forests for achieving sustainable development in Arunachal Pradesh and here lies the importance of effective forestry planning in a hilly State like Arunachal Pradesh.

In this paper, an attempt is made to study the need of effective planning for development of forestry in Arunachal Pradesh having bearing upon agricultural development. The paper is worked out mainly on the basis of secondary data.

Section I

Out of the total geographical area of nearly 83,700 sq. km. of Arunachal Pradesh, 51,540 sq. km. is estimated to be under forests. However, as per the recent estimate of the Forest Survey of India, based on satellite imagery, forest area in this State is 68,661 sq. km. which constitutes nearly 80.99 percent of the total area of the State. The detailed classification of forests in Arunachal Pradesh is shown in Table 1.

Table 1

CLASSIFICATION OF FORESTS IN ARUNACHAL PRADESH IN 1990-91 (LEGAL STATUS)

Sl. No.	*Legal Status of Forest*	*Area in sq. km.*	*% of Total Forest Area*	*% of Total Geographical Area*
1.	Reserve Forests	19,236.55	37.32	22.97
2.	Anchal Forests	256.08	0.05	0.30
3.	Protected Forests	7.79	0.01	0.01
4.	Unclassed State Forests	32,039.00	62.17	38.27
	Grand Total		100.00	61.55

Source: Compiled from Arunachal Pradesh Forests, Environment and Forest Department, Government of Arunachal Pradesh, 1993.

Table 1 shows that the reserve forests constitute nearly 37.32 percent of the total forest area of the State which is much less than the all India average of 52.2 percent. There is a steady increase in reserve forest area as compared to 1950, when there was only 526 sq. km. (11.9 percent of total forest area of the State) and in 1979-80, it increased to 11,422 sq. km. (22.17 percent of total forest area of the State). However, the question is that such an extension of reserve forests may have an impact on the Jhumias of the State who may be forced to shift to other places as it happened in the case of Tripura (Chakravarti, 1986, p. 39).

The important thing to observe from Table 1 is that there is a vast area of forest which is known as Unclassed State Forest (U.S.F.) (62.17 percent of total forest area of the State). This is the forest on which local people claim absolute right and the State also claims ownership rights. The official position with regard to land in jhum cultivation is embodied in Jhum Land Regulation of 1947. The Act has recognised customary rights of the tribals over land. The fact has an important bearing on the ownership of forests and forest land not being used for Jhuming. However, the Government amended the Forest Act in 1955 and recognised the rights of local tribesmen to collect fuelwood, bamboo, cane, etc. even from reserve forests as well as limited rights in hunting and fishing. In this connection it should be noted that these ownership of land and forest in Arunachal Pradesh which varies from tribe to tribe can be broadly divided into three categories: *(i)* land owned by individuals, *(ii)* land owned by clan, and *(iii)* Community owned village land. In Arunachal Pradesh, large tracts of land and forest are under community ownership. However, vast tracts of land are now being claimed as individual property where even other villagers are denied entry (Roychowdhury, 1992). For example, in the Apatani valley forest land has become increasingly privatised, local tribes are now asserting hereditary ownership rights over forest area.

Finally Anchal Reserve Forests covered only 256.08 sq. km. (only 0.50 percent of total forest area). Such forests are managed by Forest Department with the provision for sharing the net revenue in the ratio of 50:50 (share of village: share of Government). Thus, the creation of Anchal Reserve Forest in 1975 has intensified the overall management of forestry in Arunachal Pradesh because such schemes are expected to provide both direct and indirect benefits to the local people and scientific coverage of forest management to wastelands as well as Anchal Samity Lands.

Section II

Forest plays an important role in the socio-economic life of the people of the State. This is evident from the fact that the contribution of forestry to the Net State Domestic Product (NSDP) is much higher 8.47 percent than the all India average of less than 2 percent in 1991-92 at 1980-81 prices. The contribution of forestry to the NSDP went up quite high in the early eighties but since then the contribution has been decreasing which may be due to conservation-oriented policy of natural resources, inadequate funds for creating man-made forestry, etc.

The development of forestry at the national level did not receive much attention during the first two plans. The main thrust of national forestry planning during the next four five year plans was mainly on: *(a)* large scale plantation of industrially valuable species; *(b)* enlargement of social forestry including farm forestry; and *(c)* linking forestry development with the economy of the people.

Forestry planning in Arunachal Pradesh slowly evolved out of forestry planning enunciated at the national level. Before the Third Plan, no serious attempts were made for the development of forestry in Arunachal Pradesh. However, attempts were made during these three plans to control deforestation and to restore the forest by afforestation but the efforts were rather modest. From the sixth Five Year Plan, stress was laid on social forestry, farm forestry etc. Social forestry is basically a people's movement because the growing of trees on land, not held by Forest Department, depends on the people's response to it. The concept of 'Apna van' scheme received wide and enthusiastic acceptance upto 1992-93, a total area of 6,106 hectares of plantation have been raised under this scheme with a target of 1650 hectares in 1993-94 (Government of Arunachal Pradesh, 1993; p. 39).

Section III

It has been found from the experience in the context of Arunachal Pradesh that, the private goods which the forests yield get more priority particularly at the initial stage. This may be due to the fact that the public goods which the forests yield are of such a nature that the benefits of their presence, or the harms caused by their absence are felt slowly and only in the long run (Bhattacharjee, 1985, p. 56). At the same time it should also be noted that Forest has externalities but essentially it is a resource (Ganguly, 1986, p. 126). Even as forests must be protected to conserve soil, environment, wild life and genetic pool, at the same time resources yielded by forests should be used in growing quantum for satisfying direct human wants and requirements of industries and constructive activities which are expected to grow along with economic development. So, an effective forestry planning should try to minimise the conflict between the demand for private goods and that for public goods from the forests. Therefore, effective planning of forestry for sustainable development of agriculture assumes greater significance in view of the fact that the population of the state has been growing at a rapid rate, the annual exponential rate of growth of population being more than three percent. The per capita income of the state is increasing at a moderately high rate. These two factors—a growing population and a rising income—are mainly responsible for the rapid expansion of the demand for both agricultural and forest products. Naturally, the demand for land is on the increase. Consequent escalation of land prices has acted as incentive to convert forest land into agricultural land—both jhum and permanent.

Conclusion

The analysis has made it clear that there is a conflict between agricultural expansion and forestry development. The resolution of the conflict warrants that alternative sources of income for growing population should be explored so that pressure on land as a source of income is minimised. Eco-friendly industries such as electronics, watch making, etc. should be developed. Appropriate training should be imparted to the local people so as to equip them with necessary skill so that they can be employed in such industries. So far as the forest management is concerned, Joint Forestry Management (JFM) system should be introduced and the role of NGOs should be recognised.

References

1. Bhattacharjee, P.R. (1987): Forest and Economic Development: The Problems of Goal Conflicts in North-East India, Datta, Rau, B. (ed) *North East India*; 2000 A.D. Deep and Deep Publications, New Delhi.
2. Chakravarti, M. (1986): Forestry in Tripura: Its Past and Present, Das Gupta, M. *et al.*, (eds): *Forestry Development in North-East India*, Omsons, Publications, New Delhi.

3. Chatterjee, S.K. (1986): *Emergence of a Dynamic Economy,* Associated Publishing House, New Delhi.
4. Ganguli, J.B. (1986): Planning for Forestry Development in the North-Eastern Region: The Approach. Das Gupta, M. *et al., Forestry Development in North-East India,* Omsons Publications, New Delhi.
5. Government of Arunachal Pradesh (1990): *Arunachal Pradesh Forest Statistics.* Forest Department, Itanagar.
6. Government of Arunachal Pradesh (1993): *Economic Review of Arunachal Pradesh,* Directorate of Economics and Statistics, Itanagar.
7. Government of Arunachal Pradesh (1993): *Arunachal Pradesh Forests:* Environment and Forest Department, Itanagar.
8. Government of Arunachal Pradesh (1992): *Draft Eight Five Year Plan (1992-97).* Planning and Development, Itanagar.
9. Government of India (1993): *The State of Forest Report* , Forest Survey of India; Dehra Dun.
10. Malhotra, K.C. (1995): People and Biodiversity. *Mimeographed paper presented at Eleventh Foundation Day Lecture,* Arunachal University, Rono Hills, Itanagar.
11. National Commission on Agriculture (1976): *Report.* Volume IX, New Delhi.
12. National Council of Applied Economic Research (1967):*Techno-Economic Survey of N.E.F.A.,* New Delhi.
13. North-Eastern Council (1994): *Basic Statistics of North-Eastern Region,* Shillong.
14. Roy Chowdhury, A. (1992): Chopping Down the Future, *The Sunday Sentinel,* Vol. X, No. 19, August, Guwahati.

CHAPTER 28

Ethnogeography and Traditional Agricultural System of the Apa Tanis of Arunachal Pradesh

❑ ARUN KUMAR SINGH

Introduction

Human societies organise the use of their surrounding resources not according to the total knowledge of ecological reality but through knowledge limited by three factors: cultural filters representing the set of shared terminologies, categories, knowledge and beliefs passed from generation to generation by the process of enculturation, concurrent learning process or knowledge becoming, but not yet incorporated as, a part of culture; and individual and collective levels of insight and aspiration (Knight: 1974-61). The agricultural system of the Apa Tanis is the reflection of the cultural knowledge which they have gained or gathered through the passage of time, know-how modified and adapted through contact with their neighbours or other alien sources and also through progressive learning of the environment occupied by them. The primary task of this paper is to understand how the Apa Tanis have developed their agricultural system keeping in view the ecological conditions in which they are placed. Emphasis is also being made to understand the Apa Tanis' environmental knowledge from their perspective. The data base for this analysis is the long fieldwork undertaken by the author in the Apa Tanis' land and also through querries and interviews of the Apa Tanis on household level.

Environmental Risks and Uncertainties

Traditional agricultural system is riddled with many environmental risks and uncertainties. The societies try to understand it and cope with at their own level. However the Apa Tanis failed to recall when they had experienced the last famine. Though it is a general feeling that the North-Eastern states experience famine one in twelve years which is also related with the flowering of the bamboo. But in the land of Apa Tanis only male bamboo is found and the question of flowering does not arise. However, for the better understanding of the issue we can divide the environmental risks and uncertainties into three broad categories which are as follows:

Biological Uncertainty

The Apa Tanis failed to provide with broad data related to biological uncertainty. But they recognise that there are some insects which do extensive damage to the paddy crops. The State agricultural department at Ziro also could not provide a detail account on the biological uncertainty prevailing in the Apa Tanis' agriculture but it did mention three general types of insects/pests which are common in the Apa Tanis' land. They are steam borer, rice bug and blast. It has been reported that these insects/pests do considerable damage to the crops grown by the Apa Tanis. However, Apa Tanis do not use pesticides but they perform various types of puja/ritual for the betterment of the paddy crops. Apart from insects/pests rat is also a menace to the paddy and millet crops. Apa Tanis try to kill the rats after the harvest is over so that their population is reduced to some extent. Birds and wild animals also do considerable damage to the paddy crops. To overcome this problem the Apa Tanis individually or sometimes jointly fence the field specially at places where the paddy fields meet the rim of the highland/forest land etc. These fences are repaired tightly before the crop is sown. For taking care of the birds Apa Tanis build watch hut (Pudi Lankha/Pudi Pubyi) in the paddy field and do continuous vigilence so that the grains of the paddy and millet are not damaged.

Climatological Uncertainties

Among the climatological uncertainties the Apa Tanis are very much concerned with the heavy rainfall which lashes the Apa Tanis' land from June to September. Heavy rainfall occasionally results in flood and excessive damage is done to the paddy fields as well as to the crops. Apart from this due to heavy rainfall the main rivulets and their sub-channals discharge sand in huge quantity and along with the water sand gets spread into the paddy fields which in turn reduces the fertility rate and thus hampering the production of paddy. All these constraints have made the Apa Tanis to put maximum attention towards this climatological phenomenon and they have developed elaborate water-management system so that the excess water of the plateau is properly drained without damaging the paddy fields as well as the paddy and millet crop. Apart from heavy rain-fall Apa Tanis have also to cope up with forest. The whole agricultural calendar revolve round the frost free days available to them. After October when frost becomes severe no agriculture is done in the Apa Tanis' land. Storm, hailstones and lightening also damage the paddy crop. The Apa Tanis are helpless in this regard and they try to cope up with this situation by offering prayers/puja known as 'Yapung'. 'Yapung' is a ritual performed to the sky god to prevent the crops from thunder, hailstorms and frost. This ritual starts in the later part of August and continues till the paddy crop is harvested. In this context it must be noted that due to lack of frost free days wheat crop failed to come up in the Apa Tanis' land.

The third uncertainty which the Apa Tanis are very much concerned with is the evil forces. After the month of July a small structure made of bamboo shavings is planted in the paddy field which is known as 'Iyu Piiroh'. The main ritual function of 'Iyu Piiroh' is to protect the young paddy crops from the bad eyes.

Agricultural Implements

The Apa Tanis do not use plough or any form of animal power. The whole agricultural operation is performed with the help of manual labour and few agricultural implements.

The principal traditional implement of the Apa Tanis is long handled iron spade (Dipe). Before the arrival of ironspade long handled wooded type implement was used to dig the soil. Spade is used for digging as well as for other earthworks like levelling, preparing and repairing the bunds, irrigational channels etc. The second important tool is a flat wooden oval shaped tray known as 'Sampya'. This is used for carrying the mud/soil from one end of the ricefield to the another end so that the ricefield becomes level.

Apart from 'Sampya' a wooden levelling stiick (Huita) is also used to level the ricefields. During the time of weeding a hook like implement made of bamboo shaves known as 'Pale' is used. 'Kale' a small bamboo shaved stick is used to weed the grass and undergrowth from the paddy field. Sickle (Tagi) is used to harvest the crops. Baskets (Yagi) made of cane or bamboo is used for carrying purposes. As no animal energy is used in the whole agricultural operation these agricultural implements are very useful for the Apa Tanis and they take a lot of care to maintain them.

Crops

The major staple crops of the Apa Tanis are rice and millet. Among these two crops rice is the single most important crop grown by the Apa Tanis. Rice is a wet crop and is grown in the well maintained irrigated rice fields but millet is a dry crop and is grown on the rice fields bunds as well as in the dry fields specially prepared for millet. Apart from these two main crops Apa Tanis also grow maize in their dry land and kitchen garden. Wheat was tried but it failed to come up. Among the root crops potato and sweet potato are new entry in the Apa Tanis agriculture though space marked for these two crops is very limited. A good number of vegetables and leafy vegetables are grown in the kitchen garden. Among fruits trees apple has been introduced with little success.

Evolution of Rice Cultivation

The corner stone of Apa Tanis' agriculture is the cultivation of rice on irrigation terraces. Rice is the staple food, and all other crops are grown mainly to provide variety of died and to utilize those portions of land not suitable for irrigation. Rice too is the principal item in the Apa Tanis' export (Furer—Haimendorf: 1946:29). The whole economy, social and ritual pattern revolve round rice cultivation. But the question of origin of Apa Tanis rice cultivation remains unanswered by the early writers (Furer—Haimendorf: 1946, 1955, 1962, 1980; Bower: 1953, Elwin: 1957). From the interviews with many Apa Tanis it was found that during their course of migration they did not bring rice with them. It seems that they brought millet (Eleusine Coracana), maize, pines (Pinus excelsa) and bamboo. These crops and trees vary from the crops and trees cultivated and grown by the neighbouring tribes—Nishis and Miris.

However, it can be assumed that Apa Tanis settled down in a valley which was a marshy land (Iard: 1951) and rice might have been growing in its wild form. Apa Tanis might have developed the present variety of rice from the local wild rice during their long occupation of the valley. Looking at the geographical situation of the valley it can also be presumed that there were no option for the early Apa Tanis settlers but to develop rice crop. The millet and maize which were brought by them from the place of migration were not suited to the marshy land. This belief that rice is a local crop gets more confirmed if we look at the map prepared by Tadaya (1985: pp. 33-39) to demonstrate the geographical origin of cultivated rice. He also confirms that rice cultivation originated in the Assam-Yunnam Zone and spread to the various countries of South-East Asia, China and Japan. It is also found that nearly all the tribal population of North-Eastern States in general and Apa Tanis' neighbouring tribes—the Nisis (Shukla: 1959) and the Hill Miris (Chowdhury: 1970) in particular grow rice in their Jhum fields. Looking at the rice cultivation system of the Apa Tanis one can easily feel that rice cultivation is being practised by them since time immemorial. The ecological conditions also help and support rice cultivation and Apa Tanis have excelled in it.

Ecology and Rice Cultivation

Rice as we have noted earlier, the most distinctive crop grown by the Apa Tanis is cultivated intensively but to a great extent on subsistence level in the fragmented but well maintained fields. On the success or failure of rice depends the whole household economy of the Apa Tanis. About 90% of the arable land is under rice cultivation. Whenever land is suitable and water is available rice is being grown.

Among the ecological factors affecting rice cultivation availability of water is very important. The field has to be submerged under approximately 6" of fresh and slowly moving water for at least 75 days. If rainfall is not regular fields have to be properly irrigated. Keeping the water requirement of rice in mind the Apa Tanis pay maximum attention towards this aspect. Development of better water management and irrigation system have helped the Apa Tanis to grow better crop of rice in their field. Apart from water rice requires approximately 70° F temperature during the growing season for nearly 4-6 months. Clay soil is also necessary so that the surface water should not runaway by seepage. The Apa Tanis valley fulfills all these ecological conditions. Located at the altitude of 1600 meters Apa Tanis valley receives nearly 2000 mm. of rainfall per annum and that also coming in 4-5 months (last of May to October) by the South West Monsoon. Heavy rainfall helps the Apa Tanis to submerge their rice fields with 5"-6" water. However, heavy rainfall creates some problems like flooding.

Types of Rice Fields

The importance of rice fields (Ajee) is extremely high in Apa Tanis society because from here comes the bulk supply of food. Rice field is also a symbol of social prestige. The richer and highly placed Apa Tanis have a sufficient number of rice fields under their command. Land is the source of wealth and all other and less permanent possession are mainly valued as a means of acquiring land (Furer-Haimendorf: 1946:82). Each and every Apa Tanis desires that he should acquire more rice fields. Here he differs from the neighbouring tribes—the Nisis and the Hill Miris—because in other societies land is not a personal property as it is in the Apa Tanis' society.

The geographical layout of the valley has laid a strong impact on the pattern and type of rice fields of the Apa Tanis. Furer-Haimendorf (1962:22) has classifieds the Apa Tanis' rice field into two categories: in first category fall those rice fields which are kept permanently under water for most part of the year where as in the second category those rice fields fall which are occasionally flooded with water. However, our observation is that the rice fields of the Apa Tanis may be classified into two broad categories and these two broad categories may again be subdivided. These classifications are as follows:

(1) ***Aha Ajee :*** In this category there are two sub-categories which are as follows:

(a) *Lango Ajee :* The rice fields which are located very near to the village are termed as Lango Ajee. These rice fields receive the outlet water (discharge) from the village. The discharge water of the settlements carries a lot of waste which is decom-

RICE FIELDS (AJEE)

- Aha Ajee
  - Lango Ajee
  - Arambo Ajee
- Asang Ajee/Kombu Ajee

posed and increases the fertility of the rice fields. This type of rice fields are not more and there is extreme competition among the Apa Tanis to acquire more and more Lango Ajee. In Lango Ajee Pyaping and Emo varies of rice are grown.

(b) *Arambo Ajee:* If we proceed from the settlement the valley becomes more and more wider. The rice fields located in this area are called Arambo Ajee. The size of the rice fields becomes larger than the Lango Ajee. These rice fields are often flooded and each and every year new soil is added. However, it has been reported that its fertility is less than the Lango Ajee. Apa Tanis women carry house hold waste like rice husk (Puina) and ash (Mubu) and spread them in these rice fields. It is a common scene in the morning of an Apa Tanis village where women can be seen carrying 'Puina' and 'Mubu' to the rice fields after the paddy crop is harvested. These waste materials add manure to the rice fields. It is important to note that Apa Tanis do not use fertilizer of any short.

(2) ***Asang Ajee/Kombu Ajee:*** This type of rice fields are located to the upper areas of the valley in between the hillocks (Putu) and he hills (Pango). Here the rice fields become smaller and narrower because the valley itself becomes narrower. The rice fields situated in these areas are less fertile because soil contains boulder and sand. Due to upper elevation run off rate of water is also high which affects the rice production.

Method of Rice Cultivation

Understanding of the rice cultivation method is important because the type of rice grown in different types of rice fields differs. Preparation of rice fields also differs according to their type and location. Preparation of rice fields takes major part of the Apa Tanis agricultural labour. Throughout winter and spring season Apa Tanis repair the embankments and bunds of the rice fields. Women, children and also men do this job. Wherever it is necessary small boulders are placed with the help of bamboo poles. The second job in this process is the repair of water channels so that each and every fields get sufficient water.

Apa Tanis have conserved their traditional mode of tilling the land. The main focus of the method is absolutely no use of animal energy. Even at this stage of development plough is not used. There are different methods of tilling the land and these vary according to the nature of the rice field. The rice fields which are submerged under water throughout the year are not tilled. Roots and stems of the previous year crop is left and during the current season seedlings are planted in between the old roots and stems. This is a character of a marshy land. In these type of rice fields late growing variety of rice is grown. The second category is those rice fields which remain wet throughout the year but before the agricultural season starts some time in late winter, water is drained and the fields is allowed to be dried up. The with the help of spade field is thoroughly dug up and water is released. Before transplantation the rice field is again puddled by young men and women till the soil is fully churned to a smooth thick paste. Afterwards seedlings are planted. The last category of rice fields which are located on the uplands are dug with spade, submerged under water and seedlings are transplanted. In the above two types of rice fields early growing variety rice is grown.

Nursery beds are located very near to the settlement and care is taken throughout the year to maintain the nursery plots. The bunds are regularly repaired and fields are irrigated properly. Ash is regularly spread in the nursery bed so that the fertility is maintained. For each and every variety of rice separated nursery beds are prepared. By the end of March the rice plants in the nursery bed grow upto 6" to 8" and by the first week of April seedlings are ready to be transplanted in the rice fields. Generally 60-75 days old seedlings are transplanted.

Apa Tanis grow basically 3 broad types of rice such as Empu Aarean early variety rice, Empu Hate-late variety rice and Elang-a red variety rice. This is again further subdivided, Empu Aare is a combined name of a group of rice which are known as early growing rice in the Apa Tanis' agricultural system. In Empu Aare there are mainly 2 varieties of rice such as Pyate and Pyaping. Each and every seedling is planted at the interval of 8" approximately. The first variety to be planted is Pyate which is followed by Pyaping. By the middle of April transplanting of early growing rice is completed.

After the early growing rice Empu Aare, Empu Hate is transplanted. In this category there are two varieties of rice—Empu and Rade. These varieties of rice are grown on the permanently wet rice fields which are marshy in nature.

Apart from these two varieties of white rice Apa Tanis also grow a red variety of rice which is known as Elang or Pyare. Elang or Pyare variety of rice is grown mainly in Kombu Ajee. Most of the rice beer of the Apa Tanis is prepared with Elang or Pyare variety of rice. Weeding of rice fields are done with utmost care. Generally 4 times weeding are done after transplanting but this differs from rice field to rice field.

The first rice to be harvested is Pyare in early August. While harvesting stems are not cut but the grains are stripped from the ear by hand (Furer-Haimendorf: 1962-30). After Pyare the next rice to be harvested is Pyate. But the main harvest starts in October. Men, women and children labour hard atleast for two to four weeks to complete the job. The rice grain is out with the help of sickle and the stem is left in the field to get dried up and later on it is decomposed to become manure. After the harvest the crop is threshed on a wooden plank. Afterwards the grain is carried to the granary house (Nasu) for storing. The straw is left near the thrashing ground or stacked near the house/dry field/kitchen garden or thrown in the rice fields. In the granary house rice grains are separated for seeds and for eating purpose.

Water Management

Through generations Apa Tanis have learned the art of water management and today their system has no parallel in whole of North-East. The basic factor in Apa Tanis water management is the use of bamboo for construction of small dams and also from water distribution system.

Every small or big streams which rises from the wooden high hills surrounding the Apa Tanis plateau are trapped and water is taken to various rice fields with the help of contour. Sometimes, the stream is dammed at the upper head with the help of bamboo sticks, pine planks and poles so that the water level is elevated and afterwards with the help of distributary channels water is taken to the rice fields. This system is known as "Mugo Sigang Siling". Sometimes water is overflowed in a controlled way with the help of bamboo holes (Hubru) from one field to another. However, 'Hubru' is placed after cutting the rice field bund. On the discharge end of the 'Hubru' two pine planks are placed at an interval of half foot which is called 'Pading', 'Pading' checks the current of the water discharged with the help of 'Hubru' and thus minimises the soil erosion. This system is used when the slope between the two rice fields are little higher say two to three feet. But if the two rice fields have negligible slope the bund is simply cut.

After winter season the irrigation system is thoroughly repaired so that it can last for 5-6 months when there is a heavy flow in the streams due to heavy rain. Care is also taken so that no rice field gets flooded and damaged. The whole water management of the Apa Tanis revolves around three important factors: mutual distribution of water, prevention of flood and soil erosion.

Dry Crop Cultivation

Though dry crops do not rival rice in importance the same meticulous care which an Apa Tanis lavishes on his rice terraces characterises his treatment of millet, maize and various vegetables. Many of these crops are grown in gardens and the methods employed in their cultivation are these of the horticulturist rather than of the farmer (Furer-Haimendorf: 1946:34). The importance of dry crop for the Apa Tanis is also mainly due to the fact that it is a major source in preparing the household beer without which the Apa Tanis cannot survive in the severe cold of the high Himalayas. Among the dry crops millet (Ebusine coracana) is the most popular crop and it is grown exclusively on the plateau where ever suitable land is available. Apart from millet, maize is also grown by the Apa Tanis but on a low scale.

Millet as we have noted earlier is the main source of rice beer for the Apa Tanis. It is grown at two places—firstly on the rice bunds and secondly in the dry fields specially prepared for it. If we observe the agricultural land use map then we will notice 3 important zones of millet. The first zone is located in the far south eastern end of south of Hong village. The second zone which is also the biggest according to area is located on the north-eastern portion of Hong village and runs upto north east of Hari-Bula villages. The third zone is located on the north western portion of the plateau close to old Ziro. Geographically the dry fields are located in between 1600 meter to 1800 meters. Dry fields are located on the meeting point of the paddy fields and the rising hills. Many fields are tightly fenced but some fields are open and here the spread is much. However, in the fenced dry fields along with millet maize is also grown.

Millets are of two types and accordingly they are grown at two locations. The first type of millet is called 'Sarpu' and is an early growing variety. This type of millet is grown on the bunds (Agro) of the paddy fields. The second variety is known as Sarto and is a late growing variety millet. This type of millet is grown in the millet fields known as 'Lyappo'. In the month of February millet seeds are shown in the millet nursery bed called 'Papu'. By the end of April the millet samplings are about 4" to 5" in height and are ready to be transplanted in 'Lyappo' and on the 'Agro'. By the middle of April transplanting of paddy is over and after this only Apa Tanis pay attention towards the millet. The millet samplings are carried in basket and are planted on the bunds of the paddy fields by the help of Hoe. It is a laborious job and women take extra care so that the bunds of the paddy fields are not damaged. Not a single square foot land is left on the bunds of the paddy fields where 'Sarpu' is not transplanted. 'Sarte' is transplanted a little later sometimes in the middle of May. The dry field is well prepared by digging the soil and then it is well soaked in the rain water so that the soil gets loose. In the dry field also transplanting of millet is done by the women. One important point is to be noted is this that immediately before transplanting the top of the seedlings are chipped so that the growth is thick and also the plant grow in a bushy way.

The harvest of 'Sarpu' starts in the middle of October and ends by last week of October. 'Sart' is also harvested by the end of October. In the granaries they are spread and heaped on the floor. Millet is not sold but sometimes Apa Tanis buy millets from their Nisi friends.

The next important dry crop grown by the Apa Tanis is maize, (Tanyi). It is of two varieties: the first variety which is also an early growing variety maize is called 'Nyre'. 'Nyre' is sown in the last week of February and is harvested in the early part of September. The second or late growing variety maize is called 'Nyt' which is sown in the last week of February and harvested in the last week of September. Maize is grown in the kitchen garden 'Yarlu' along with other root crops like 'Tape' a sweet potato, 'Taku' cucumber and 'Enge' a small roots. Potato is being grown by the Apa Tanis but on a small scale. Gujang—a leafy vegetable is grown in the kitchen garden 'Yarlu' throughout the year except in the severe winter months.

Conclusion

The Apa Tanis' agriculture is very complex in nature because they have taken pain in controlling the fertility of soil with the help of elaborated water management and land tilling system supported by cropping pattern most suited to their environment.

References

1. Adams, Jnez, 1948: Rice Cultivation in Asia, American Anthropologist: L: 256-282.
2. Blaut, J.M., 1961: The Ecology of tropical farming systems, Revista Geographia. 28:47-67.
3. Bower, Ursula Graham., 1953: The Hidden Land, John Murry. London.
4. Chowdhury, J.N., 1970: The Hill Miris of Subansiri, Shillong.
5. Chowdhury, J.N., 1973: Arunachal Panorama: A study in Profile. Shillong.
6. Colby, B.N., 1966: Ethnographic semantics, Current Anthropology, 7:27-61.
7. Conklin, H.C., 1961: The Study of Shifting Cultivation, Current Anthropology, 2:27-61.
8. Frake, C.O., 1964: Notes on queries in anthropology, American Anthropologist. 66.3 Part 2: 132-145.
9. Furer-Haimendorf, C.Von, 1955: Himalayan Barbary. John Murry. London.
10. Furer-Haimendorf, C.Von, 1962: The Apa Tanis and their neighbours (A primitive civilization of the eastern Himalayas.) Rout Ledge & Kegal Paul, London.
11. Furer-Haimendorf, C.Von, 1980: A Himalayan tribe from cattle to cash, Vikas Publishing House Pvt. Ltd., New Delhi.
12. Knight, C.G., 1971: Ethnogeography and Change, Journal of Geography, 70:47-51.
13. Knight, C.G., 1974: Ecology and Change: Rural Modernization in an African Community, Academic Press. London.

14. Singh, Arun Kumar, 1991: Techniques of food production among the Apa Tanis of Arunachal Pradesh, J. Anthropological Survey of India, 40: 109-115.

15. Singh, Arun Kumar, 1992: Ecology and rice cultivation among the Apa Tanis of Arunachal Pradesh. In the ecology of agricultural system. Edited by Noor Mohammad. 267-281. New Delhi: Concept Publishing Company.

16. Singh, Arun Kumar, 1992: From agriculture to fishculture: An example from highlanders of Arunachal Pradesh. In Agriculture and economic aspects of tribal landscapes. Edited by G.P. Gupta. 36-49, Jaipur: Arihant Publishers.

17. Singh, Arun Kumar, 1994: Cultural Landscapes of the Apa Tanis of Arunachal Pradesh, Journal of the Indian Geographical Foundation, Volume 1, Winter, pp. 1-13.

18. Singh, Arun Kumar, 1994: Apa Tanis: A Study in Ecology and Change (unpublished Report), Anthropological Survey of India, Calcutta.

19. Sturtevant, W.C., 1964: Studies in Ethnoscience, American Anthropologist. 66.3 Part 2: 99-131.

20. Sukla, B.R., 1959: The Dafla of the Subansiri Region, Shillong.

21. Tatung, Taniyang, 1987: Apa Tanis Calender, Ziro Hutco. 16-17, Ziro.

22. Tado, W., 1985: Origin and Dispersal of Rice in Asia. East Asian Cultural Studies, XXIV (No. 1-4): 33-40.

23. Izzard, R., 1951: The Hunt for the Bru, London.

Acknowledgement

I would like to express by deep sense of gratitude to Dr. R.K. Bhattacharya, Director, Anthropological Survey of India, Calcutta for his kind guidance and help. I am grateful to Mr. Hage Tado, Mr. Hage Kojin, Mr. Lord Kojin, Mr. Tasso Sai and Mr. Hage Hinda of Hari village, Mr. Arup Ganguly the then District Statistical Officer, Zero and Dr. Mihir Kanti Paul, MBBS, M.D. of District Hospital Ziro for their help and cooperation during my fieldwork among the Apa Tanis.

Index

B

C

G

H

I

J

K

L